The Social Order of a Frontier Community

The Social Order
of a Frontier Community

Jacksonville, Illinois
1825-70

DON HARRISON DOYLE

University of Illinois Press
URBANA CHICAGO LONDON

Publication of this work was supported in part by grants
from the Mobil Foundation, Incorporated, the Carnation
Company, and the city of Jacksonville

Library of Congress Cataloging in Publication Data

Doyle, Don Harrison, 1946–
The social order of a frontier community: Jacksonville,
Illinois, 1825–70

Bibliography: p.
Includes index.
1. Jacksonville, Ill.—History. 2. Frontier
and pioneer life—Illinois—Jacksonville. I. Title.
F549.J2D68   977.3'463   78–5287
ISBN 0–252–00685–2

To my Mother,
and to the memory
of my Father

Contents

List of Maps

Preface

THIS BOOK ANALYZES the process of building a new community in the nineteenth-century American Midwest. I have adopted a broad definition of "frontier" to define not the cutting edge of initial settlement, but the long struggle of a town's first generation to achieve urban greatness and construct a viable social order. I hope the citizens of Jacksonville, and other Illinoisans, enjoy my efforts to dissect their collective past, but I also want the book to reach students and scholars interested in the new methods and theories emerging in urban and social history, and the general reader interested in community life in America.

As a native of California, I know, perhaps better than others, the problem of building communities amid a culture that exalts individualism, mobility, and freedom. Still, I am far more impressed with the persistent and ingenious efforts of Americans to construct new forms of community, adapting them to a changing environment whenever necessary. The powerful communitarian tradition of American culture has been too long obfuscated by a popular myth of the frontier that depicts hearty pioneers escaping the constraints of a closed society in the East for the liberation of an open, individualistic society in the West. I hope this study of community-building in a young town striving to gain urban status and to mold a social order will help us to see the American frontier experience in the context of broader forces of urbanization, mobility, and immigration at work within a rapidly expanding capitalist society.

The problems involved in writing this book have at times seemed no less demanding than the ones Jacksonville's pioneers confronted. I have enjoyed the special pleasure of belonging to a community of scholars, and their allies, whose help, criticism, and friendship have made my task less difficult. This book began years ago as a graduate research seminar paper at Northwestern University. George Fredrickson first suggested doing a historical community study to test the Elkins-McKitrick thesis, and all along he has encouraged me to wrestle with the subject on my own terms, now and then gently guiding me toward the central questions before me. Robert Wiebe helped me with the earliest stages of research in his seminar, and he later brought his insights into American community life to bear on a thorough criticism of my dissertation, which strongly influenced the final product. In a more general way, both men have served as models of the inquiring historical mind; I am grateful for all that they have done for me.

I am also indebted in more tangible ways to several institutions for their financial support while the book was in the making. Northwestern University and its department of history supported me during the early stages of research; the Woodrow Wilson Fellowship Foundation awarded me a dissertation-year fellowship and research funds; the Horace C. Rackham School of Graduate Studies at the University of Michigan offered a faculty fellowship and research funds in the summer of 1973, while I was employed by the University of Michigan–Dearborn. Finally, the Vanderbilt University Research Council has provided essential support in the last stages of this book's preparation by awarding a faculty summer grant in 1975 and providing funds for research assistance, microfilm, typing, and photocopying.

At various times my task was made easier by the help of research assistants. I am grateful to Tom Jones, Lynn Bohmer, Janice Purdue, and especially Lorraine Parrish Herwig, for their help. Thanks also to Jo Tabereaux, whose typing skills magically transformed my messy draft into a polished manuscript. I am deeply indebted to Jeanne Christian for her careful reading of the page proofs.

The staff of the Illinois State Historical Library was most helpful to me; I especially want to thank Paul Spence, Roger

Bridges, and Mildred Schulz. I am also grateful to the North-western University Library; Chicago Historical Society; Illinois Historical Survey; Jacksonville Public Library; Robert Lovett of the Baker Library at Harvard; and the Joint University Librar-ies at Vanderbilt University. Lois Griest, at the latter institution, was particularly expeditious in securing interlibrary loans of needed materials. Finally, Richard Pratt, head librarian at Il-linois College, was extremely cooperative and congenial in as-sisting my research at the Tanner Library.

I came to Jacksonville an objective outsider, with a youthful eagerness to cut through the mythology that enshrouds local history. But, I confess, my acquaintance with the town and its people over the years has developed into a genuine fondness. Jim Davis of Illinois College was very helpful in turning up new sources and allowing me to test some of my ideas on his stu-dents. Pauline Newport, the city clerk, generously opened the city records to me and has given her enthusiastic support to my project all along. I am also grateful to the members of The Club and the Literary Union, two of Jacksonville's oldest literary societies, for giving me a wonderful opportunity to share my research with an audience of interested laymen. Dozens of other people in Jacksonville's churches, businesses, and frater-nal lodges took time out from their busy schedules to aid my work and share their own knowledge of the community's past. Above all, I am grateful to Charles Frank for the kind hospital-ity he and his wife, Dorothy, afforded me during visits to Jack-sonville, and for all his devoted efforts to see my labors come to fruition. In a wonderful display of the "Jacksonville Spirit," Charles Frank also boosted my book at community club meet-ings and persuaded local industry to lend its support to the cause of history. Special thanks to the people of the Plastics Division of the Mobil Chemical Company in Jacksonville, the Carnation Company, and the City of Jacksonville, whose generous grants helped make this publication possible.

A good many colleagues have helped me in the research and writing of this book. John Drodow gave generously of his time and thought during the early stages of my work. Bill Klecka patiently introduced me to the mysteries of computer processing. Kermit Hall, Jeff Hantover, and Terry Calvani helped me with their advice, encouragement, and friendship during the crucial final summer of writing. Charlie Zucker has read and criticized each stage of my work and has given both his knowledge of Illinois history and his friendly encouragement to complete the project—I have valued both enormously. Robert Dykstra, whose own book, *The Cattle Towns*, charted much of the territory I explore here, read my dissertation and offered criticisms. Robert Church, Jon McKenna, Samuel P. Hays, and Stephan Thernstrom also read my dissertation, and their comments aided subsequent revisions. Sam McSeveney shared his extensive knowledge of American political history and ethnicity, which I hope I have put to good use in this book. Eugene Tobin gave his thoughtful comments on two important chapters. One of the most helpful experiences in sharpening my interpretation of Jacksonville's social order has come from my efforts to teach American urban and social history to Vanderbilt students, and I am grateful for their assistance. Finally, I owe a special debt of gratitude to Kenneth Lockridge, whose incisive criticism improved the final product, and whose vote of confidence in my work has meant a great deal. The comments of all these people have helped me write a stronger book; I hope they forgive me for whatever weaknesses remain.

My thanks to the editors of the *Western Historical Quarterly* for allowing me to incorporate in the introduction portions of my article, "Social Theory and New Communities in Nineteenth-Century America," which appeared in their April, 1977, issue. A part of the seventh chapter also appeared in *Social Science History,* Spring, 1978, as "The Social Functions of Voluntary Associations in a Nineteenth-Century American Town," and I am grateful to the editors for allowing me to publish portions of that article here.

I hope Jacksonville's boosters forgive the fact that their history is published by the state university which was "stolen" from them back in 1867. Richard L. Wentworth, editor and associate director of the University of Illinois Press, and Ann Lowry Weir, who copyedited the manuscript, have "made amends" to the town by their helpful attention to the publication of this book.

My family deserves a special note of thanks for their patience during my long sojourn in nineteenth-century Jacksonville. My daughters, Carrie and Kelly, have grown up with this book and have taken a lively interest in its progress, offering on several occasions to edit the manuscript with their crayons and to reorganize my notes and computer cards. My nearly liberated wife, Marilyn, requests me to announce that she aided in none of the editing or typing, but I hope she won't mind if I thank her instead for her confidence in me and the life we share—that helped me write this book as much as anything.

D. H. D.

Introduction:
The Problem of Community

> Jacksonville was then a new world, socially em-
> bryonic, genetic, in a period demiurgic, constantly
> engaged with primordial problems which required
> dealing with and handling, re-examining and testing
> first principles, philosophic and organic, social, polit-
> ical, institutional, educational, and religious. The
> stimulus imparted to those thus engaged was intense
> and profound. Most of us, also, were in life's morn-
> ing, with an indefinite kaleidoscopic future through
> the vague glittering scenery of a world yet in genesis
> and magnificent mystery and therefore highly
> idealized. The excitement and activity of enterprise
> and speculation were universal; I felt most intently
> and deeply the impress of this genetic genius of a new
> world.
>
> —TRUMAN POST[1]

"OLD AMERICA SEEMS to be breaking up, and moving westward. We are seldom out of sight, as we travel on this
grand track towards the Ohio, of family groups behind, and
before us. . . ."[2] Morris Birkbeck was en route to the Illinois
frontier in 1817 when he recorded this scene of nineteenth-
century America in motion. A recent English immigrant, Birkbeck may have exaggerated the former solidity of "old
America," but he understood clearly that the new America was a
society of movement, expansion, and change.

Birkbeck's vision of the disintegration of "old America" an-

1. Truman Augustus Post, *Truman Marcellus Post: A Biography Personal and Literary*
(Boston, 1891), pp. 51-52.
2. Morris Birkbeck, *Notes on a Journey in America* (Philadelphia, 1817), p. 34.

1

ticipated by three-quarters of a century the historian Frederick Jackson Turner's interpretation of the frontier experience. Turner saw this westward movement as a central force giving shape to what he called "the first period of American history" before the closing of the frontier in the 1890s. For Turner, the frontier offered Americans liberation from the restraints of the civilized, class-ridden, fixed society to the east. On the frontier individualism, democracy, and acquisitiveness found unrestrained freedom. "The early society of the Middle West was not a complex, highly differentiated and organized society," he wrote. "Almost every family was a self-sufficing unit, and liberty and equality flourished. . . . American democracy came from the forest, and its destiny drove it to material conquests. . . . Both native settler and European immigrant saw in this free and competitive movement of the frontier the chance to break the bondage of social rank, and to rise to a higher plane of existence."[3] These free-floating pioneers on Turner's frontier gradually succumbed to the layers of civilization that built up after the first wave of settlers, but the original experience of individualism and democracy "still persisted . . . even when a higher social organization succeeded."[4]

Ever since Turner's eloquent exposition on "The Significance of the Frontier in American History" in 1893, historians have squared off with one another to exchange blows attacking or defending the Turner thesis. The most heated battles have been over the degree of political democracy and economic opportunity in the West. For those still willing to join the fray, there is ammunition for both sides in this book. But I have chosen to quietly sidestep this battle, without even so much as an encouraging cheer to either of the weary contestants, and to proceed toward what I see as the central problem of an expansive, mobile society—the problem of community.[5] Turner's adulation of frontier individualism notwithstanding, I am convinced

3. Frederick Jackson Turner, *The Frontier in American History* (New York, 1920), pp. 153-54.

4. Ibid., p. 37.

5. Ray Allen Billington, *America's Frontier Heritage* (New York, 1966), pp. 1-22, 288-91; Gene M. Gressley, "The Turner Thesis—A Problem in Historiography," *Agricultural History* 32 (1958): 227-49.

that the really pressing problems of this new society had to do not with egalitarian democracy or individual opportunity per se, but with how to fashion new communities compatible with these ideals in a nascent capitalist society.

The problem of building new communities was on one level purely material. The eager efforts of the booster to promote colleges and railroads in the western town have become a celebrated part of the American past, but we know less of the countless thousands of failures and false prophecies in small towns and ghost towns than we do of the triumphs of big city boosters who, in a sense, wrote their own history. The problem of building new communities was social as well as economic. It involved the constant influx of uprooted newcomers, the clash of unfamiliar cultures, and the early difficulty of defining status and leadership in an unformed social structure. For community leaders and property-owners, the problems of social disorder were ultimately intertwined with the overriding concerns of promoting the town's economic future.

This book explores the problem of building new communities in the Old Northwest by focusing on the history of a single community, Jacksonville, Illinois, from its founding as the seat of Morgan County through 1870, when its struggle for urban prominence finally ended, with local boosters yielding to its fate as a small town. I have used the term "frontier" rather loosely to define that period when the first generation of town boosters fought to seize a leading place in an open, rapidly developing, and as yet unfixed region. Because a fundamental assumption of the case-study method is that the chosen community exemplifies broader patterns typical of communities within a given period, region, or some other category of size or age, this study of Jacksonville has been informed by research on other Illinois towns. However, I chose to focus exclusively on Jacksonville to bring out the rich texture and complexity of one locale whose history has been lovingly preserved by its citizens. The basic patterns of culture and social structure with which this study is concerned seemed sufficiently similar in the other towns to warrant the conclusion that, in fundamental ways, Jacksonville was typical of many new communities in Illinois.[6] Indeed, the very name "Jacksonville" suggests the kind of pretentious pseudonym, like "Middletown" or "Jonesville," that a social scientist might have given to a case study of community life in Jacksonian America. Jacksonville, I readily admit, was not America in microcosm (and I have resisted the facetious suggestion of a friend that the book be entitled "The Age of Jacksonville"). All communities have unique features that defy the term "typical," but this one did exemplify a large and important segment of community life in the nineteenth century.

First, Jacksonville was a new community that sprang from nothing to become a medium-sized city of close to 10,000 people by 1870. New communities popped up almost overnight in the nineteenth century, some in the East, but most in the developing regions of the West. In 1800 the census reported 33 "urban" places with at least 2,500 population. By the end of the century there were 1,737 urban places; three-fourths were under 10,000, and another 2,128 had at least 1,000 people.[7] Historians' growing interest in our urban past has rarely touched upon this central phenomenon of new towns in the nineteenth century; the older, well-established, large cities of the East and the successful metropolises of the West have usually occupied the center of attention. A standard theme in many of the recent studies in American urban history has been the impact of urbanization, industrialization, and immigration upon community traditions—the old order being slowly swallowed by the new.[8]

The study of new communities as arenas of social change offers special opportunities to examine the freshest expression of the values and institutions that gave shape to nineteenth-century community life. This does not mean that migration to

6. Two other Illinois towns, Vandalia and Galesburg, were originally part of my research project, but neither had records as rich or complete as Jacksonville's.

7. U.S. Census Bureau, *Historical Statistics of the United States from Colonial Times to the Present* (Washington, D.C., 1957), series A 181-94.

8. See, e.g., Stephan Thernstrom, *Poverty and Progress: Social Mobility in a Nineteenth-Century City* (Cambridge, Mass., 1964), and Michael H. Frisch, *Town into City: Springfield, Massachusetts, and the Meaning of Community, 1840-1880* (Cambridge, Mass., 1972).

the West suddenly released people from the burden of history to shape society anew. Rather, in new communities the dead weight of tradition and entrenched interests were less cumbersome, and here institutions and values could be molded to the new needs of a mobile, competitive society. At the same time, the unsettled nature of the new community, produced by the continual influx of newcomers and the clash of strangers, created a more acute need to define some form of social order as a prerequisite for growth and progress. No community, not even a utopian colony, could be completely new. Indeed, Jacksonville's early history saw strenuous efforts to transplant traditional institutions from the East and South. I overstate the importance of newness to argue a less ambitious point: that the struggle of new communities to define a social order reflected, perhaps in sharper form, a more general problem of social organization in a mobile, rapidly changing society that seemed constantly to create disorder.

Jacksonville was typical of most new towns in that it aspired to urban greatness with only moderate success. Despite frequent trumpeting about the need to study the lives of common people, urban historians have, with rare exceptions, focused on the history of the few cities that managed to make it toward the top of the urban hierarchy.[9] Yet for every Chicago, St. Louis, or even Springfield, there were hundreds of Jacksonvilles whose ambitions for urban prominence were betrayed by the conspiracies of nature, politics, and fate. Their failures were usually not for want of spirit. Local boosters struggled valiantly to make Jacksonville the educational capital of the state as the self-proclaimed "Athens of the West" (later modestly reduced to the "Athens of Illinois"). They also tried to win the state capital; they promoted railroads to tap the agricultural hinter-

9. Some important books that deal with smaller communities are: Lewis Atherton, *Main Street on the Middle Border* (Bloomington, Ind., 1954); Page Smith, *As a City upon a Hill: The Town in American History* (New York, 1966); Robert R. Dykstra, *The Cattle Towns* (New York, 1968); Herman R. Lantz, *A Community in Search of Itself: A Case History of Cairo, Illinois* (Carbondale, Ill., 1972). Stuart M. Blumin, *The Urban Threshold: Growth and Change in a Nineteenth-Century American Community* (Chicago, 1976), was published after my manuscript was completed, but it is a very perceptive analysis of the evolution of Kingston, N.Y., that complements most of the themes I discuss in Jacksonville.

land of central Illinois; they beat the drums for more manufacturing and commerce.

Boosterism provided powerful energy to a rising young town, but what happened when the prophecies of future greatness clearly failed? How did towns like Jacksonville justify their failures? In the end, the boosters retreated to nurture the image of a quiet, genteel midwestern town, the home of two small private colleges and a constellation of state charitable institutions. Jacksonville's apologists smugly pretended they had never wanted any other destiny.

Despite its compact size, Jacksonville was also a complex society made up of diverse cultural groups. Its location in central Illinois drew migratory streams from the upper South, the Middle Atlantic states, and New England, thereby producing sectional tensions that erupted repeatedly from the very beginning. The conflict between Yankees and Southerners probably did not have the overriding importance that post–Civil War local historians claimed, but it was sufficient to create real strains within the community, particularly in its early years. By the 1850s these sectional divisions were overshadowed by the sudden influx of Irish, German, and Portuguese immigrants, joined in the 1860s by a stream of southern blacks. Together these minorities comprised almost 40 percent of Jacksonville's population by 1870.

How did this struggling frontier community, with its mobile and heterogeneous population, hold together? How did it define some workable social order in an environment that seemed destined to spawn nothing but social disorder? Since Frederick Jackson Turner many historians have wrestled with these questions, and two fairly distinct schools of interpretation have emerged. The first, put forth in 1954 by Stanley Elkins and Eric McKitrick in their article "A Meaning for Turner's Frontier," was essentially Turnerian in its conclusions.[10] But Elkins and McKitrick discarded Turner's notion of frontier individualism and insisted the frontier experience was fundamentally a process of community-building. Borrowing a conceptual

10. Stanley Elkins and Eric McKitrick, "A Meaning for Turner's Frontier," *Political Science Quarterly* 69 (1954): 321-53, 565-602.

framework from Robert Merton's sociological study of World War II housing projects, and employing historical evidence from county histories and pioneer memoirs (including some from Jacksonville), Elkins and McKitrick describe the community-building process in the Old Northwest as a response to the challenges of the frontier. New communities were beset by a multitude of problems, ranging from the individual's needs for food and shelter to the collective struggle of nascent towns to gain a solid economic base. These very problems, confronted by a young, homogeneous population without an established structure of leadership, stimulated intensive cooperative interaction in politics and voluntary associations as the pioneers met the challenges of community-building collectively. Elkins and McKitrick's purpose was to reconfirm the essence of Turner's connection between the frontier experience and American democracy, but they did so by focusing on the central problem of town promotion, instead of emphasizing Turner's frontier primitivism. For Elkins and McKitrick, boosterism was the key mechanism for social integration in new communities; participative democracy and cooperation were a "brutal necessity" in ambitious western towns, not an abstract ideal. Boosterism created the crucial nexus between the individualism of frontier capitalism and the social bonds of community.

A similar interpretation of new western communities, one that is clearly indebted to Elkins and McKitrick, is found in Daniel Boorstin's *The Americans: The National Experience*.[11] The first half of Boorstin's sweeping survey of the nineteenth century deals with forms of community devised by a mobile, expansive people. Boorstin brings to his interpretation of the past a Tocquevillean view of America as an atomistic, formless, transient society, capable nonetheless of quickly adapting organizations to meet specific ends. He is fascinated with the paradox of individualism and mobility fitting into uniquely American forms of community. Boosterism plays a central role in Boorstin's interpretation of new communities, because it joins the interests of ambitious individuals to the collective interests

11. Daniel J. Boorstin, *The Americans: The National Experience* (Chicago, 1965), pp. 113-68.

of the upstart towns they promoted. Although Boorstin's town promoters float from one western city to the next, they throw themselves completely into the business of boosting their communities wherever they alight. Except for Sinclair Lewis, perhaps no one has captured the spirit of American boosterism better than Daniel Boorstin; or it may be that Boorstin is the one who has been captivated by the spirit of American boosterism. In either case, his felicitous style helped make this interpretation of the frontier experience as instant community the most popular view of the past.

Was every western migrant a booster? Did all own stock in the future of their community? Did all agree on what was progress for the town? Critics of the Elkins-McKitrick-Boorstin camp have answered these questions without the sanguine optimism the Turnerian tradition evokes. Allan Bogue's "Social Theory and the Pioneer," published in 1960, was a frontal assault on the Turnerian interpretation of frontier community-building.[12] Like the Elkins and McKitrick thesis, Bogue's analysis was informed by a number of modern case studies of new towns, many of them created during the New Deal. But from these studies Bogue extrapolated a very different model of pioneer communities. "In portraying communities reacting in unified fashion to common problems," Bogue wrote of Elkins and McKitrick, "these Neo-Turnerians may have paid too little attention to another element in social dynamics—the politics of conflict and community power structure." "Their theory of social behavior," he added, "is basically the Turnerian one of simple response to the opportunities and challenges of the physical and economic environment."

Instead of unity, collective problem-solving, and participative democracy, the studies reviewed by Bogue seemed to reveal a consistent pattern of volatile social conflict and instability, a characteristic which Bogue concluded was inherent in the ex-

12. Allan Bogue, "Social Theory and the Pioneer," *Agricultural History* 34 (1960): 21-34. Richard C. Wade, *The Urban Frontier: The Rise of Western Cities, 1790-1830* (Cambridge, Mass., 1959), also attacked the Turnerian approach by stressing the early presence of cities in the West and their rapid transfer of eastern urban ways. However, Wade did not share Bogue's premise that frontier settlements experienced special problems of social organization.

perience of building new communities. Migrants to the frontier, he theorized, came in order to improve their economic and social status, and they usually brought with them high expectations of success. Most pioneers were torn out of a familiar network of kinship and friendship. They often settled amid a population from diverse regional and national origins, each with different cultural values, which impeded the development of new group ties. The absence of any preconceived structure of political or social authority encouraged greater political participation, as Elkins and McKitrick had assumed. But Bogue concluded that this political activity more often took the form of fierce competition among potential leaders striving for unclaimed rewards in an open social and political structure, thus exacerbating the tendency toward conflict and instability. By stifling the emergence of a commonly agreed-upon structure of leadership to guide the community, this divisive competition perpetuated the unstable and contentious atmosphere of a new settlement where the institutional framework was already weak or absent. All of these tendencies toward conflict and instability were further aggravated by economic uncertainties, inherent in frontier community development, which often left the hopeful migrants disappointed.

Bogue's hypothetical model received empirical support in Robert Dykstra's *Cattle Towns*.[13] Dykstra was keenly aware of the theoretical framework through which he studied a group of Kansas towns, and in an appendix he directly confronted the Elkins-McKitrick thesis. One of the central themes of Dykstra's analysis was the incessant conflict that attended the decision-making process within these struggling frontier towns. One faction's cattle trade bonanza was another's invitation to a Sodom and Gomorrah of cowboy revelry. Not even the boosters' grand prophecies of riches and greatness were enough to unite the contentious citizens of Dykstra's cattle towns.

Bogue and Dykstra's theory of frontier society argues that the process of community building entailed real problems of conflict, problems that were more than mere stimuli for social harmony and collective progress. The absence of a well-defined

13. Dykstra, *The Cattle Towns*, pp. 355-78.

structure of leadership and the uncertain economic future of new towns aggravated the problem of social conflict, instead of surmounting it as Elkins and McKitrick argued. Dykstra does not go as far as Bogue in depicting anomic social disorder; rather, he sees the cattle town's citizens coalescing into competing factions, each defining its claim on the community's future. Still, the polarity between Elkins and McKitrick's instant community of expectant boosters and the contentious atmosphere of Bogue and Dykstra's frontier communities is clear enough. Bogue and Dykstra's theory touts the advantage of a test against empirical historical evidence in *The Cattle Towns*, whereas Elkins and McKitrick relied primarily on scattered accounts in local histories and pioneer memoirs which (as Dykstra shrewdly observes) were organs of boosterism intended to project false images of harmony and progress.

Though my debts to Elkins and McKitrick's analysis of boosterism will be evident to readers of this book, Bogue and Dykstra's model offers the more plausible framework for understanding the social behavior of new communities. I share their appreciation for the real problems of social discord that flared behind the boosters' rhetorical veil of unity and collective progress, and I have been especially sensitive to the unsettling forces of migration that kept Jacksonville's population churning. The constant movement of people through the community and the fact that so many met as strangers made social cohesion problematic at best. In Jacksonville the diversity of regional and ethnic cultures, social classes, religions, partisan loyalties, and personalized factions provided fuel for a multitude of conflict situations. The clash of sectional cultures was repeatedly aggravated by the politics of slavery and the Civil War. The tension between middle-class natives and the foreign born became a symbolic contest over prohibition. The competition of religious denominations manifested in several local schisms made Jacksonville, in the words of one disheartened observer, "a sea of sectarian rivalries." Finally, the fierce partisanship of nineteenth-century politics was all the more intense in Jacksonville because of its location in an important swing county.

Southerners caning Yankees, vigilante mobs chasing

abolitionists, Christians battling over the doctrine of infant baptism, police raiding Irish grog shops, angry citizens demonstrating for and against the Civil War—all evoke an image of this frontier town as a Hobbesian jungle of violent social discord. Yet I fear the stress on conflict and instability may exaggerate the impression that these new towns were overwhelmed by social disorder, obscuring the social organization that did crystallize quietly beneath all the tumult. The danger lies in a temptation to equate conflict with social disorganization, thereby implying that a normative model of the nineteenth-century community is one which is fully integrated, where all conflict was resolved through the legitimate process of politics and government. Dykstra warns against this temptation in *The Cattle Towns* by emphasizing that "social conflict was normal, it was inevitable, and it was a format for community decision making."

To elaborate on this point, we should consider some of the insights offered by students of contemporary social conflict. Sociologist Lewis Coser advises that, instead of viewing conflict as a disruptive event signifying disorganization, we should appreciate it as a positive process by which members of a community ally with one another, identify common values and interests, and organize to contest power with competing groups.[14] Different manifestations of social conflict should also be considered as measures of social organization. When Jacksonville's Colonel W. B. Warren publicly horsewhipped and caned a newspaper editor who had dishonored his family's name, he clearly perceived and expressed conflict in highly personalized terms. In contrast, the propensity to organize conflict through vigilance societies, political parties, or voluntary associations signified a more sophisticated form of conflict that integrated local society as it defined social boundaries. Furthermore, one line of conflict often had the effect of diminishing others. The influx of Irish and Germans into Jacksonville in the 1850s, for example, caused middle-class Southerners and Northerners to join in defense of their interests in temperance and law enforcement. Political, sectarian, sectional, and class cleavages all crossed the community at slightly different angles. The very

14. Lewis Coser, *The Social Functions of Conflict* (New York, 1954).

multiplicity of conflict, Coser tells us, has the effect of binding the community as long as "multiple lines of conflict cross one another and prevent basic cleavage along one axis." Across each of these social divisions angry words and bitter enmity might flow, but the forces pulled in so many directions that the very heterogeneity of the community could create a certain stability and cohesion.

More than countervailing forces were involved in Jacksonville's emerging social order. To understand this order, we must dissect the intertwining elements of cultural values and social structure. Culturally, the social order was enforced by the rhetoric of boosterism and local pride that placed high value on internal cohesion and sacrifice for the community's progress. Though it ostensibly appealed to a higher level of allegiance, nationalism was celebrated in ways that further reinforced the ideals of local unity and common purpose; it, too, helped check local sectional and ethnic divisiveness. The cultural basis of the social order was also apparent in the ethos of self-discipline, temperance, improvement, and respect for authority, values which were taught in a multitude of formal institutions, from public schools and churches to voluntary associations. All of these institutions served as training agencies that instilled social discipline and taught their pupils to control conflict, live by the rules, and defer to the authority of elected leaders.

The structural foundations of Jacksonville's social order appeared in the patterns of migration that tended to select residents according to their economic function and stage in the life cycle. These selective forces allowed many people to merely pass through the town, while others remained part of a stable core with deep roots in the community. Within this transient population the family, kinship, and the household unit also served as important bases of social organization.

The most important structural innovations in the social order of Jacksonville appeared in a multitude of formal institutions. Churches, political parties, and a whole series of lodges, reform societies, literary clubs, and other voluntary associations came to serve the special needs of a mobile, heterogeneous community. Together they comprised the essential framework of what I have called the voluntary community. This concept is similar in certain respects to sociologist Morris Janowitz's notion of a "community of limited liability."[15] Though he applies it to social arrangements in urban neighborhoods, Janowitz's model helps our understanding of the new form of community that emerged in the nineteenth century. As his felicitous metaphor implies, the community of limited liability allows its members to share common institutions and to promote common interests with only limited "social and psychological investment." It is not a community of "completely bureaucratized and impersonalized attachments"; nor is it a community with deep primordial bonds of kinship, neighborhood, or ethnicity as prerequisites for membership. The community of limited liability is at once more adaptable than the premodern community to accepting new "investors," and it allows easier withdrawal by transient and dissatisfied members. Joining and withdrawing from the community, or its institutions, is often a matter of the member's voluntary choice, decided according to individual goals of social mobility or other personal and family benefits; "his relation to the community is such—his investment is such—that when the community fails to serve his needs, he will withdraw."

In Jacksonville the individual choices to invest in the community and its institutions took place within certain well-defined barriers of ethnicity and class. Churches and voluntary associations served to help define individual status and demarcate social boundaries in a loosely structured young community. Still, within each ethnic segment of the community a set of institutions, similar in form and function to those of the dominant native American population, were quickly created to integrate the members of each subcommunity. The social bias that tended to exclude the lower classes from participation in some of the fraternal lodges and other voluntary associations had as much to do with the instrumental needs of different occupations and with the transient character of unskilled workers as it

15. Morris Janowitz, *The Community Press in an Urban Setting: The Social Elements of Urbanism*, 2nd ed. (Chicago, 1967), pp. 210-13; cf. Gerald D. Suttles, *The Social Construction of Communities* (Chicago, 1972), pp. 44-81.

did with any conscious decision to banish the lower classes from participation. Within these limits of ethnicity and class, the institutions of the voluntary community were open to those who chose to join them (with only a few exceptions among the elite lodges and literary societies). Political parties transcended the boundaries of class and ethnicity to serve as one of the broadest integrative institutions of the voluntary community.

Intermeshed with the community's structural framework of voluntary institutions were equally strong coercive mechanisms for social control. Most of the churches, lodges, and other voluntary associations enforced a rigorous code of personal discipline that proscribed sins ranging from intemperance to sexual immorality, quarreling with the brethren, and unethical business practices. Voluntarism ruled the individual's decision to join or leave these institutions, but as a member one was subject to the discipline of the fellowship. The functions of these churches, lodges, and other voluntary associations as moral police in the community contributed in no small way to the social order that took shape in Jacksonville. There were other institutions designed to extend a similar moral discipline to those who lived outside the sanctions of the church or voluntary association. Here the expansion of municipal government provided the control which town leaders sought to impose upon the community. The creation of public schools also became an important method of extending social control beyond the limits of voluntarism. The simultaneous enactment of prohibition and anti-vice ordinances, enforced by a new municipal police force, was the fullest expression of this effort to impose order and social discipline upon the whole community.

The repressive control of the small community over its members is a familiar theme in American culture. Page Smith's insightful survey of the town in American history traces this tendency to the covenanted community of Puritan New England. This tradition no doubt helped shape the migrant New Englanders' impression upon Jacksonville, but the ethos of temperance and social discipline was in no way the special property of the Yankees. Rather, the understanding and enforcement of this social discipline was defined by the conditions of nineteenth-century America: the rise of *laissez-faire* capitalism and the middle-class cult of social mobility; the renewed fervor of pietistic Protestantism; the surge of movement stemming from westward expansion, immigration, and rapid urbanization; and a new liberal faith in the capacity of properly engineered institutions to improve society and control the forces of disorder that seemed to threaten the community and nation.[16]

The social order that evolved in Jacksonville ultimately took shape in a series of contradictions. It exalted communal values of loyalty to Jacksonville and the Union; at the same time, each cultural minority within the town worked determinedly to mark off distinct social boundaries. It was a social order that allowed enormous turnover within the population; yet it maintained continuity through a set of formal institutions and a small core of stable residents. Its institutions affirmed the nineteenth-century faith in voluntarism, social mobility, and democracy while they imposed a strict regimen of collective discipline upon their members. A fervent ideological faith in *laissez-faire* capitalism and individual self-reliance guided the same citizens who tried to impose a communal standard of morality and personal behavior. These were only some of the contradictory elements that coexisted within the concept of community that molded nineteenth-century Jacksonville. In the end this community was neither the harmonious band of boosters depicted by the Turnerians, nor the disordered anarchy of strangers portrayed by their critics. In its paradoxical combinations of mobility and stability, voluntarism and collective discipline, Jacksonville's social order seemed to strike a workable compromise between the chaos of an expansive capitalist society and the enduring human need for community.

In the chapters that follow I have analyzed the interacting elements of the community's culture and social structure as both evolved over time. The arrangement of chapters is essentially thematic but within a chronological framework. "The Infant Community" begins with the founding of the town and the peculiar marriage of the boosters' interest in rising land values

16. Smith, *As a City upon a Hill.*

15

with the New England missionaries' dream of a spiritually enlightened and homogeneous West. "Unpeaceable Kingdom" explores some of the early sources of social conflict in this contentious young town. "The Booster Ethos" continues the story of the town's economic development up to the Civil War and discusses boosterism's function as an antidote to internal divisiveness and as a partial solution to the problem of community. The limits to this solution are revealed in "Citizens and Strangers," which shows how only a small core of the community were stable citizens who lived amid a constant stream of transients. Both groups moved, or stayed, in response to the unspoken logic of individual opportunity, the tempo of the local economy, and the cycle of life. And both groups organized their lives around the institutions of family, kinship, and household.

From the fifth chapter onward the book deals primarily with the period after 1850, when a number of forces converged to shape Jacksonville's new social order. One of those forces was the influx of foreign immigrants and blacks. "The Boundaries of Culture" describes the social boundaries that demarcated these ethnic groups, along with regional cultures already coexisting in Jacksonville. The seventh chapter applies the concept of "The Voluntary Community" to three types of institutions: church, political party, and voluntary association. It describes how these institutions were designed to integrate and order a transient community, and how they enforced the values of social discipline in their members. "Moral Government" explores what we might call the "coercive community," dealing with the expansion of public authority over private behavior, and with the growing faith in the institution of government to invest order in the physical and moral environment. Fire control, street paving, public schools, and prohibition were all different expressions of this shift in the uses of local government. Also examined are the social backgrounds of the men who guided the expansion of public authority in the municipal government. The concluding chapter, "Localism as Nationalism," takes Jacksonville through the Civil War and probes the uses of nationalism as a source of local cohesion. It also covers the last desperate efforts of Jacksonville's boosters to rescue their community from its fate as a small town, and closes with a discussion of how boosterism was inverted into a local history tradition that justified that fate.

The Infant Community

The conflict which is to decide the destiny of the
West, will be a conflict of institutions. . . .
—LYMAN BEECHER[1]

AMONG THOSE ACTUALLY involved in building the new towns
of the nineteenth century, the problem of community was
understood in economic and moral terms, and both were faced
with a remarkable sense of optimism. Amid an unformed wilderness, the boosters of each ambitious hamlet prophesied the
beginnings of a great metropolis—if only enough capital, political manipulation, and human spirit could be brought to bear.
Though not oblivious to the dictates of geography and natural
resources, these town-builders implicitly rejected theories about
the natural evolution of cities, instead promoting their towns as
aggressive competitors within a booming western marketplace.

Those who saw themselves as responsible for the moral environment of new communities likewise interpreted the problem
as one requiring the quick construction of a proper set of
institutions. Though not altogether unburdened of their ancestors' obsession with original sin and divine authority, the
community-builders of the nineteenth century placed far more
responsibility on human institutions and ideas to mold the
moral environment. These goals of economic prosperity and
social morality were seen as inseparable, if not always compatible. This chapter will demonstrate how, in the very early years
of the town's history, the booster's speculative dream of urban

1. Lyman Beecher, *A Plea for the West*, 2nd ed. (New York, 1835), pp. 11-12.

18

success was married to the reformer's zealous plan to uplift and enlighten the West. In subsequent chapters the tension between the goals of growth and moral order will reveal itself as a recurring theme in the problem of constructing new communities.

BEGINNINGS

The new understanding of community as the deliberate product of human will was implicit in the very founding of Jacksonville as it was staked out by surveyors in the midst of a sparsely settled wilderness. Central Illinois began attracting settlers soon after Illinois became a state in 1818. The population grew as the threat of hostile Indians receded northward and as the strange, treeless prairie proved its abundant fertility.[2] Soon after the creation of Morgan County in 1823, local politicians began coalescing into factions to contest which of two or three nascent settlements along the Illinois River would become the new county seat. A long squabble finally ended when the county commissioners decided the only fair compromise would be to plant a new town in the center of the county and make that the county seat.

A site for the proposed town was approved in the winter of 1825. The government land upon which the county seat was to be platted was sold at auction, and two nearby settlers were quick to recognize a wise investment. They bought eighty acres at $1.25 per acre and shrewdly donated half their purchase to the county. With this inducement the county quickly platted the town on the eighty-acre site.[3]

The only criterion for the location of the town was that it be in the center of the county. The Mauvaise Terre River, just east of the town site, wound its way to the Illinois River twenty miles

2. Arthur C. Bogess, *The Settlement of Illinois, 1778-1830* (Chicago, 1908); Solon J. Buck, *Illinois in 1818*, 2nd ed. (Urbana, 1967), pp. 61-117; Theodore Calvin Pease, *The Frontier State, 1818-1848*, The Centennial History of Illinois, vol. 2 (Chicago, 1922), pp. 1-32; George Flower, *History of the English Settlement in Edwards County, Illinois* (Chicago, 1909).

3. Donnelley, Loyd & Co., *History of Morgan County, Illinois: Its Past and Present* (Chicago, 1878), pp. 334-35; John C. W. Baily, comp., *Sangamon County Gazetteer . . . with City Directories of Springfield and Jacksonville . . .* (Springfield, 1866), p. 320.

to the west, but not even the most hopeful booster could have imagined that this shallow, muddy stream could be made navigable. So there, stranded in the center of a sparsely settled wilderness, a town was platted. The plan, which was laid out in a standard grid pattern around a public square, could have been borrowed from any of a hundred similar towns in the South or Midwest. In the square would be the county courthouse. Main Street bisected the town on the north-south axis, while State Street divided it along the east-west median. The original plan provided sixty square blocks surrounding the central square, each with uniform lots that could be surveyed and transferred with minimal complication in what the town's early promoters hoped would be a booming real estate market. Later many of the minor streets would be renamed in honor of illustrious citizens who marked the town's early history. But at this point it was a town without citizens, prominent or otherwise. Street names like State and Main lent a certain air of dignity and promise to the town, while its name, Jacksonville, paid homage to the immensely popular "Hero of New Orleans."[4]

Despite the commonplace, utilitarian grid plan, the site itself was fortuitously an attractive one. The square rested on a gently rising knoll just northeast of Diamond Grove, an abundant forest of oak and walnut. A small brook flowed south of the square into the Mauvaise Terre. Rising to the west of the square was a thickly wooded hill from which the town's anxious promoters could look out upon the undulating prairies as they began to thicken with settlers.

Jacksonville grew slowly as a few hopeful businessmen established stores and taverns to serve the surrounding rural population and to profit from the flow of people who came to the county seat each Saturday to pay taxes, attend a hearing, trade, or socialize with distant neighbors and join with them in politicking, horse racing, wrestling, and, eventually, drinking whiskey. Among the town's first business establishments were three taverns; they enjoyed a thriving trade, serving food and drink

4. William F. Short, ed., *Historical Encyclopedia of Illinois . . . Morgan County* (Chicago, 1906), pp. 679-80; Donnelley, *History of Morgan*, p. 335; John W. Reps, *Town Planning in Frontier America* (Princeton, 1969), p. 427.

and providing lodging to visitors in crude log buildings clustered around the public square. George Hackett and J. M. Fairfield, both former peddlers in Morgan, established the first general store. There clothing, tools, seed, and other provisions could be bought—or, more often, bartered for furs, beeswax, honey, and produce. A log meetinghouse was erected by 1826 to house a subscription school and newly formed congregations of Methodists and Presbyterians. All the early buildings were made of logs, with rough puncheon floors and stick chimneys. Later a row of small frame structures went up on the west side of the square to house a variety of stores and offices for Jacksonville's growing legion of frontier lawyers as they flocked to the county seat.[5]

As news of Morgan County's rich soil spread, the land swarmed with new settlers. The main flow still came from the south, but an increasing number began to arrive from the northeast. Between the state census of 1825 and the federal census of 1830 the county population more than tripled, from a little over 4,000 to nearly 13,000. Jacksonville grew from a handful of families to 446 people.[6]

This was an encouraging rate of growth, but hardly enough to satisfy the expectations of local promoters. Those who owned a stake in Jacksonville's future were anxious that their town move quickly to outdistance its rivals, particularly Springfield, thirty-odd miles to the east. Within two years of the town's founding several local boosters fixed upon a plan to bring a "seminary of learning" to Jacksonville. Here was an institution that would both uplift the moral and intellectual environment of the crude frontier community and enhance the material prospects of the town by drawing tuition, philanthropy, and "respectable citizens" eager to educate their children. All of these would help inflate land values, which, in turn, would improve the personal fortunes of the seminary's promoters.[7]

The need for education in frontier Illinois had been dis-

5. Donnelley, *History of Morgan*, pp. 335-38, 350.
6. *Western Observer*, July 17, Oct. 9, 1830; Mar. 19, 1831. (Unless stated otherwise, all newspapers cited were published in Jacksonville.)
7. Louis B. Wright, *Culture on the Moving Frontier* (Bloomington, Ind., 1955), pp. 81-122, 223-24.

cussed publicly for some time. New Englanders were especially sensitive to this issue, though men of wealth and standing throughout the state shared their concern. Since the fall of 1825 a Yankee agent for the American Home Missionary Society, John M. Ellis, had been trying to channel this interest in education into a movement for a seminary in the West. Because many saw in Ellis a lucrative avenue to eastern charity, he found himself being wooed by the advocates of several competing towns who understood both the moral and material advantages of an educational institution.[8]

Ellis and his committee, appointed by the Missouri Presbytery, arrived in Jacksonville in January, 1828. They were entertained by eager boosters as though they were visiting royalty. A group of prominent property-owners in Jacksonville promised Ellis that local residents would offer not only enthusiasm for the proposed seminary but, more important, ample subscription funds, if only their town were selected. Ellis was pleased with Jacksonville's attractive physical setting as well as with the interest and support of its citizens. His hosts took him out to the hill overlooking the town from the west. There, as he gazed out on the crude beginnings of Jacksonville and the rich farmland surrounding the town, Ellis was impressed both with the view and with his hosts' promise that the site would be given to the proposed seminary if Jacksonville were chosen.[9]

Ellis's committee went on to visit Springfield but found it could "furnish no parallel." Afterwards the group returned to "the charming hills" of Jacksonville and declared their decision to begin the seminary there. Here Ellis exceeded the authority delegated to him by the Missouri Presbytery, and by doing so he lost both official approval and financial support which the new seminary would desperately need. Jacksonville's champions quickly reassured Ellis that strong local support would pour forth. When Ellis canvassed Morgan County for subscription funds in the spring of 1828, the response was indeed encourag-

8. David Dimond, "Memoir of Rev. John M. Ellis," *The Presbytery Reporter* 5 (1859): 637-51; Charles Henry Rammelkamp, *Illinois College: A Centennial History, 1829-1929* (New Haven, 1928), pp. 1-9.

9. Rammelkamp, *Illinois College*, p. 9-14, 44; William Coffin, *Life and Times of Hon. Samuel D. Lockwood* (Chicago, 1889), pp. 120-27.

ing; local residents had pledged a total of nearly $2,000 and two tracts of land. But most of the pledges were gifts of books, labor, supplies, and produce; less than $800 was promised in cash. The rudimentary economy of Illinois was at this point based largely on subsistence farming, and it generated very little capital. To build a seminary for higher learning, Jacksonville would have to appeal to eastern charity for financial support. When the proposed seminary's new board of trustees met in November, 1828, they made plans to proceed with the construction of a large, two-story brick building as a demonstration of their commitment to open the institution. At the same time they authorized a representative to go east and appeal to the philanthropy of "friends of science and religion," whose generosity they were now counting on to help fill their proposed building with teachers, students, and books.[10]

THE NEW ENGLAND MISSION

Already Jacksonville's pleas for eastern charity had found a friendly audience among a group of earnest young Yale graduates. After reading an article in the *Home Missionary* describing Ellis's plans for a seminary in Illinois, they quickly wrote to tell him of their resolve to enter missionary activity in the West; they even offered their services in behalf of the seminary, on the condition that they would control its development. After conferring with the trustees, Ellis welcomed the "cooperation of the friends at the East" and promised them "all the control of the institution they could desire if they would furnish the funds."[11] The "Yale Band," as they came to be known, accepted Ellis's invitation and prepared for their mission in the West. Organized formally as "the Illinois Association," they signed a written compact which stated their concern for the salvation of the Western pioneers in piously solemn terms:

> Deeply impressed . . . with the destitute condition of the western section of our country and the urgent claims of its inhabitants

10. Coffin, *Lockwood*, p. 127; Rammelkamp, *Illinois College*, pp. 14-17.
11. Rammelkamp, *Illinois College*, pp. 21-23.

upon the benevolent of the East, and in view of the fearful crisis evidently approaching, and which we believe can only be averted by speedy and energetic measures on the part of friends of religion and literature in the older states, and believing that evangelical religion and education must go hand in hand . . . [we] hereby express our readiness to go to the State of Illinois for the purpose of establishing a seminary of learning. . . .[12]

The Yale Band brought the seminary $10,000 in donations from New Englanders who shared their sense of an urgent mission in the West. More money subsequently came from the East through agencies like the American Home Missionary Society and the Society for Promotion of Education in the West.

The missionary fervor that persuaded the Yale Band to dedicate their lives as missionaries in the West and prompted thousands of donations from the purses of Easterners was just one manifestation of a general revival of evangelical religious enthusiasm that flowed into a broad movement to reform all aspects of antebellum America. This energy, emanating primarily from New England, gave life to Jacksonville's seminary and in many ways shaped the community itself.

For the zealous young members of the Yale Band and those who joined them in Jacksonville, a mission in the West was at least in part a personal solution to several dismal career alternatives. Most of these men came from declining rural towns of New England. To go to Yale they had left behind dwindling inheritances and poor, rocky farms. After graduation most went on to a theological seminary (at either Yale or Andover) to fulfill callings to the ministry, a profession that expanded rapidly with the revivals of the "Second Great Awakening" in the 1820s. But by the end of that decade the New England clergy faced what historian Daniel Calhoun has described as a crisis of oversupply. The number of educated clergy simply outstripped demand by 1830; this was especially true among

12. Ibid., pp. 23-24. Two recent dissertations deal with the New England mission in Jacksonville and the West: Daniel Thomas Johnson, "Puritan Power in Illinois Higher Education prior to 1870" (Ph.D. dissertation, University of Wisconsin, 1974); Travis Keene Hedrick, "Julian Monson Sturtevant and the Moral Machinery of Society: The New England Struggle against Pluralism in the Old Northwest, 1829-1877" (Ph.D. dissertation, Brown University, 1974).

Congregationalists, who were losing ground to the Baptists and Methodists across New England. For many young ministers, like those who joined the Yale Band, the solution lay in migration to the West, either to new pulpits or, more frequently, into new ministerial roles administering a whole range of new church-related institutions, from western seminaries to national benevolent societies.[13]

Missionary work in the West not only absorbed the oversupply of clergy; in addition, it gave expression to a deepening fear of social and moral disorder which clergymen warned was threatening American society from the West. By the time the Yale Band started out for Jacksonville, New England clergymen and other reformers were depicting the West as a symbol of social chaos—an idea that harked back to the Puritan's notion of the covenanted community threatened by the savage wilderness that surrounded it. Proof of western social disorder was supplied in abundance by traveling Easterners, who returned to civilization to publish accounts filled with scenes of a society gone awry.[14]

Most eastern visitors complained about the crudeness of western manners, but the lack of refinement was only the outward manifestation of what the Yankee missionaries perceived as deeper, more serious flaws in western society. What bothered them especially was the weakness of fundamental social institutions (the family, church, school, civil government, and community itself), all of which, in their view, instilled order and cohesiveness in New England life. Moreover, these very weak-

13. Biographical sources on the Yale Band and their associates include the following: *Julian M. Sturtevant: An Autobiography*, ed. J. M. Sturtevant, Jr. (New York, 1896); George Frederick Magoun, *Asa Turner: A Home Missionary Patriarch and His Times* (Boston, 1889); Julian M. Sturtevant, *The Memory of the Just: A Sermon Commemorative of the Life and Labors of the Rev. William Kirby* . . . (New York, 1852); Julian M. Sturtevant, *Sketch of Theron Baldwin* (Boston, 1875); Mary Turner Carriel, *The Life of Jonathan Baldwin Turner* (1911; reprinted, Urbana, 1961); Truman Augustus Post, *Truman Marcellus Post: A Biography Personal and Literary* (Boston, 1891). See also Daniel Hovey Calhoun, *Professional Lives in America: Structure and Aspirations, 1750-1850* (Cambridge, 1965), pp. 149-50; Edwin S. Gaustad, *Historical Atlas of Religion in America* (New York, 1962), pp. 43, 168.

14. Rush Welter, "The Frontier West as Image of American Society: Conservative Attitudes before the Civil War," *Mississippi Valley Historical Review* 46 (1960): 604.

nesses rendered the few enlightened leaders of the West incapable of reforming their own society from within, since, as Lyman Beecher lamented, "no homogeneous public sentiment can be formed to legislate into being the requisite institutions."[15]

These same institutional foundations may have been suffering in New England communities, but there was little mention of this in the missionary literature. On the contrary, missionaries now called upon New England society, by virtue of its superior moral order and strong educational institutions, to lead the mission to save the West from chaos. The disorder of the western wilderness that once was seen as a threat to the internal cohesiveness and exclusiveness of New England, now came to be understood as a challenge that urgently called upon New England to extend the strength of its moral vision and its institutions—in short, to mold the West in its own image.[16]

The immediacy of this call was emphasized repeatedly and was explained through two lines of argument. The first built upon the metaphor of the family, warning of the need for careful parental nurturing of the "infant" West during its impressionable years. According to a circular requesting donations to the seminary in Jacksonville, "The claims of the new states upon the old are the claims of children upon their parents. They are sensible of their need, and now ask for aid. Let parental sympathy extend to them the means for education, and you secure their gratitude and affections forever— withhold these means and the children grow up in ignorance and alienation, and forget the institutions of their fathers, and cease to venerate their character and to cultivate their virtues."[17] This idea complemented new theories of child nurture by stressing that, given the proper institutional guidance and moral support in its formative years, western society would mature into a self-reliant entity. The West's need for eastern support, it followed, was only temporary, and the emphasis

15. Beecher, *Plea for the West*, pp. 15-16.

16. Welter, "Frontier West," pp. 593-614; James M. Banner, Jr., *To the Hartford Convention: The Federalists and the Origins of Party Politics in Massachusetts, 1789-1815* (New York, 1970), pp. 84-89, 110-12.

17. Untitled circular for donations to Illinois College [1829?], in Sturtevant-Baldwin Letters, Tanner Library, Illinois College.

was upon creating the proper institutional foundations, schools in particular, which thereafter would produce teachers and ministers native to the West.[18] As with children, it was extremely important to instill the necessary moral strength early if the West was to survive alone.

The missionaries warned those in the East that their beneficial influence could not wait. Just as they optimistically assumed that the West would be easily shaped by the correct institutional molds, so it could be irreparably harmed if neglected in its early years. "What is done must be done quickly," urged Lyman Beecher in his famous *Plea for the West*, "for population will not wait and commerce will not cast anchor, and manufacturers will not shut off steam nor shut down the gate, and agriculture, pushed by millions of freemen on their fertile soil, will not withhold her corrupting abundance. We must educate!" "It should be cultivated *now*," wrote an Illinoisan of the need for education, "while our communities are young and plastic, and while a direction may easily be given to the public mind."[19]

A second line of argument implied a more aggressive threat to the West and to the American republic itself. The New England missionaries pointed ominously to a European Catholic conspiracy led by "despotic" "papist" monarchs in league with the Vatican, who aimed at darkening "the light of our republican prosperity."[20] The flood of Catholic immigrants coming mostly from Ireland helped the Catholic church become the largest one in America by the mid-nineteenth century. Most of these immigrants arrived after 1840, and they concentrated in the northeastern cities. Nevertheless, the home missionaries argued that the "Romish plot" was intended to undermine the American republic at her weakest, most vulnerable point—the chaotic West. The absence of cohesive social order and religion in the West was regrettable in itself, but in face of the highly organized, international conspiracy led by "profes-

18. Ibid.; Beecher, *Plea for the West*, p. 39. See Bernard Wishy, *The Child and the Republic: The Dawn of Modern American Child Nurture* (Philadelphia, 1968).

19. Beecher, *Plea for the West*, p. 31; *Illinois Monthly Magazine* 1 (1830): 2.

20. Beecher, *Plea for the West*, p. 53; cf. Charles I. Foster, *An Errand of Mercy: The Evangelical United Front, 1790-1837* (Chapel Hill, N.C., 1960), p. 207.

sional" Catholic priests and educators, these western flaws imperiled the republic. "The West," Lyman Beecher warned, "is destined to be the great central power of the nation, and under heaven, must affect powerfully the cause of free institutions and the liberty of the world." "It is equally clear," he continued, "that the conflict which is to decide the destiny of the West, will be a conflict of institutions for the education of her sons, for purposes of superstition, or evangelical light, of despotism, or liberty."[21]

These New England missionaries feared and despised the monolithic "absolutism" of the Catholic Church, but they were not rushing West to defend its opposite, the Jacksonian ideal of unfettered individualism. On the contrary, these men saw in the emerging cult of individualism and economic acquisitiveness the ruin of traditional communal values. If the Catholic church and *laissez-faire* capitalism represented two organizational models—one international, hierarchial, and "absolutist," the other atomistic and unrestrained—the New England missionaries sought to defend a middle way in the form of a cohesive, voluntary, autonomous community.[22]

There were some attempts to transport a New England community model to the West; indeed, some twenty-eight Yankee "colonies" were established in Illinois in the 1830s alone. Gathered from the declining rural villages of New England and upstate New York, the colonists were transplanted as cohesive units into the Illinois wilderness, following a pattern reminis-

21. Beecher, *Plea for the West*, pp. 11-12, 187-88; Ray Allen Billington, *The Protestant Crusade, 1800-1860* (New York, 1938). Editor James G. Edward devoted much space in Jacksonville's first newspaper, the *Western Observer* (1830-31), to denouncing the "Romish plot" in the West.

22. Robert Merideth, *The Politics of the Universe: Edward Beecher, Abolition and Orthodoxy* (Nashville, 1968), pp. 73-125; David Tyack, "The Kingdom of God and the Common School: Protestant Ministers and the Educational Awakening in the West," *Harvard Educational Review* 36 (1966): 447-69; David Brion Davis, "Some Themes of Counter-Subversion: An Analysis of Anti-Masonic, Anti-Catholic, and Anti-Mormon Literature," *Mississippi Valley Historical Review* 47 (1960): 205-24. Davis argues that the fear of conspiracy was a paranoid reaction in defense of the "dominant values" of "Jacksonian democracy and the cult of the common man" (p. 208). The missionaries certainly saw the Catholic "plot" as a threat to the American Republic, but they also believed that the unfettered individualism of the age made the nation, particularly the West, vulnerable to subversion.

cent of their Puritan ancestors.[23] Southern migrants already in Illinois criticized what they saw as the snobbish exclusiveness of these Yankee colonies, but one defender of the New England experiment pointed to the dangers of unplanned frontier communities:

> We have seen a family remove to our new States, and take up their abode among neighbors collected from every quarter of the world, of every sect in religion, and every grade of mental and moral cultivation, agreeing, in short, neither in opinions, manners, nor feelings; with no common bond, no common standard of character, duty, or interest. In consequence of this discordance of views, sentiments, and habits, no united and effective efforts are used to establish those religious and literary institutions which are so important to the well being of society.

The transplanted community, he then argued, avoided these difficulties: "Now a compact body of people settling as a colonized community . . . have at once a school, a church, etc. in which they cordially unite. This society is a model to the country round. . . . And then, after the difficulties of founding and perfecting their own community are overcome, they naturally proceed to aid in the improvement of their less privileged and advanced neighbors."[24]

What these Yankee colonists were proposing was a frontier version of the Puritan "city upon a hill." It would be an "organic community," a homogeneous, stable, miniature society with its own church and school that embodied the community's collective values. This model of society would have been difficult enough to apply to New England in the nineteenth century; in frontier Illinois, with its diverse, mobile population, it was an impossible dream.

If stable social institutions required as their prerequisite a homogeneous, orderly community, then the West was destined to drift in chaos. But the New England missionaries now ex-

23. Hermann R. Muelder, *Fighters for Freedom: The History of Anti-Slavery Activities of Men and Women Associated with Knox College* (New York, 1959), p. 109; Page Smith, *As a City upon a Hill: The Town in American History* (New York, 1966); Lois K. Mathews, *The Expansion of New England* (Boston, 1909); Steward H. Holbrook, *The Yankee Exodus: An Account of Migration from New England* (New York, 1950).

24. *Illinois Monthly Magazine* 2 (1831): 112-14.

plained their purpose in the West by neatly turning this relationship around. If churches, schools, and the basic institutions of
social discipline could not spring naturally from coherent communities, then these very institutions would be imposed from
without to *create* the needed social homogeneity and order.
Social institutions, now conceived as autonomous, transportable
entities independent of the organic community, would be exported from New England, where they thrived in abundance, to
the West, which was unable to spontaneously generate strong
institutions. It was as though the proper building, prefabricated
in the East, would somehow create its own strong foundation.
With this new understanding of the role of formal social institutions as molders of social order came a whole new era of institutional reform that touched not only Jacksonville but also nearly
every part of nineteenth-century American life.[25]

For missionaries like the Yale Band, the central focus came to
rest upon the school as a major agent of social reform. This
nicely complemented the notion that the Northeast had a parental duty to educate the "infant" West. Though efforts were
made to instill morality and enlightenment in the adult population through voluntary reform associations, the logic of the
familial metaphor argued that the necessary moral values and
cultural homogeneity required for proper social order in the
West must be created in children. This would require the intervention of the school and college, along with religious influence,
to provide for the child an environment which the indigenous
family and social institutions in the West could not supply
alone.[26]

The school could also reach the public across denominational barriers that limited the range of reform through the
church. To the extent that school reformers succeeded in
identifying their cause with secular values of enlightened
democracy and individual economic opportunity, the school
would enjoy even broader appeal in the West. In Illinois the

25. See David J. Rothman, *The Discovery of the Asylum: Social Order and Disorder in
the New Republic* (Boston, 1970), for a discussion of similar logic which underlay the
development of asylums in Jacksonian America.
26. Tyack, "Common School," p. 469.

reformers urged that a system of public common schools, open to children of all classes, should be established to serve as the primary agent of mass education. Colleges and seminaries would be introduced by the churches, with support from eastern charity. An ingenious plan for student self-support would also open these institutions to worthy students of all classes. The "manual labor system" adopted by Jacksonville's new college involved a workshop and nearby farmland; there the students worked a few hours each day "for the promotion of health, and for the purpose of bringing the benefits of the institution within the reach of numerous youth of promise to whom, otherwise, it would be inaccessible." Colleges or seminaries were tied into the scheme for mass education by serving as institutions to train teachers (and ministers) who were natives of the West. "Our hope for the success of Foreign Missions," explained a circular for the seminary at Jacksonville, "depends on the schools that are raising up native teachers and native preachers for the work. It must be so at the West if we would preserve our institutions."[27]

Unfortunately, as the Yale Band was shocked to discover, many western parents were openly hostile toward the intrusion of "meddling Yankees" into what they considered the sovereign realm of the family.[28] But this hostility was, after all, what the Yankee missionaries had gone West to overcome, and it was all the more reason for them to push for the early establishment of schools in Illinois. As Julian Sturtevant, one of the Yale Band, explained: "There are portions of our country—it would perhaps be invidious to name them—where the founding of colleges in their infancy was neglected. Some of them are communities not wanting in wealth, general intelligence, active enterprise, and even religious principles." But, he went on, "the ideas—the felt wants, which created that Institution [Amherst

27. Untitled circular for donations to Illinois College [1829?], in Sturtevant-Baldwin Letters.

28. Rammelkamp, *Illinois College*, pp. 116, 201; Paul E. Belting, "The Development of the Free Public High School in Illinois to 1860," *Journal of the Illinois State Historical Society* (hereafter *JISHS*) 11 (1918): 269-369; Donald F. Tingley, "Anti-Intellectualism on the Illinois Frontier," in *Essays in Illinois History in Honor of Glenn Huron Seymour*, ed. Donald F. Tingley (Carbondale, Ill., 1968), pp. 3-17.

College] are not there, and the best time for generating them is past long since."[29] Sturtevant was referring to the South, citing that region's example as one his fellow Yankees would work hard to avoid in Illinois.

"ATHENS OF THE WEST"

The Yale Band hastened to Jacksonville with a keen sense of the New England mission. The small brick building which was to house the seminary had not even been finished when Julian Sturtevant began instructing nine students in January, 1830. At the first meeting he and his students helped the carpenters put up a stove to warm the classroom from the winter cold which seeped through the yet unplastered walls. The Yale Band wasted no time in pursuing their errand in the Illinois wilderness.[30]

Below College Hill lay the rude frontier village of Jacksonville, separated from the campus by open fields and farms with only a muddy trail connecting them. Some townspeople may have felt skepticism or even hostility toward the Yale Band's "moral edifice" on College Hill, but most could also see the college as a material asset to the town's growth. The whole county enjoyed a boom which continued through the early 1830s, bringing the population from 13,000 in 1830 to 25,000 within four years, according to one estimate. "Morgan County," J. M. Peck's *Gazetteer* of 1834 predicted, "is destined to become one of the richest agricultural counties in the state. . . . Emigration in a few fleeting years, has changed a region that we have seen in all the wildness of uncultivated nature, into smiling villages and luxuriant fields, and rendered it the happy abode of intelligence and virtue."[31]

Jacksonville had more reason to smile than most villages in Illinois, given its prime location in a booming agricultural

29. Julian M. Sturtevant, *An Address in Behalf of the Society for the Promotion of Collegiate and Theological Education at the West* (New York, 1853), p. 10.

30. Rammelkamp, *Illinois College*, pp. 21, 39, 41-49, 64-65; Merideth, *Politics*, pp. 73-79; Sturtevant, *Autobiography*, p. 178.

31. John M. Peck, *A Gazetteer of Illinois . . .* (Jacksonville, 1834), p. 148; *Western Observer*, June 26, Oct. 9, 1830.

county and the cherished prize of Illinois College. "Few towns have risen so rapidly as Jacksonville," wrote John Ellis in 1829. "About a dozen frame buildings finished in good style have gone up the last year. I have not counted the temporary buildings going up daily almost."[32] Indeed, the population growth was outstripping the construction of new dwellings, and the town's first newspaper editor lamented the overcrowded conditions in 1830. Capital was still in short supply, and much of it was invested in high-interest loans to new farmers, rather than in improvements for the town.[33] Truman Post, who came to Jacksonville in the summer of 1833, was also struck by the crowded conditions. "I found it a huddle of log cabins clustered around a public square where [there] was a rude courthouse in a rectangle of mud and dirt. The village contained about 3,000 inhabitants [an overestimate] crowded into these cabins, where each apartment, often quite narrow, had frequently to suffice for the accommodation of an entire separate household."[34]

William Cullen Bryant was more concerned about the aesthetics of Jacksonville than with its growing pains. "It is a horridly ugly village," he observed during his visit in 1832, "composed of little shops and dwellings stuck close together around a dingy square, in the middle of which stands the ugliest of possible brick courthouses, with a spire and weathercock on its top."[35] Fortunately, comments like this did not often find their way into print. Besides, the claims of Jacksonville's boosters rested not on what the "ugly village" actually was, but on what its future promised. In the early 1830s, when the boosters began dubbing the town the "Athens of the West" (or the "Western New Haven," as the proud Yale alumni who taught on College Hill would have it), they referred to Jacksonville's obvious potential as a major educational and cultural center in a frontier society full of promise.

32. Quoted in Franklin D. Scott, ed., "Minutes of the Session of the First Presbyterian Church in Morgan County, 1827-1830," *JISHS* 18 (1925): 150n.
33. *Western Observer*, Oct. 23, 1830. The housing shortage was also exacerbated by the severe shortage of skilled artisans to build dwellings; see Rammelkamp, *Illinois College*, p. 41.
34. Post, *Post*, p. 49.
35. Quoted in Frank J. Heinl, "The Bryants at Jacksonville," *JISHS* 18 (1925): 218.

That potential was soon reinforced by a number of supportive institutions and enterprises. The Jacksonville Female Academy opened in 1833 as an adjunct to Illinois College, and local women also founded a "Ladies' Association for Educating Females" to raise funds for the support of needy women seeking education.[36] The community soon spawned a whole host of literary and reform societies, including a lyceum and branches of the American Tract Society, American Temperance Society, American Education Society, and American Colonization Society—all hallmarks of an "enlightened community," as its boosters proclaimed tirelessly. In addition, there were five thriving churches, two newspapers, and a nascent publishing industry.[37]

Jacksonville's dubious status as the "Athens of the West" would certainly have to rest upon more than these struggling institutions. Real fulfillment of this claim would depend a great deal on external events (the creation of a public-supported common school system, in particular) if Illinois College and its adjunct institutions were going to serve genuine statewide needs. A public common school system would supply trained students for the college and help instill the proper respect for education in the people; equally important, it would create an enormous demand for trained teachers which Illinois College was, of course, eager to fill.[38] Jacksonville's editors and politicians actively campaigned in behalf of a public system of common schools, but they met with strong resistance. Morgan County's representative, Joseph Duncan, passed a Free School Act through the state legislature in 1825, but it was immediately

---

36. *Semi-Centennial and Anniversary Exercises of the Jacksonville Female Academy* (Jacksonville, 1880); Donnelley, *History of Morgan*, p. 387; *The Sixth Annual Report of the Ladies' Association for Educating Females* (Jacksonville, 1839); Margaret King Moore, "The Ladies' Association for Educating Females 1833-1837," *JISHS* 31 (1938): 166-87; Rammelkamp, *Illinois College*, p. 74.

37. *Western Observer*, June 12, Sept. 11, 1830; Feb. 26, Mar. 12, 1831; Oct. 27, 1832; *Sangamon Journal* (Springfield), Dec. 8, 1831; *Gazette and News*, Feb. 4, 1836; Frank J. Heinl, "Jacksonville and Morgan County, An Historical Review," *JISHS* 18 (1925): 8-9, 23; Heinl, "Newspapers and Periodicals in the Lincoln-Douglas Country, 1831-1832," *JISHS* 23 (1930): 371-438.

38. Rammelkamp, *Illinois College*, pp. 56, 66. Robert Wilson Patterson, *Early Society in Southern Illinois* (Chicago, 1881), pp. 5-6; Pease, *Frontier State*, pp. 22, 66-68, 429-32.

repealed. Illinois communities continued to depend on private "subscription schools," usually staffed with poorly paid, untrained teachers. Though it would be a long uphill battle, Jacksonville's representatives in the legislature pushed hard for common school education. At stake were the reformers' goals of universal education in Illinois and the material interests of their town.[39]

Jacksonville's stature as a center of education and culture relied also on its less tangible image as an island of refined gentility on the crude frontier, an image that local promoters carefully cultivated very early in the town's history. Jacksonville, one proud resident wrote to a local paper, contains a "state of society" that is "moral, agreeable and correct."[40] Jonathan Baldwin Turner, a young professor at Illinois College, directed his boosterism at his fiancée, who was reluctant to leave the civilized East: "You cannot find a village east of the Hudson of the same number of inhabitants possessing so many men of literary eminence and moral worth, or a community of greater refinement in taste and manners." Another advertisement for Jacksonville's advanced civilization claimed that eastern visitors who expect to see the primitive frontier will ask, when they arrive in the refined environment of Jacksonville, "Where is the West?"[41]

This contrived image of genteel refinement coexisted, without the slightest hint of contradiction, with Jacksonville's brazen boasts about its material growth and economic prosperity. Indeed, the transformation of the town had been impressive. By 1835 many of the rustic log cabins around the public square had been replaced by frame and brick buildings to house new businesses and offices. The Methodists had built their own brick church, and the town constructed a large brick public market house, with stalls in which local farmers and butchers could sell their products. The neoclassic brick courthouse, proud symbol of Morgan County government, added an imposing presence to

39. Rammelkamp, *Illinois College*, pp. 4-6; Heinl, "Jacksonville," pp. 19-21; *Western Observer*, May 22, 1830.

40. *Patriot*, May 11, 1833; Peck, *Gazetteer*, pp. 148-49, 265.

41. Carriel, *Turner*, p. 14; *Patriot*, May 11, 1833.

the square as well. Many of the streets were also improved and more clearly defined; the former muddy walkways around the square were now paved with brick. Neat picket fences around many of the residential yards provided a more fastidious appearance while helping to keep at bay the multitude of pigs, stray dogs, and other livestock which roamed the streets. In short, "a finer more elegant life was becoming manifest."[42]

Local boosters were very conscious of the neat, impressive appearance their town enjoyed, and they would have been delighted to read visitors' favorable comparisons of Jacksonville with neighboring rival Springfield. "Jacksonville contains about the same number of souls as Springfield, but is superior in buildings, arrangements and situation," wrote one traveler in 1835.[43] Peck's *Gazetteer*, an influential guide for Illinois immigrants, also gave Jacksonville high ratings. An informal census of the town's assets included sixteen stores, two druggist shops, two taverns or hotels, and "several respectable boarding houses" (no mention of any unrespectable boarding houses). Peck also listed a steam flourmill and sawmill, a manufactory for cotton yarn, a distillery, two oil mills, two wool-carding factories, a tannery, and three brickyards. "Few towns," he summarized, "exhibit a finer prospect than does Jacksonville. . . ."[44]

In the mid-1830s Jacksonville seemed destined to become a city of major importance in Illinois, as settlers poured into the central and northern parts of the state. There were several foundations upon which the hopeful town could begin to build its future as a great city. One would be its role as a market, processing, and transportation center for the rich and rapidly growing agricultural hinterland of central Illinois. The sudden growth in the number of stores and mills had already demonstrated the potential of these functions. A second promising possibility was implicit in the town's claim to the title "Athens of

42. Peck, *Gazetteer*, p. 265; Charles M. Eames, *Historic Morgan and Classic Jacksonville* (Jacksonville, 1885), p. 45; Donnelley, *History of Morgan*, p. 351; *Patriot*, July 13, 1833.
43. Patrick Shirreff, *A Tour through North America* (Edinburgh, 1835), p. 251; Heinl, "Jacksonville," pp. 6-7; James Stuart, *Three Years in North America* (Edinburgh, 1833), II, 377-87.
44. Peck, *Gazetteer*, p. 264.

the West," a slogan to promote Jacksonville as the home of what many residents hoped would become the major university of the state, a producer of teachers and ministers to enlighten the entire West. Around the college a constellation of academies, publishers, and educational societies would thrive.

Beyond these goals were the unbounded hopes of future greatness, including the very real possibility of becoming the new state capital. As the northern portions of Illinois began to fill with settlers, Illinois legislators grew dissatisfied with the capital's location in the slow-growing town of Vandalia; they began to talk about bringing the capital northward as early as 1832. Jacksonville, with its central geographic location, its status as the seat of a flourishing county, and its remarkable economic growth and educational development, was obviously in contention—along with Springfield—as an alternative site.[45] Jacksonville's potential as a political center was already evident to several ambitious young politicians, including Supreme Court Justice Samuel Lockwood and Governor Joseph Duncan, who came there to live. They were joined by dozens of lawyers in the early 1830s, among them a young Vermont migrant named Stephen Douglas. All were anxious to hitch their careers to Jacksonville's political and cultural star. "Everything which had political ambition behind it," wrote one of Stephen Douglas's biographers, "pointed to Jacksonville."[46]

Within a few years this aspiring little community had been forged out of a wilderness by a strange combination of political fiat, speculative interest, and Yankee missionary zeal. The goals of material prosperity and moral reform were to this point compatibly joined in Jacksonville, but there were inherent tensions in the marriage. Growth would inevitably bring more diverse groups and discordant values into the community. Jacksonville's visions of educational prominence would also soon compete with, instead of complementing, hardheaded schemes of commercial and industrial greatness; in addition, the illusions of urban success would eventually be clouded by the claims of rival towns in the unpredictable scramble for

45. Pease, *Frontier State*, pp. 201-4.
46. Quoted in Heinl, "Jacksonville," p. 6.

bigness. But, in the meantime, a fragile harmony rested on the hope of a young frontier town full of promise.

"There is a figure of rhetoric adopted by the Americans, and much used in description," wrote Illinois pioneer Morris Birk-beck. "It simply consists in the use of the present indicative, instead of future subjunctive: it is called *anticipation*. By its aid, what *may be* is contemplated as though it were in actual existence."[47] Jacksonville's early claims to urban prominence were sheer anticipation, and the town's potential greatness was always far easier to envision than the disappointments that would spoil the boosters' dream.

47. Morris Birkbeck, *Notes on a Journey in America* (Philadelphia, 1817), p. 44.

Unpeaceable Kingdom

> In Illinois I met for the first time a divided Christian
> community, and was plunged without warning or
> preparation into a sea of sectarian rivalries which was
> kept in constant agitation, not only by real differences
> of opinion, but by ill-judged discussions and unfortu-
> nate personalities among ambitious men.
> —JULIAN STURTEVANT[1]

THE AMERICAN FRONTIER legend persuades us to see the
adversity of town-building as a stimulus to a rough-hewn
cooperative community. But the very conditions necessary for
success in the frontier town meant that diverse cultures and
"ambitious men" would be attracted to it. The inevitable result
was a continuous round of internal conflicts, some involving
transitory personal squabbles and parochial factionalism,
others centering on more deep-seated religious, moral, and
political divisions that emanated from the larger society. The
very plurality of values and the undefined structure of local
authority at first allowed no reliable mechanisms for restraining
this conflict. Those institutional mechanisms that did emerge
were successful only when they recognized the pluralistic nature of the new community and aimed at regulating inherent
conflict, rather than instilling universal consensus.[2]

1. *Julian M. Sturtevant: An Autobiography*, ed. J. M. Sturtevant, Jr. (New York, 1896),
pp. 160-61.

2. Cf. Michael Zuckerman, *Peaceable Kingdoms: New England Towns in the Eighteenth
Century* (New York, 1970), which develops the concept of a "consensual community"
designed to repress all conflict. Though some of the values Zuckerman describes in
eighteenth-century New England persisted in Jacksonville, the drive for communal
harmony was more often based on the premise that conflict must be anticipated and
controlled through institutional mechanisms, rather than repressed altogether.

ADVERSITY AND THE FRONTIER SPIRIT

The first response was to deny internal conflict, to translate frontier adversity and cultural pluralism into social cooperation. "The little inconveniences to which we are subject . . . ," boasted Jacksonville's first newspaper editor, "make us more friendly and attached. Our society is agreeable, moral and correct."[3] Similarly, diversity of cultures was defended as the basis for a new, superior cultural synthesis. "The elements from the North and South were about equally blended," claimed one local legend, "forming a society with the virtues of both, without the vices of either; and to this fact, perhaps more than any other, Jacksonville owes her influential position among the cities of the Great West."[4] Out of hardship came cooperation and harmony; out of diversity, a new homogeneity. This formula, repeated endlessly in the press and later in local histories, became an integral part of Jacksonville's ethos of community.

A classic example of the tendency to translate adversity into community came during a devastating cholera epidemic that struck during the summer of 1833, suddenly sweeping away a large portion of Jacksonville's small population. Cholera, like any other catastrophe, was seen as a stigma, a sign of the town's sickliness, its unhealthy location, or even its moral deficiencies. All of these possibilities were eagerly publicized by rival Springfield's newspapers.[5] The local editor carried on bravely throughout the crisis, defending Jacksonville against Springfield's sniping attacks and issuing a series of optimistic reports on the town's progress in controlling the epidemic. In local histories the cholera epidemic of 1833 became a tragic but inspiring episode, wherein frontier hardships were met with the cooperative response of the new community.[6]

In their analysis of midwestern frontier society, historians

3. *Western Observer*, Oct. 9, 1830.

4. John C. W. Baily, comp., *Sangamon County Gazetteer . . . with City Directories of Springfield and Jacksonville . . .* (Springfield, 1866), p. 319; see also Charles M. Eames, *Historic Morgan and Classic Jacksonville* (Jacksonville, 1885), p. 14; *Western Observer*, Oct. 9, 1830.

5. *Sangamon Journal* (Springfield), Aug. 10, 17, 1833; Charles E. Rosenberg, *The Cholera Years: The United States in 1832, 1849, and 1866* (Chicago, 1962).

6. *Patriot*, June 22, July 6, 13, Aug. 17, 1833; Eames, *Historic Morgan*, p. 83.

Stanley Elkins and Eric McKitrick used Jacksonville's cholera epidemic as a model of the frontier "problem-solving experience." They cited the role of cabinetmaker John Henry, who responded to the crisis by adapting his skills to making coffins for the epidemic's victims. When most of the other citizens fled, he and several of his employees stayed on to help inter the dead. Henry's own account of his valiant efforts testified not only to his bravery and sense of community responsibility, but also to his remarkable quickness to take advantage of a rather macabre opportunity, one that Elkins and McKitrick plausibly suggest helped pave the way for his later career as a local politico.[7]

Other more detached sources provide a very different view of the same event. Jonathan Baldwin Turner, a young professor at Illinois College, wrote to his fiancée in the East during the cholera plague:

> As I have walked through the streets in the evening I have seen through the windows and doors, the sick and the dying, sometimes four or five in the same room in a log hut, some on the bed, others on the floor, and perhaps one or two sorrow-smitten beings crawling from bed to bed to give a cup of water or to brush away the flies. On every face was written "Woe" and on every door post "Death" and on not a few "Utter Desolation."[8]

In a similar vein, Truman Post analyzed the crisis with poignant insight:

> The distress of the town was extreme. Society was not then knit together by acquaintance and mutual kindness. The people, gathered from all quarters, had not coalescense enough for mutual helpfulness. The wild, vague terror of a disease, regarded as contagious and killing with fearful rapidity, kept men aloof from each other. Families were isolated in mutual quarantine, and doors and windows were seen by one passing along the streets, thronged with pale and tearful faces, sometimes with the

---

7. Charles Henry Rammelkamp, *Illinois College: A Centennial History, 1829-1929* (New Haven, 1928), p. 58; Baily, *Gazetteer*, p. 321; C. H. Rammelkamp, ed., "The Memoirs of John Henry, a Pioneer of Morgan County," *JISHS* 18 (1925): 54-55; Stanley Elkins and Eric McKitrick, "A Meaning for Turner's Frontier," *Political Science Quarterly* 69 (1954): 332-33; William F. Short, ed., *Historical Encyclopedia of Illinois . . . Morgan County* (Chicago, 1906), p. 671.

8. Mary Turner Carriel, *The Life of Jonathan Baldwin Turner* (1911; reprinted, Urbana, 1961), p. 20.

sick, who had no one to minister a cup of cold water. . . . Human society seemed almost disintegrated by mutual fear. . . .[9]

These haunting pictures of victims left alone to suffer and die, both coming from sources with no motive to distort reality, provide a sobering corrective to the buoyant descriptions of brave pioneers confronting hardships together.

Adversity did not always bring cooperation among discordant people, and relatively minor disagreements could rapidly escalate into intense and often violent hostilities. For example, a meeting organized by the Presbyterians to protest the Black Hawk War met with unexpectedly fierce opposition. Springfield's newspaper reported an account of the 1832 meeting at which those opposing the "peace society" threatened the speaker, a teacher at the Illinois College Academy, with physical violence. "A motion was made to the Chairman," it was calmly reported, "to tar and feather the aforesaid Professor, and ride him on a rail; which was seconded with cheers, loud and long. A tar-barrel, rails, etc. etc. were immediately produced, but the bird had flown. The house was searched from top to bottom, after which [a mob] proceeded to the College but could not find him."[10]

Similar accounts of petty disturbances, ranging from personal feuds to mob violence, crept into the local press and other sources often enough to indicate that the problem of social conflict was far more than an occasional one.[11] Most of these conflicts were relatively spontaneous and transitory, but a few produced deeper and more prolonged divisions within the community. Following is an exploration of several incidents which represent broad themes of social conflict in early Jacksonville.

THE NORTHERN CROSS AFFAIR

Several of the most vicious conflicts emerged out of the very factors that should have united the community; a case in point was the heated debate over the route of the Northern Cross

9. Truman Augustus Post, *Truman Marcellus Post: A Biography Personal and Literary* (Boston, 1891), p. 57.

10. Reprinted in *Patriot*, Jan. 26, 1832.

11. See, e.g., *Western Observer*, Sept. 25, 1830, for a denunciation of favoritism at the

Railroad. Citizens of Springfield and Jacksonville met as early as 1831 to rally support for building a railroad to the Illinois River. Although both towns were located on rivers (Jacksonville on the Mauvaise Terre, Springfield on the Sangamon), those waterways were too shallow for commercial use and were frozen closed in winter. Promoters were convinced that only a railroad would bring their "fertile tracts of country . . . into the immediate vicinity of large water courses and commercial depots, thereby rendering a ready market to the farmer and mechanic for all the surplus produce and manufactures they wish to dispose of. . . ."[12]

In 1836 this goal was partially realized when Charles Collins built a railroad with wooden tracks from Naples, on the Illinois River, two miles east toward Jacksonville. It consisted of one small wooden car pulled by a horse and was still some eighteen miles short of reaching Jacksonville's markets. At its opening the boosters expressed great expectations of growth and prosperity; however, these dreams collapsed when the railway company failed and the road was left incomplete and useless.[13]

During the 1837 legislative session the state's political leaders caught the fever for internal improvements, and Jacksonville's hopes rose again with a plan for the Northern Cross Railroad. Included as part of an internal improvements package, the rail line would link Springfield to Jacksonville and, in turn, to the Illinois River at Meredosia (the upriver rival of Naples). The new route was surveyed in November, and work began at Meredosia in the spring of 1838.[14] Except for certain Whigs, who questioned the financial wisdom of the elaborate internal improvements scheme, most everyone in Jacksonville eagerly anticipated the completion of the Northern Cross and the fulfillment of its promise of rich markets beyond Morgan County.[15]

---

local meat market and a call for a retaliatory boycott. *Illinoian*, Sept. 8, 1838, describes mob violence at an evening political rally.

12. *Sangamon Journal* (Springfield), Jan. 5, 1832.

13. Eames, *Historic Morgan*, pp. 102-3.

14. Ernest G. Hildner, *Jacksonville: A Survey of Its Past* (Jacksonville, 1966), p. 5.

15. Donnelley, Loyd & Co., *History of Morgan County, Illinois: Its Past and Present . . .* (Chicago, 1878), p. 351.

These shared hopes of growth and progress notwithstanding, the construction of the Northern Cross quickly brought on a terrific local battle over the railroad's exact route through town. At the center of this controversy was Murray McConnel, an adventurous native of upstate New York who, after various sojourns in the Southwest, had arrived in Jacksonville around 1830 to serve as the town's first lawyer. An ardent Democrat, McConnel had been appointed district commissioner of public works in 1837; his position made him responsible for administering funds for the surveys and construction of the Northern Cross. His opponents accused McConnel, who was heavily invested in local real estate, of deliberately planning for the Northern Cross to go through his property north of the public square. "Here," one of McConnel's enemies revealed, "is manifestly a design to remove the business and the trade from the public square to his own property near the line of the road."[16]

Accusations of nepotism and graft also came forth in a series of public meetings inspired and led by prominent Whig leaders, who now seized the opportunity to embarrass McConnel and the Democrats. Throughout 1838 and on into the spring of 1839, as the Northern Cross construction crew slowly worked its way east toward Jacksonville, angry citizens' meetings, scandalous exposés, public denunciations, threats of violence, and bitter personal insults erupted in rapid succession—all over a question of where the long-sought rail line would pass through town. Jacksonville's board of trustees, then dominated by Whig partisans, finally took legal action to block McConnel's northern route and stop construction altogether until the matter was settled. Referring to the "great Disapprovation manifested by the Citizens at different well conducted and well attended meetings," the board denounced McConnel, who "still persists in an obstinate course against the Known will of a larger portion of his fellow citizens in Town."[17]

With his support in Jacksonville rapidly eroding, McConnel,

16. *Illinoian*, Apr. 21, 28, May 12, 1838.

17 Minutes, Town Board (title varies), May 15, 1838, MSS in City Clerk's Vault, Jacksonville Municipal Building.

in a tactic that was to become a familiar part of Democratic strategy in later years, turned to the rural population of Morgan. He tried to whip up opposition against the townspeople, who, he alleged, wanted to gouge more taxes out of rural citizens in order to change the railroad route through Jacksonville. McConnel called a meeting in May, 1838, where he appealed to the "country people" to "put down the little selfish Jacksonville faction"; he denounced the "junto of aristocrats" in Jacksonville as "a set of loafers," "a corrupt aristocratic faction" in a "polluted den of scandal" who would impose their will against the common sense of the country folk.[18]

But McConnel's resistance was broken with the proliferation of issues and escalation of opposition. The argument was finally resolved: the Northern Cross would pass down State Street through the center of the public square, where a station would be erected. In October, 1839, the editor of the *Illinoian* reported the beginning of construction inside Jacksonville: "It is truly gratifying to see the public spirit that is manifested in making improvements in our village," he observed, with unintended irony. Public spirit there had been plenty of—but it had done more to frustrate than to encourage progress. "We regret to see . . . ," the editor who had fought so fiercely for the chosen route added, "the large embankment thrown up in one of our principal streets for constructing the railroad. However much it may be supposed for the common good, it certainly detracts from the beauty of the place."[19]

By the end of the year the train was steaming through the center of town regularly. The inconvenience of the route had only begun to dawn on the merchants around the square when its construction disrupted their business. Once in operation, the railroad brought unexpected noise and dirt through the heart of town each day. Murray McConnel's accomplice, Charles Collins, later recalled, no doubt with satisfaction, that "the public square was filled with teams [of horses], and whenever the engine steamed into the square making all the noise possible,

18. *Illinoian*, June 2, Oct. 20, 1838; Apr. 27, May 11, June 29, 1839.
19. Ibid., Oct. 5, 1839.

there was such a stampede. . . . Many of the people," he added, "were as much scared as the horses at the steaming monster as it came rushing into the square."[20]

Those who fought hardest for the route, especially merchants whose stores fronted the square, must have wondered why they had done so. The advantage of having a steam-driven locomotive belching through the center of the business district once or twice each day was much less appreciated after the fact than earlier, when it had appeared that Murray McConnel was somehow conspiring to relocate the center of business on his own property. In 1847, when a group of eastern capitalists acquired the languishing railroad, the rails were removed from the town square and replaced further north—exactly where Murray McConnel had proposed they be laid a decade before.[21]

In retrospect, the battle over the route of the Northern Cross must have seemed absurd to even its staunchest proponents. The entire dispute was inflamed by partisan interests which were made all the more sensitive by the fact that 1838 was a state election year. But the Northern Cross affair was not just the product of partisan issues or economic depression which impinged upon the local community from outside; rather, it was an eruption within a new, unsettled community where the lines of power were as yet poorly defined. Within this uncertain structure of authority, local leaders competed fiercely for power—power that, once gained, was viewed with suspicion and hostility by an untrusting constituency. The result was a series of ad hoc citizens' meetings, indignant resolutions, self-appointed committees, angry accusations, personal insults, and, in the end, irrational resolution of the conflict. However, this element of irrationality is recognized far too easily with historical hindsight. Rationally defined goals of economic progress were by no means irrelevant to the participants in the Northern Cross affair; those goals were simply perceived differently by competing factions, and were confused by suspicions and fears that were natural products of a new and quarrelsome community.[22]

20. Eames, *Historic Morgan*, p. 104.
21. George Murray McConnel, "Some Reminiscences of My Father Murray McConnel," *JISHS* 18 (1925): 97-98; Hildner, *Jacksonville*, p. 5.
22. See Allan Bogue, "Social Theory and the Pioneer," *Agricultural History* 34 (1960):

"A Divided Christian Community"

If material issues like a railroad route caused bitter divisions, spiritual differences could produce even deeper and more permanent rifts in a fragile young community. Religious disputes thwarted ambitions for the community's material progress, especially when they affected Illinois College. Religious conflict was not new to nineteenth-century America or unique to frontier towns. The energy generated by the "Second Great Awakening" excited fierce competition among evangelical Protestant churches everywhere, as each struggled to enlarge its membership and extend its influence through new colleges, missionaries, revivals, or circuit-riding preachers.

Towns like Jacksonville felt the full force of the new spirit of sectarianism which now divided local society into a multitude of separate (sometimes hostile) camps. By the 1860s, eighteen separate Protestant churches had been organized in a town of fewer than 10,000 people. Before the rise of Protestant denominationalism, the members of a small-town community church had frequently squabbled over who to appoint as minister or where to locate the new church; occasionally they had also disagreed over more substantive theological issues. Nonetheless, they had shared a common faith. In contrast, nineteenth-century communities were fragmented into a dozen or more sects, each striving at first to set itself off from the others by defining the inviolable doctrines it understood to be the truth. Most of these sectarian rivalries had their origin outside the local community, in national debates over proper ecclesiastical structure or on the slavery question. Abstruse theological schisms could also be personalized on the local level by what Sturtevant labeled "unfortunate personalities," thereby adding to the propensity for conflict within a contentious community.[23]

Even the Congregationalists, who distinguished themselves

21-34; Robert R. Dykstra, *The Cattle Towns* (New York, 1968); pp. 207-38; James Coleman, *Community Conflict* (Glencoe, Ill., 1957), pp. 21-25.

23. See Sidney E. Mead, *The Lively Experiment: The Shaping of Christianity in America* (New York, 1963), esp. pp. 103-33; William Warren Sweet, *The Story of Religion in America* (New York, 1930), pp. 223-311; and Martin Marty, *Righteous Empire: The Protestant Experience in America*, Two Centuries of American Life (New York, 1970), pp. 67-130.

theologically by their disdain for formal doctrine and ecclesiastical hierarchy, could not be safe in what one of them called "a sea of sectarian rivalries." Yankee clergymen came west under the terms of the Plan of Union, which required them to put aside their Congregational loyalties in the interests of expanding the influence of Protestant Christianity in alliance with Presbyterians. Together the "Presbygationalists," as they came to be known, founded institutions like Illinois College which deliberately tried to avoid any specific denominational affiliation in order to appeal to the broader support of a religiously divided public.

Their hope of uniting all sects in the common cause of Christian enlightenment was rudely disappointed in Jacksonville, however. Julian Sturtevant was appalled at the reception he received from his fellow Christians shortly after he arrived in November, 1829. Sturtevant was invited to deliver a sermon before the Presbyterian congregation, but when he arrived at the courthouse, where the service was to be given, he was surprised to find that, due to a mix-up in scheduling, the Methodists (largely southern in origin) were gathered to listen to their fiery circuit-riding preacher, Kentuckian Peter Cartwright. "Under such circumstances," Sturtevant expected him to deliver "a tender evangelical sermon, full of those truths which commend themselves to every Christian heart." Cartwright instead launched into a "bitter attack" on Calvinism and New England religious practices in general, which he "held up now to the ridicule and then to the indignation of the hearers." He went on to refute the whole concept of an educated ministry and denounced outright the plans for Illinois College. "I have never spent four years in rubbing my back against the walls of a college," Cartwright boasted loudly to his audience. The truth of this last statement was distressingly obvious to Sturtevant, but what worried him was the apparent popular approval of this anti-intellectual sectarianism. Even Sturtevant's Presbyterian audience was noticeably unreceptive to ponderous sermons delivered from carefully prepared manuscripts; he sensed that they wanted the same emotional spontaneity and low intellectual content that preachers like Cartwright displayed with such ease.[24]

More disturbing was the divisive sectarianism that Sturtevent found everywhere in Jacksonville. "No words can express the shock which my mind experienced," he wrote.

> The transition from those harmonious and united Christian communities in which my life had hitherto been passed, to this realm of confusion and religious anarchy was almost overpowering. . . . As large a proportion of the people around me in Jacksonville were members of Christian evangelical churches as in the other communities in which I lived; but here every man's hand was against his brother. The possibility of Christian co-operation was absolutely limited to these little cliques into which the body of Christ was divided.[25]

As if the rivalry with other denominations, like the Methodists, were not enough, the Presbyterians in Jacksonville were themselves torn by internal suspicions and disagreements. The tenuous alliance between Congregationalists and Presbyterians was beginning to show strain in the early 1830s, as Yankee Congregationalists led the vanguard of missionary activity in the Old Northwest. This tension became manifest in the rivalry between the American Home Missionary Society, led by Congregationalists and based in New York City, and the Presbyterian Assembly's Board of Missions, based in Philadelphia. The latter organization watched with suspicion as the Home Missionary Society and its Congregational adherents rapidly extended their influence westward through their dominance in several institutions, such as Illinois College in Jacksonville.[26]

Fearing a Congregational conspiracy in Jacksonville, the Philadelphia Board of Missions sent an agent to a nearby pastorate to watch over the Yale Band's activities at Illinois College. "We immediately felt a disturbing element in our community," Sturtevant recalled. That feeling was justified early in 1833, when charges of heresy were brought against Illinois College

24. Sturtevant, *Autobiography*, pp. 159-63.
25. Ibid., p. 163.
26. Ibid., p. 183.

President Edward Beecher, Sturtevant, and one other professor. The apparent purpose was to eject the accused from the Presbyterian Church, thereby either dealing a death blow to the "heretical" college or allowing more loyal Presbyterians to take over its leadership from the New England "Presbygationalists." Though the defendants were ultimately found not guilty, the heresy trial of 1833, as Sturtevant recalled, "added to all the other elements of unrest then existing among us."[27]

The feeling of alienation among the New England element of Jacksonville's Presbyterian Church was aggravated by the heresy trial; by the end of the year a local schism resulted in the establishment of a Congregational Church in Jacksonville, in direct defiance of the Plan of Union. This movement was not led by Beecher, Sturtevant, or any of the others associated with Illinois College, though their leadership was sought. Sectarianism already threatened to undermine the college, and both Beecher and Sturtevant pleaded in vain with their disaffected New England brethren not to split with the Presbyterians.[28]

Within a few years the Plan of Union dissolved on a national scale, ending a disappointing attempt to rise above the spirit of sect in the interests of advancing Protestant influence in the West. At the same time, the Presbyterian church was wracked by internal divisions; this national schism found expression in a local rift in 1838, when the Presbyterian church of Jacksonville was split once again. On this occasion the more liberal New School faction prevailed, and the Old School minority was forced to leave and found a separate church.[29]

These, and several other local schisms and interdenominational rivalries, had serious repercussions on Jacksonville's material progress. Illinois College, the key to Jacksonville's claim to educational prominence in Illinois, now rested on a fragmented religious foundation. The college became a target for the Pres-

27. Ibid., pp. 183-84.
28. Ibid., pp. 195, 204-9; Julian M. Sturtevant, *Origins of Western Congregationalism* (Jacksonville, 1884); Carrie P. Kofoid, "Puritan Influence in the Formative Years of Illinois History," Illinois State Historical Society *Transactions* 10 (1905): 297-98.
29. Donnelley, *History of Morgan*, pp. 369-70; Eames, *Historic Morgan*, pp. 99-100; Kofoid, "Puritan Influence," pp. 298-99.

byterian hierarchy suspicious of Yankee Congregationalists, and for a conservative public hostile to the liberal theology it felt certain was emanating from the college faculty.[30] The college was recognized by most boosters as a major asset to the hopeful community, yet these divisive sectarian rivalries excited jealousies that crippled the college, and to some extent the town itself, during their formative years.

THE SLAVERY QUESTION

The slavery issue also intruded into the local community, where it excited intensely personal forms of conflict. A movement to legalize slavery in Illinois had been defeated in 1824. Morgan County's scattered settlers formed the antislavery Morganian Society at that time, "for the dissemination of political knowledge and the maintenance of the inalienable rights of Man." These were Southerners, for the most part from Kentucky and Tennessee, who had little sympathy for the slaveholding class and even less for blacks. Their class antagonism toward the planters and their racial animosity toward blacks, rather than moral objections to slavery alone, inspired them. At the same time, Southerners in Illinois could fiercely oppose the movement to abolish slavery in the South, in part because it threatened racial homogeneity in Illinois. Antislavery also came to be identified with Yankee reformers who poured into Illinois during the 1830s, precisely when the national antislavery movement was heightening its demands for immediate and total abolition.[31]

30. *The History of Presbyterianism in Morgan County, Illinois, 1827-1967* (Jacksonville, 1967); Sturtevant to Theron Baldwin, Illinois College, Nov. 22, 1844, and Nov. 26, 1845, Sturtevant-Baldwin Letters, Tanner Library, Illinois College; Sturtevant, *Autobiography*, pp. 160-61, 233-38, 266-68; Rammelkamp, *Illinois College*, pp. 39-194. Some of the public attacks on Illinois College are reported in *Patriot*, May 4, 1833; *Illinoian*, Nov. 24, 1838; Feb. 2, Sept. 21, 1839; *Illinois Statesman*, Dec. 4, 11, 18, 1843.

31. Merton L. Dillon, "The Anti-Slavery Movement in Illinois, 1809-1844" (Ph.D. dissertation, University of Michigan, 1951). Eugene H. Berwanger, *The Frontier against Slavery: Western Anti-Negro Prejudice and the Slavery Extension Controversy* (Urbana, 1967), explains the apparent paradox of dual opposition to slavery and abolitionism. See also Theodore Calvin Pease, *The Frontier State 1818-1848*, The Centennial History of Illinois, vol. 2 (Springfield, 1918), pp. 363-82. Charles N. Zucker, "The Free Negro Question: Race Relations in Ante-Bellum Illinois, 1801-1860" (Ph.D. dissertation, Northwestern

Not until 1837, when Elijah Lovejoy was murdered by an anti-abolitionist mob in Alton, Illinois, did the tension of the slavery issue surface in Jacksonville. Lovejoy, an earnest young missionary turned newspaper editor from New England, was driven out of St. Louis for publishing antislavery editorials. To his surprise, he found an equally inhospitable audience across the Mississippi River in Alton. Lovejoy called for an antislavery convention there for November, 1837, and he pleaded with Edward Beecher in Jacksonville to lend the prestige of his name and office as chairman of the convention. Beecher, acutely conscious of the anti-abolitionist sentiment around him, reluctantly agreed to chair the convention but insisted that it be open to all "friends of free discussion" who might want to debate the issue of slavery and Lovejoy's right to publish an antislavery newspaper in Alton. Unfortunately, Beecher found few "friends of free discussion" there, and what he had hoped would be an enlightening, rational debate among thoughtful men rapidly dissolved into an angry mob scene climaxed by the infamous murder of Elijah Lovejoy, who died defending his printing press. Beecher now found events pushing him into a league with the "unpopular and despised minority" of antislavery sympathizers.[32]

Despite his caution at Alton, Beecher returned to Jacksonville to face a college president's nightmare. A large meeting of indignant students and townspeople met on the campus to protest the murder of Lovejoy and the violation of freedom of the press—an issue which now attracted many who previously had been indifferent to the issue of slavery alone. A local student of southern origin, Billy Herndon, addressed the crowd and spoke out against the suppression of freedom in Alton. According to Herndon's account, his irate father blamed the

---

University, 1973), and personal conversations with Professor Zucker have been helpful to my understanding of race and the slavery issue in Illinois.

32. Edward Beecher, *Narrative of the Riots at Alton: In Connection with the Death of Rev. Elijah P. Lovejoy* (1838; reprinted, New York, 1965); Merton L. Dillon, *Elijah P. Lovejoy: Abolitionist Editor* (Urbana, 1961); Robert Merideth, *The Politics of the Universe: Edward Beecher, Abolition and Orthodoxy* (Nashville, 1968), pp. 104-5.

college for poisoning his son with abolitionism and angrily disowned him.[33]

The identification of the college with radical abolitionism was mistaken but, nonetheless, deeply felt, and the public outrage against the college intensified after the Lovejoy incident. "There was evident danger," Sturtevant recalled, "that a ferocious mob would make an immediate attack upon the head of the institution and upon the college buildings . . . the very existence of the college was endangered." The resentment toward the college was harbored not only by "the mob," but also by "many individuals of wealth and social standing and even of religious reputation." Student meetings and orations were thereafter attended "by certain men of ruffianly habits and pro-slavery prejudices who wished to act as self-constituted guardians of the moral and social proprieties of the occasion."[34] Goals of community progress, which hinged in important ways upon the success of the college, were once again obfuscated by internal conflict.

Below College Hill many previously moderate antislavery sympathizers now discovered a deeper commitment to the cause. About the time of Lovejoy's murder a Kentucky couple with two slaves arrived in Jacksonville to visit relatives. Slave-owning was by no means unprecedented in Illinois, or in Jacksonville; but the presence of these slaves, brought in by Southerners at a time when the whole community was agitated by the Lovejoy murder, stirred some antislavery men into a bold act of defiance. They convinced the two slaves, Bob and Emily Logan, that they were legally free in Illinois and helped them flee from their masters and take refuge with a local black family.[35]

The slaves' owners and their Jacksonville kin determined not to let the abolitionists get away with this. Later they found Bob

33. Frank J. Heinl, "Jacksonville and Morgan County, an Historical Review," *JISHS* 18 (1925), 15-16; cf. David Donald, *Lincoln's Herndon* (New York, 1948), pp. 11-14. William Herndon was later Lincoln's law partner and biographer. Donald explains the dubious validity of Herndon's account of the Illinois College incident.

34. Sturtevant, *Autobiography*, pp. 224-26; see also *Gazette and News*, Nov. 16, 1837; Heinl, "Jacksonville," p. 14; Post, *Post*, pp. 91-92; Carriel, *Turner*, pp. 51-53.

35. *Illinoian*, Aug. 4, 1838. The editor blamed Josiah Lamborn, a Democratic political opponent, for aiding the Logans, but this is not confirmed in any other sources.

Logan cutting wood outdoors; in broad daylight, they jumped him and quickly returned him to Kentucky, and to slavery. The remaining fugitive slave, Emily Logan, soon became a cause célèbre among Jacksonville's antislavery sympathizers. Yankees in the Congregational church raised funds to provide for her, took her into the church as a full member, and arranged to support her fight for freedom, which she eventually won in 1840.[36] "The shock to the whole community occasioned by this outrage is beyond description," wrote Julian Sturtevant after Bob Logan's kidnapping. "From that time onward there was in our community a slow but steady progress in the antislavery sentiment."[37]

After the Logan affair Jacksonville's growing reputation as a bastion of abolitionism helped establish it as a frequently used station on the Underground Railroad, a loosely organized effort to help escaped slaves northward to Canada. For the most part, the debate over slavery was a battle of words and abstract principles. But the full human reality of slavery came home to Jacksonville in several incidents of desperate runaways knocking on doors in the middle of night, and bounty-hunters prowling about the houses of suspected Underground Railroad activists.

The most explosive incidents, though, involved the slaves of Southerners who came to visit relatives in Jacksonville. The Logan affair of 1838 should have made it clear that slaves could not safely be brought into Jacksonville, but the amenities of personal service were not easy to leave behind. Soon after Emily Logan's trial a wealthy visitor from St. Louis hired out her slave girl, Lucinda, to earn some pin money for her mistress. Lucinda dutifully went from door to door asking if anyone wished to employ her; she finally came to the residence of Julius Willard, a Yankee milliner who passionately opposed slavery. The Willards told Lucinda that slavery was illegal in Illinois and convinced her to sue for her freedom in court. They recommended Murray McConnel as a lawyer with the necessary political connections; McConnel (in characteristic style) agreed to take

36. Ibid.; Heinl, "Jacksonville," pp. 17-18.
37. Sturtevant, *Autobiography*, p. 228.

Lucinda's claim for human freedom through court in exchange for two years of her service. McConnel won the case with apparent ease, and Lucinda was given her freedom to serve in her champion's kitchen.[38]

Lucinda banged on the Willards' door late one night in February, 1843, and begged them to aid her friend, a young slave girl in flight from her master. The runaway was a slave of Mrs. Lisle of Louisiana, who had been visiting her sister in Jacksonville and planned to leave on the stage the next morning. The young slave was hiding with black friends in town when Willard's son, Samuel, found her and led her away to a farm owned by Eb Carter, a fellow Yankee and strong antislavery advocate. Two days later Julius Willard took the runaway from the Carter farm and headed across icy roads toward Greenfield, some twenty-five miles south of Jacksonville, where some of his friends agreed to escort the girl north to Canada.[39]

Meanwhile, Mrs. Lisle's brother-in-law, William Branson, formerly of North Carolina, gathered a posse of outraged fellow Southerners to hunt down the runaway slave. The gang immediately searched the "negro part of town" southwest of the public square and frightened a resident into informing on the Willards. Samuel Willard was taken into custody and, in effect, held hostage while Branson and his posse tracked down the elder Willard and the slave girl. Once caught, the girl was hastily returned South to slavery, and the Willards were thrown in jail with exorbitant bail set at $2,500. Antislavery friends put up the money for their release, and the Willards sent out letters across the state pleading for financial support to carry their case through the courts. "The excitement growing out of this case," Julius Willard wrote to one supporter, "has brought out sundry friends of the slave, who were not before known as such, and stirred up the good feelings of others who have been before deemed such."[40]

---

38. Samuel Willard, "My First Adventure with a Fugitive Slave: The Story of It and How It Failed," typewritten MS, n.d., p. 1, Illinois State Historical Library, Springfield.

39. Ibid., p. 6.

40. Julius A. Willard to Rev. W. J. Allan, Jacksonville, Mar. 30, 1843, Willard Collection, Illinois State Historical Library, Springfield.

Unfortunately, the Willard case stirred up feelings on the other side of the fence as well, and the Willards now found themselves the target of threatened violence. "Many, I understand, have been the threats of tar and feathers, and rails and lickings," wrote the father before the trial.[41] One of the Willards' friends was chased through the streets of Jacksonville by a Branson gang member who brandished a huge club. When Augustus Ayers, another friend of the Willards, tried to interfere, he was cruelly bludgeoned by the assailant. Other plots to assault the Willards never came to fruition: one quiet Sunday evening following the Lisle incident "a group of worshippers" in the Old School Presbyterian Church "put their heads together and discussed the question whether it would not be a good thing to mob the Willards and inflict tar and feathers or some form of personal punishment."[42]

As the Willards prepared for a prolonged legal battle, their enemies did not wait for the courts to defend their own principles. They threw up notices all over Jacksonville announcing a mass protest meeting on February 23, 1843. One purpose of this meeting was to publicize a strong opposition to "negro stealing" as a way of assuring Southerners that "the citizens of Jacksonville will . . . extend the hand of friendship and hospitality to their acquaintances in the South and will be . . . ready at all times and on all occasions promptly and efficiently to aid and protect them in the enjoyment of their property."[43]

A well-publicized account of the meeting made it clear that, although most were southern-born, not all were proslavery. The first resolution stated explicitly that "we do not consider this a question of slavery or anti-slavery, of abolition or anti-abolition. . . . Many of us believe that slavery as an institution, is one which has been, and will be a curse upon the nation." What they did oppose unanimously was the illegal *modus operandi* of those who would "steal" slaves away from their masters. Nor were they content to merely condemn those in-

41. Ibid.
42. Willard, "First Adventure," pp. 17-18.
43. "News—Extra" handbill, Willard Collection.

volved in this most recent incident of slave-stealing. They proposed organized, ongoing vigilance against the antislavery movement. The second of several resolutions passed at the meeting read as follows: "Having reason to believe that there are regular bands of abolitionists, organized with depots and relays of horses to run negroes through our state to Canada, and that one of them is in this town, we will form an Anti-Negro Stealing Society, as we heretofore formed an Anti-Horse Stealing Society, and that we will, in this neighborhood, break up the one as we broke up the other."[44]

The response to the Willards' antislavery activities took on a form typical of frontier towns: a citizens' meeting was called, a series of angry resolutions passed, and inevitably some new ad hoc organization emerged to carry out the sense of the meeting—in this case, a vigilance committee to derail the Underground Railroad. But whatever strong sense of purpose informed the founding of the Anti-Negro Stealing Society, the group never met a second time and quickly faded from the historical record. Their opposition to abolitionists by no means waned, but antagonism toward antislavery activity in Jacksonville was only rarely channeled into formal institutions. Typically, the battle against antislavery forces was fought with more personal forms of harassment, threats, and occasional violence. Recollections of antislavery men reveal a strategy of controlled terrorism at work against them. Timothy Chamberlain, a New Yorker who made no secret of his sympathy for runaway slaves, found his wagon stolen whenever his enemies saw it unguarded. Dr. M. M. L. Reed, another reputed Yankee abolitionist, felt threatened by every dark shadow and always walked down the center of the street when venturing out at night. Arsonists tried to destroy Reed's house one night, and he never opened his door again without fear. In the 1850s merchants suspected of antislavery sympathy were boycotted by townsmen and rural visitors who opposed their views. One of the Yankee merchants, J. O. King, recalled bitterly the treatment he and his antislavery friends suffered: "We were the most hated and despised of men

44. Ibid.

. . . and were almost socially ostracized. . . . The best and otherwise worthiest people of the town united in deeming us fanatics and revolutionists. . . ."[45]

The rhetorical attack on abolitionism exaggerated both the scale and the effectiveness of antislavery organization, but it did accurately identify a preference for institutional channels to fight slavery. The antislavery movement did not just "steal Negroes" away from their masters; it also appealed to the courts to establish legal precedents which would grant freedom to slaves entering Illinois, and it put together a network of local antislavery societies to issue propaganda and exert pressure on state and federal governments. When the antislavery movement turned to direct political action following Lovejoy's dramatic murder, Jacksonville's abolitionists agitated for the Free Soil party; they made certain that a poll was opened for their party on election day and that citizens heard their message, even if few voted in support of it. Elihu Wolcott, one of Jacksonville's most prominent antislavery spokesmen, forced the slavery issue into the congressional election of 1846 by running on the Free Soil ticket against moderates Abraham Lincoln and Peter Cartwright. These efforts were successful in arousing public awareness and in establishing the bare beginnings of a foundation upon which the Republican party would quickly rise in 1854, when the Kansas-Nebraska Act jolted the nation. Jacksonville was among the first places in Illinois to foster a local unit of this new political alliance which would sweep into national power six years later.[46] Through the political process, slavery was eventually lifted from the parochial realm of personal and sectional squabbles to a level where it could be debated in more lofty ideological terms, and within the constraints of established political institutions.

The Republican position that slavery must be restricted, if not abolished outright, gave voice to an idea that had been funda-

45. Eames, *Historic Morgan*, pp. 143-47, 136. On the boycott, see *Sentinel*, June 20, July 11, 1856. See Leonard L. Richards, *"Gentlemen of Property and Standing:" Anti-Abolition Mobs in Jacksonian America* (New York, 1970), pp. 155, 168.

46. *Journal*, Aug. 7, 1846. Samuel Willard to Father and Mother, Illinois College, Oct. 31, 1840, and Samuel Willard to Julius Willard, Jacksonville, Sept. 28, 1840, Willard Collection, both describe antislavery political activities. Heinl, "Jacksonville," pp. 27-28, claims that the nucleus of Jacksonville's Republican party organized in 1853.

mental to the antislavery crusade from its very beginnings in Illinois. It was based on the assumption that the slavery question could not be answered by the private individual or family. The community, state, and finally the federal government had the right—indeed, the moral duty, in the Republican view— to prohibit slavery wherever it conflicted with the community interest.[47]

The Democratic party in Illinois desperately tried to defend the position that slavery was an individual prerogative. After the rise of the Republican challenge, Illinois Democrats retreated to an ambiguous compromise which defined slavery as a local issue. Jacksonville's Murray McConnel, by then a leading Illinois Democrat, stated his party's uncomfortable stand in revealing terms during his 1856 congressional campaign: "The power to legislate upon private rights and relations, as they exist between one citizen and another, was never granted to the general government. . . . The question of domestic servitude or slavery, is clearly a municipal regulation. It is the relation that one person bears to another in the community. It is as clearly a matter of private right and domestic relation as that of parent and child, husband and wife, master and apprentice. . . ."[48]

By 1858, during his famous debates with Lincoln, Stephen Douglas staked out a position very similar to McConnel's in his controversial Freeport Doctrine. This tortured position of Illinois Democrats was dictated by the hatred for both slavery and abolitionism among their constituents. Simply stated, Democrats held that slavery, whether right or wrong, was essentially a private matter not to be decided by distant government. But their admission that local communities could also decide on the propriety of slavery within their boundaries led to a fundamental contradiction: if slaveowners were subject to the will of the community, then the principle was lost. Slavery could not be both a private and a community decision.

Even if the local community possessed the power to decide on

---

47. Eric Foner, *Free Soil, Free Labor, Free Men: The Ideology of the Republican Party before the Civil War* (New York, 1970), pp. 55-58, 310-11; Harry V. Jaffa, *Crisis of the House Divided: An Interpretation of the Issues in the Lincoln-Douglas Debates* (New York, 1959), pp. 347-62.

48. *Sentinel*, June 6, 1856.

slavery, this hardly insured a peaceful solution to the question. Both McConnel and Douglas had witnessed enough in Jacksonville alone to realize that the local community, whatever its size, could not be counted on to share a common moral sentiment on an issue as divisive as slavery. In a social environment where families shared a set of common values and generations of experience, an issue like slavery might be more easily resolved. But in towns like Jacksonville there was no community consensus on slavery, or on a whole range of other fundamental issues. The principle of local option settled nothing.

As a social institution, slavery had little effect upon the daily life of Jacksonville; nevertheless, as a symbolic issue it shaped the community in two important ways. As a persistent source of division, the slavery issue added to the town's atmosphere of contentiousness. Equally important, the slavery question helped to define two opposing concepts of community. Antislavery forces seemed willing to redefine certain areas of behavior like slaveholding (as well as temperance and education, which became linked with antislavery reform in the Republican ideology) into something more than private matters. In appealing to the local, state, or federal governments to restrict slavery they accepted a new definition of community, not as a network of self-regulating personal and family relationships, but as a collection of individuals subject in some areas to the regulation of public institutions. They were willing to assign to formal institutions the kind of moral leverage that had formerly inhered solely in the family or church. In retrospect, this understanding of community seems more appropriate to the conditions and needs of a new, mobile, and culturally diverse town, one that shared neither the traditions nor the common values to spawn a less formal social order. But the tension between these two divergent views of community surfaced later, over other issues (e.g., temperance), and continued to shape Jacksonville's development as a community.[49]

The slavery issue, sectarian rivalries, and the Northern Cross dispute were only some of the more prominent examples of social conflict in Jacksonville's early history. The lines of cleav-

49. See pp. 94-126.

age crossed the community in several directions, sometimes following the divisions between regional cultures, other times tracing the boundaries between denominations, political parties, social classes, neighborhoods, and kinship factions. That these multiple lines of conflict so often crossed, rather than reinforcing one another, helped prevent any single line of cleavage from irreparably dividing the community.[50] Still, these fractures could suddenly open; when that happened, little adhesive tradition and few institutional controls were there at first to impede and regulate the ensuing conflict. One solution, adopted in Jacksonville, was to transfer to the political arena divisive moral questions that arose from regional, ethnic, or religious diversity. There issues like slavery and temperance would be debated fiercely, but the institutional constraints of the political process helped to control and depersonalize community conflict, even if they did not diminish its presence.

New Englanders like Sturtevant and his colleagues on College Hill saw the plague of social conflict as a temporary aberration of a communal norm. Since the organic basis of a consensual community was lacking, the Yankees sought to mold common values through schools, churches, and other formal institutions. Out of this "chaotic confusion," Edward Beecher prophesied, "a moral edifice will arise, complete and harmonious in all its parts, and resplendent with beauty and glory."[51] But more perceptive men soon realized that the quarrelsome nature of community in Jacksonville was more than a transitory prelude to homogeneity.

Instead, conflict was an integral and permanent aspect of a pluralistic community in which no single hierarchy of authority and values could instill consensus. To some, the very ethos of mobility, competition, and democracy inherent in nineteenth-century capitalism (and exaggerated on the frontier) seemed to deny the very possibility of a consensual community. Others realized that a new definition of community would have to be constructed within an unsettled and forever contentious society.

50. See Lewis Coser, *The Social Functions of Conflict* (New York, 1954); James S. Coleman, *Community Conflict* (New York, 1957).
51. Quoted in Merideth, *Politics of the Universe*, p. 79.

The Booster Ethos

In promoting the prosperity of our city and county
persons of all shades of political opinion, sectarian
sentiments, clique or faction, in [the] community may
unite and operate together upon the platform of a
common and mutual interest.

—*Illinois Sentinel*[1]

"HITHERTO, TO OUR SHAME we acknowledge it, we have been too much divided among ourselves." This admission in Jacksonville's *Illinois Statesman* in 1844 was balanced by a more optimistic vision of the future: "We think we see better days ahead. . . . Then fellow citizens one and all let us be united in the interests of Jacksonville and our country."[2] These pleas for unity were recited *ad nauseam* in the town's strife-ridden early history. In them was a partial solution to the problem of community, for the booster ethos could effectively link goals of individual opportunity to the collective destiny of the town. Despite all the vaunted individualism and unsettling transience of laissez-faire capitalism in the nineteenth century, it was capable of generating an intense spirit of community.

The ethos of boosterism equated social unity with progress and warned of the evil fruit born of a divided community. An underlying assumption of this ethos was that urban prominence was not decided by geographic location and natural resources alone; rather, it was decided by the collective will of the community or "public spirit"—a favorite expression in the booster's

1. *Sentinel*, Nov. 30, 1855.
2. *Illinois Statesman*, May 6, 1844.

lexicon. The virtues of communal energy, enthusiasm, and enterprise would somehow find their just reward in what the boosters repeatedly referred to as the "open race" of competing towns striving toward growth and progress. The prizes to be grabbed in this frenzied race—the county seats, colleges, railroads, mail routes, and state asylums—were the makings of great cities. They would be won by aggressive lobbying and pork-barreling in the halls of government, by vigorous fund-raising, and by local donations of land, all aimed at luring the unclaimed asset to the ambitious town. The race was quick-paced because so many of these prizes were awarded only once. If a community was rapidly established as a prominent city, it was sure to reap the bounty that fell upon the early leader.

The booster ethos flowed naturally from the nineteenth-century ideology of individual social mobility, which promised that industrious young men of good character, if unobstructed by artificial barriers of class or monopoly, would inevitably be rewarded in the "race of life." Compared to the cult of individual success, with its vision of unlimited opportunity, the ideology of boosterism was pragmatic: it recognized that one town's success took place at the expense of its rivals. Accordingly, the local press devoted much attention to deliberately discrediting rival towns, rejoicing over their failures and misfortunes, and jealously denouncing any unfair advantage they had gained in a race where only a few winners would be recognized. But the essential impetus behind these rivalries was the parochial pursuit of local interests, compelled by the faith that enough enterprising "public spirit" would inevitably boost the community toward a self-determined future of prominence.

A necessary corollary to the booster's equation of unity and progress was the warning that factionalism and jealousy, whether sectarian, political, or personal, would lead to disgrace and failure. Local editors, playing their crucial role as coaches for the boosters, were torn between their obligation to criticize internal dissension and lassitude and their duty to veil the town's faults and project the appearance of a "wide awake," united citizenry. Of course, if they failed to point out internal problems, neighboring editors were eager to make up for their omissions.[3] Boosterism defined a strong, tangible incentive to community harmony while it disciplined internal conflicts.

To see how this rhetoric of progress and unity applied to the knotty problems of community-building, we must return to Jacksonville's economic development from the early 1830s to the Civil War. One theme emerges clearly: Jacksonville's boosters understood the problem of town promotion as a matter of consciously working out a collective strategy for economic growth and image-building. At the same time, there was not always agreement over what that strategy should be. Furthermore, the booster ethos provided only a partial solution to the problem of community, because so few shared a genuine interest in the community's destiny.

GREAT EXPECTATIONS DISAPPOINTED, 1833-44

In its very early years, Jacksonville had every reason to believe the negative lessons of the booster ethos. Before 1845 a series of disasters all but shattered the hopes of the town. In the middle 1830s, after a decade of promising development, Jacksonville could realistically look toward a time when it would enjoy unrivaled status as an educational center of Illinois, as a major market center for a rich agricultural region, and as the state capital. This last possibility was clearly Jacksonville's most ambitious goal at the time. As early as 1833, when Springfield's politicians began beating the drums to remove the state capital from Vandalia, Jacksonville's boosters put forth their own town as a likely alternative site. By 1834 the pressure for removal had mounted, and the competition involved a growing number of towns. The question was now put before the people of Illinois. Jacksonville, along with Springfield, Peoria, Alton, Vandalia, and (a familiar compromise) the geographic center of the state, were all on the ballot, but the vote was too small to be decisive.[4] The cholera epidemic which had swept through Jacksonville the previous summer hurt its position in the race; not only did it

3. See, e.g., the attack by the Alton *Telegraph* reprinted in *Journal*, May 19, 1853.
4. *Patriot*, June 8, 1833; Theodore Calvin Pease, *The Frontier State, 1818-1848*, The Centennial History of Illinois, vol. 2 (Chicago, 1922), p. 202.

reduce the population in the short run, but it also left the more enduring stigma of a reputation for being "sickly." As though this damning label were not enough, Springfield newspapers made a point of publicizing a local doctor's opinion that "moral causes have more to do with spreading cholera than physical."[5]

Despite the ominous warnings in Jacksonville newspapers, Springfield somehow escaped the cholera plague, and that summer the town used its momentary advantage to win an important mail route that bypassed its hapless rival.[6] Springfield's triumph was consolidated during 1837, when the legislature finally decided that Springfield would be the new location of the state capital. The Sangamon County delegation, known as the "Long Nine" because of their extraordinary height, included Abraham Lincoln. Through their shrewd political dealings Lincoln and his cronies were able to include the capital relocation in an elaborate internal improvements package. Some local historians have argued that, in their bid for support from Morgan County, the Long Nine offered Jacksonville a station on the Northern Cross Railroad and, later, several state institutions as consolation prizes.[7] But if a political arrangement was made, it certainly was not done with the popular approval of Jacksonville's promoters. The *Illinois Patriot* wasted no time in denouncing the Morgan County representative, Stephen Douglas, for selling out Jacksonville to further his own career. Indeed, Douglas immediately won appointment as register of the land office at Springfield, and he was seen seated among the guests of honor at a banquet given by grateful Springfield boosters to celebrate the Long Nine's victory. The records show that Douglas voted for Jacksonville to the bitter end, but how else to explain the town's failure except by citing a political conspiracy beyond control of local virtue?[8]

5. *Sangamon Journal* (Springfield), Aug. 10, 1833.
6. *Patriot*, Aug. 31, Sept. 14, 1833; *Sangamon Journal* (Springfield), Sept. 7, 1833.
7. Carl E. Black, untitled, unpublished MSS, n.d., in "Morgan County History" file, Morgan County Historical Society Collections, Jacksonville Public Library; Black, "Origin of Our State Charitable Institutions," *JISHS* 18 (1925): 190-91; cf. Paul Simon, *Lincoln's Preparation for Greatness: The Illinois Legislative Years* (Norman, Okla., 1965), pp. 42-105.
8. Allen Johnson, *Stephen A. Douglas: A Study in American Politics* (1908; reprinted,

After losing the contest for the state capital, Jacksonville might have settled back to nurture its status as an educational center, but events of 1837 brought uncertainty to this goal as well. The involvement of Edward Beecher in the antislavery convention preceding Lovejoy's murder that November tainted Illinois College with the unpopular cause of abolitionism. The controversy over slavery seriously frustrated the growth of the college during its formative years, and this problem was exacerbated by the ruinous effects of the Panic of 1837. The $100,000 in subscriptions which local supporters had pledged to the college endowment were now worthless promises, and the college's land fell in value or became altogether unsalable. The harried institution survived public opposition and financial crisis only through the sacrifices of loyal faculty who taught for several years with little or no pay. Even in 1844, when Sturtevant took over as president, the college remained deeply in debt and plagued by public animosity over the continued agitation of the slavery question, as well as by sectarian jealousies. By that time the college found itself in stiff competition with a number of other small church-related colleges that had sprung up in Illinois during the 1830s. Each of these institutions competed with the others for eastern money. The Society for the Promotion of Collegiate and Theological Education in the West, organized in 1843, coordinated and centralized eastern fund-raising, but it also divided resources which had previously flowed largely to the coffers of Illinois College. This combination of developments conspired to dwarf the college in irreparable ways, and to cast unspoken doubts on Jacksonville's ostentatious claim as "Athens of the West."[9]

The local effects of the Panic of 1837 reached far beyond the

---

New York, 1970), pp. 34-35; Pease, *Frontier State*, pp. 204-5; Paul M. Angle, *"Here I Have Lived:" A History of Lincoln's Springfield, 1821-1860* (Springfield, 1935), pp. 54-58. Douglas's rebuttal is in *Patriot*, May 8, 1837, reprinted in Illinois State Historical Society *Transactions* 6 (1901): 111-12. See Robert W. Johannsen, *Stephen A. Douglas* (New York, 1973), pp. 54-56.

9. Charles Henry Rammelkamp, *Illinois College: A Centennial History, 1829-1929* (New Haven, 1928), pp. 102-3; *Julian M. Sturtevant: An Autobiography*, ed. J. M. Sturtevant, Jr. (New York, 1896), pp. 233-38; Sturtevant to Theron Baldwin, Illinois College, Oct. 6, 1845, Sturtevant-Baldwin Letters, Tanner Library, Illinois College.

walls of Illinois College. The speculative land bubble that had risen in Morgan County suddenly burst, and prices fell from $20-$40 to $7-$15 per acre, where they remained as late as 1846.[10] In Jacksonville "every branch of business [was] prostrate"; farmers had no market, businessmen few customers, and a branch of the state bank that had just opened in 1835 was forced to an early demise. Jacksonville's population, estimated at 2,500 just before 1837, was reported at only 1,900 in the 1840 federal census.[11]

As a station of the Northern Cross Railroad, Jacksonville was at the same time one of the few communities to gain from the overly ambitious internal improvements scheme that collapsed in the wake of the Panic. Local boosters hoped the railroad would reinvigorate Morgan County agriculture and business by providing cheap transportation to the interior of central Illinois.[12] However, the Northern Cross proved to be a disaster. Slowed by a series of political scandals, the road took years to complete, and strict budgeting required cheap strap-iron rails and an inefficient wood-burning engine. Angry farmers boycotted and sabotaged the railroad to protest high freight rates; passengers, if they were not skewered by a curling iron "snakehead" through the car floor, soon wearied of walking miles to fetch water for the boiler. The state finally turned the Northern Cross over to private contractors. By 1846 the road was used only to haul an occasional carload of freight behind two plodding mules. The ill-fated railroad by then had fallen into total disrepair, a dilapidated symbol of Jacksonville's unfulfilled hopes.[13]

10. Charles M. Eames, *Historic Morgan and Classic Jacksonville* (Jacksonville, 1885), p. 106.

11. John C. W. Baily, comp., *Sangamon County Gazetteer . . . with City Directories of Springfield and Jacksonville . . .* (Springfield, 1866), p. 321; William F. Short, ed., *Historical Encyclopedia of Illinois . . . Morgan County* (Chicago, 1906), p. 691; *Sangamon Journal* (Springfield), May 13, 1842; John M. Peck, *A Gazetteer of Illinois . . .* (Jacksonville, 1834), p. 229.

12. *Patriot*, July 20, 1937, in John H. Krenkel, *Illinois Internal Improvements, 1818-1848* (Cedar Rapids, Ia., 1958), pp. 94-98, 102; Ernest G. Hildner, *Jacksonville: A Survey of Its Past* (Jacksonville, 1966), p. 5.

13. Angle, *Lincoln's Springfield*, p. 146; *Illinois Statesman*, Nov. 27, 1843; Krenkel, *Internal Improvements*, pp. 104-9; H. J. Stratton, "The Northern Cross Railroad," *JISHS*

A City of Institutions, 1845-53

By 1845 Jacksonville aimed its sights considerably lower, and in new and innovative directions. The town's recovery depended heavily on its ability to win a whole string of state charitable institutions: a school for the deaf and dumb in 1845, a hospital for the insane in 1845, a school for the blind in 1848. These sprang up in Illinois in imitation of models created in older, more urbanized states like Massachusetts and New York; behind them lay a new liberal faith in the perfectability of the human condition and a rejection of Calvinist assumptions of innate depravity. Deviant behavior was now assumed to be the product of a disordered social and moral environment—an argument easily transferred from the slums of eastern cities to the unsettled frontiers of the West. Another force propelling these institutional reforms in every state was an aggressive group of physicians and other interested professionals who persuaded state legislatures that the repair of society's defectives was possible, albeit only within large, professionally staffed institutional environments open to all classes.[14]

These new theories expounded by the champions of reform were vitally important, but their arguments would have fallen on deaf ears had it not been for the intensity of politics and boosterism in the West. A sense of pride could inspire Illinois to prove itself a progressive, enlightened state by imitating the latest eastern models of institutional reform; in addition, individual towns competed fiercely to bring these institutions into their own local economies. Insane asylums, penitentiaries, and schools for the blind served as modern symbols of progress— but they were also brick and mortar manufactured by local firms, buildings constructed by local contractors, wages spent in local stores, and markets for food and clothing. In dozens of other ways these charitable institutions were seen as rich foun-

---

28 (1935): 5-52; George M. McConnel, "Recollections of the Northern Cross Railroad," Illinois State Historical Society *Transactions* 13 (1909): 145-52; Eames, *Historic Morgan*, pp. 102-5; *Illinoian*, Jan. 6, Mar. 17, 1838; June 22, 1839; *Gazette and News*, July 6, 1837; Baily, *Gazetteer*, p. 321.

14. David J. Rothman, *The Discovery of the Asylum: Social Order and Disorder in the New Republic* (Boston, 1971), pp. 57-129.

tains of public largess flowing into the local economy. The politicians who created them probably understood the language of the boosters far better than they did the high-minded theories of the reformers. The question of whether Illinois needed state institutions for the insane or blind was quickly subordinated to consideration of a more immediate question: Which town would win the prize? For more than two decades, the voice of Jacksonville proved loud and persuasive in deciding this latter issue, and the whole future of the town became intertwined with the course of institutional reform in Illinois.[15]

The new state institutions built upon Jacksonville's image as the "Athens of the West," an outpost of eastern civilization there to reform the frontier. Before state charitable institutions were created, there was only the most meager recognition of a formal public responsibility toward the poor, the disabled, and the insane. Those who could not be cared for by their families were generally categorized as paupers, as were poor orphans and widows. According to the provisions of the state constitution of 1818, these people were "farmed out at a public vendue or outcry," a practice which invited untold exploitation and cruelties.[16] In Jacksonville the county commissioners grew sensitive to the inadequacy of this practice and in 1839 they made plans to establish "a system for the better regulation, maintenance and support of the paupers of this county." By 1840 they opened a poor farm, on the east side of town, where the poor would work for their support.[17] But in Morgan County and elsewhere there was still very little differentiation among paupers, orphans, widows, and the mentally ill.

A pioneering step toward more careful categorization of dependents took place in 1839, when a state law established an institution for the deaf and dumb. This prize went to Jacksonville, whose citizens had raised almost $1,000 to purchase

15. Black, "Charitable Institutions," p. 175.

16. Morgan County Commissioner Court Records, vols. A-E, 1828-35, Morgan County Courthouse, Jacksonville; Donnelley, Loyd & Co., *History of Morgan County, Illinois: Its Past and Present* . . . (Chicago, 1878), pp. 260-61. Numerous advertisements in local newspapers for runaway indentured servants, most of them young boys, testify to the absence of benign paternalism in many of these arrangements.

17. County Records, vol. B, Sept. 9, 1835, p. 15; Eames, *Historic Morgan*, p. 49.

seven acres of land for it just northwest of the Illinois College campus.[18]

Though slow and limited in its effect on the lagging economy, the Deaf and Dumb Asylum pointed to a whole new course of development for Jacksonville. The town's advantage in the competition for state institutions seemed to cumulate. No sooner had the Deaf and Dumb Asylum opened in 1843 than another prize was bestowed, a state hospital for the insane. A principal mover behind this institution was Dr. Edward Mead, who came to Jacksonville in 1845 to join the faculty at Illinois College's new medical school. Mead brought with him a deep concern for the treatment of the insane, and he found an eager group of boosters and politicians whose interests in advancing their town seemed in full accord with his medical interests in the treatment of insanity. Together they began a vigorous campaign to establish a state institution to rehabilitate the mentally ill. While Mead traveled the state explaining the needs of the insane to citizens and professional medical groups, Jacksonville promoters began working to serve their town's needs.[19]

Since it was clear that only the state could sponsor such an institution, local promoters, represented by William Thomas and the "Jacksonville Crowd," prepared for a vigorous campaign to enact legislation and extract funds from budget-minded, skeptical politicians. Meanwhile, Jacksonville citizens carried out an impressive effort to educate legislators and the public on the conditions of the insane. J. O. King, a local merchant, persuaded Dorothea Dix to come to Illinois and investigate the needs of the insane. Already famous for her reform activities on behalf of the insane in the East, Dix made a well-publicized tour of Illinois and exposed the wretched condition of the insane and disabled. King ushered her from town to town in his buggy as she investigated the county jails and poorhouses and prepared detailed newspaper reports describing the grisly facilities and their unhappy inmates. When the legislative ses-

18. Phillip G. Gillett, *History of the Illinois Institution for the Education of the Deaf and Dumb*, in vol. 1 of *Histories of American Schools for the Deaf, 1817-1893*, ed. Edward Allen Fay (Springfield, 1892), pp. 3-9; Minnie Wait Cleary, "History of the Illinois School for the Deaf," *JISHS* 35 (1942): 368-89.

19. Black, "Charitable Institutions," pp. 183-84.

sion convened in December, 1846, Morgan County's Senator William Thomas also arranged for her to have private talks with small groups of legislators on the need for an institution for the insane.[20]

As the bill to create a state hospital came before the legislature, Jacksonville's promoters found themselves locked in battle with Peoria and Chicago, two aggressive upstate rivals. For a time, the many efforts of Jacksonville's boosters seemed in vain. When the question was called on the location of the new institution, the Senate defeated the proposal for Jacksonville, and upstart Peoria was graced with the prize.[21]

The issue of location still had to be settled in the House. While the politicians were squabbling over the question of location, a Springfield newspaper gave lengthy accounts of the debates and published arguments strongly in favor of Jacksonville. Historians can barely appreciate the full meaning of nineteenth-century boosterism without reading each rival town's arguments for its unique qualifications to host an insane asylum. The Jacksonville proponents pointed to the ill health of Peoria's location on the Illinois River, the advantage of Jacksonville's proximity to the seat of government, and the fact that Jacksonville "was the first to make a movement in this important matter, and its citizens have shown a deep interest in its success." There must have been other persuasive forces at work as well, for when the bill came back to the House William Thomas and the "Jacksonville Crowd" were able to amend the bill to locate the institution in Jacksonville. The "Jacksonville enthusiasm," as one resident referred to it, had rescued the institution, which promised to be not only a lucrative source of income from the state but also the most prominent component of what came to be recognized as a "city of institutions."[22]

20. Donnelley, *History of Morgan*, p. 407; *Sangamon Journal* (Springfield), May 6, 1847.

21. *Journal of the Senate of the Fifteenth General Assembly of the State of Illinois, 1846-47*, pp. 79, 98, 100, 120, 196, 197, 216, 217, 285, 295-96, 301, 302, 311.

22. *Sangamon Journal* (Springfield), Feb. 25, Mar. 4, 1847; *Journal of the House of Representatives of the Fifteenth General Assembly of the State of Illinois, 1846-47*, pp. 532-33, 535; Black, "Charitable Institutions," pp. 184-90; C. H. Rammelkamp, ed., "Memoirs of John Henry," *JISHS* 18 (1925): 64-65; Eames, *Historic Morgan*, pp. 120-23; Donnelley, *History of Morgan*, p. 406; Sturtevant to Baldwin, Illinois College, Feb. 7, 1849,

Even before they secured the State Hospital for the Insane, Jacksonville's promoters were busy laying the groundwork for a third state institution, this one for education of the blind. They invited a teacher of the blind, Joseph Bacon, to come to Jacksonville in 1847. The next year Bacon opened a school for six blind students; it was supported solely by student fees and private donations from Jacksonville citizens. These meager beginnings were part of a shrewd strategy to avoid another battle over location. Richard Yates, who championed the bill for an institution for the blind in the General Assembly, was able to point to an already established institution and ask only for state recognition and funding. Yates successfully acquired state support for Jacksonville's school; furthermore, his bill included a special fund of one-tenth mil on each dollar of taxable land, in addition to a $3,000 appropriation to begin construction of the building.[23]

Similar efforts to strengthen public support were soon extended to all three institutions. The Illinois Institution for Education for the Deaf and Dumb (its name was changed from "Asylum for the Deaf and Dumb" in 1848) appealed for a special tax for its funding, instead of relying on appropriations of a sometimes fickle legislature. "There is," according to one trustee's report, "a degree of uncertainty and instability necessarily connected with this method of supporting the institution." Legislation calmed this anxiety by establishing a special fund of one-sixth mil per dollar of taxable property in the state to support the institution. By 1850 the General Assembly passed similar legislation for funding the State Hospital for the Insane.[24]

In a few short years Jacksonville had dramatically reversed the demoralizing decline and stagnation that had lingered after 1837. Now, with the new state institutions, the town discovered a stable and very promising foundation for further development. Compared to private institutions like Illinois College,

Sturtevant-Baldwin Letters; Paul Russell Anderson, "Hiram K. Jones and Philosophy in Jacksonville," *JISHS* 33 (1940): 479.

23. Black, "Charitable Institutions," p. 191.

24. Gillett, *Deaf and Dumb*, pp. 20-21.

which continued to suffer from the uncertainties of divided and volatile private support, the state institutions stood as proud symbols of progressive reform and generally found abundant financial support. State funds now poured into Jacksonville to construct and maintain new buildings, to pay staff, and to finance programs for the growing numbers of ill and disabled who crowded into Jacksonville's new facilities. In 1846 a thirty-two-room building was constructed, for some $12,000, to serve the deaf and dumb. The cynics who at first scoffed at this "State's Folly," warning that it would remain empty, watched as it quickly filled to capacity and then overflowed into a frame house which had been moved up from town. An elaborate program for academic education, industrial training, and physical exercise subsequently required major expansion of the facilities.

By 1853 the Institution for the Education of the Blind had its own three-story brick building erected on East State Street.[25] But most impressive of the three institutions was the State Hospital for the Insane, which purchased a vast plot of land south of town; where an enormous four-story brick building went up, with two long wings connecting to equally large buildings on either end. These facilities opened in November, 1851, and soon were overflowing with patients. By 1858 over 500 people were under treatment, and the staff was forced to discharge several dozen "incurable" patients to make room for new ones, who were brought to the overcrowded hospital in increasing numbers. A $200,000 program of expansion began that year; new buildings were erected, a new steam-heating system was installed, and other facilities were developed to handle the growing needs of the state's mentally ill. The mental hospital soon became the most prolific source of building contracts, payrolls, and other state revenues for Jacksonville's local economy.[26]

These state charitable institutions seemed to reinforce and

25. Ibid., pp. 206-7; *Illinois Institution for the Education of the Blind: Report, 1857*, in *Reports to the General Assembly, 1857*, pp. 180-90.

26. *Illinois State Hospital for the Insane, Sixth Biennial Report, 1858*; Andrew L. Hoekstra and Lois Wells, "A Short History of the Jacksonville State Hospital" (unpublished paper, 1973). My thanks to the authors for sending me a copy of their paper.

build upon the town's prior reputation as an educational center. In many ways the state institutions shared the same intellectual foundations and reform goals that originally inspired Illinois College. Each sought to transform individuals and society through institutions; each stressed the advantage of immediate treatment for those in need and the value of open access for all social classes. But the college depended on the uncertain foundation of private charity. After years of struggling just to survive, the college administrators must have looked with wonder at the magnificent buildings, well-paid professional staffs, and abundant financial resources these institutions enjoyed.

The college made a bold attempt at expansion when it opened the first medical school in Illinois. This department quietly folded in 1848 due, in part, to inadequate faculty salaries and to a controversy over the use of human cadavers in the anatomy course. Disappointed in their efforts with the medical school, the college trustees abandoned plans to develop schools of law and theology, and the college sank further into debt.[27]

However, some local academicians had been inspired by the success of Jacksonville's state institutions, and they began looking seriously at the possibilities for public support for the college. Jonathan Baldwin Turner began a battle to introduce a plan for a state-supported "industrial university." Since Turner resigned from his professorship at Illinois College in 1847 under strong pressure from the administration, which disliked his unorthodox political and religious views, he felt less remorse than his former colleagues about admitting the failure of sectarian education in the West. His plan, outlined in 1850, envisioned a system of higher education to serve the "industrial classes," providing a thorough education in "practical knowledge," particularly agricultural science. The university, according to Turner's bold design, would be endowed by state funds but administered independently by trustees "responsible to no legislature, sect or party."[28] By 1852 Turner's Industrial

27. Rammelkamp, *Illinois College*, pp. 95-100, 142-45, 570; Sturtevant, *Autobiography*, p. 267.

28. J. B. Turner, "A State University for the Industrial Classes," speech delivered before Illinois Teachers Institute Annual Meeting, Griggsville, Ill., May 13, 1850,

League, organized to promote his idea, was looking toward federal support; its efforts finally came to fruition in the Land Grant College Act of 1862 and the founding of the Illinois Industrial University in 1867. Although this latter prize proved elusive to Jacksonville's boosters, Illinois College began working toward some form of public support. Only by that means would the floundering college enjoy the kind of security and growth that had been so impressively displayed in Jacksonville's three state charitable institutions.

In this same period Jacksonville broadened its reputation as an educational center by creating the Illinois Conference Female Academy of the Methodists. By offering $100 scholarships to families in the region, the Methodists raised sufficient funds to erect a three-story brick building on a large plot of land on East State Street by 1850. From the time when classes were first opened in 1848, the academy was overwhelmed by the numbers of young women who entered. In 1851 it was reincorporated as a college, the first institution in Illinois devoted to the higher education of women.[29]

Another, less successful, attempt at expanding Jacksonville's educational resources was sponsored by the Church of Christ in 1853. Led by Jacksonville's congregation, the Christians quickly raised some $30,000 to purchase land and erect a large brick structure on the east side of town. Berean College was chartered in 1855 and operated only a few years before it dissolved following an 1859 schism in the local congregation.[30]

---

reprinted in Mary Turner Carriel, *The Life of Jonathan Baldwin Turner* (1911; reprinted, Urbana, 1961), pp. 68-85.

29. The establishment of the academy also opened a serious rift between Methodists on the east and west sides, each of whom wanted the school at their end of town. The "East-Enders" won, but Jacksonville's Methodist church later split into "East Charge" and "West Charge" congregations. Frank J. Heinl, *Centennial: J. Capps & Sons, Ltd.* (Jacksonville, 1939), p. 13; Mary Watters, *The First Hundred Years of MacMurray College* (Springfield, Ill., 1947); Clarence P. McClelland, "The Morning Star of Memory," *JISHS* 40 (1947): 253-66; C. P. McClelland, "The Education of Females in Early Illinois," *JISHS* 36 (1943): 378-407; Dr. J. R. Harker, "Progress in the Illinois Conference, 1824-1924," *JISHS* 18 (1925): 159-74; Harry E. Pratt, "Peter Cartwright and the Cause of Education," *JISHS* 28 (1936): 271-78.

30. *History of the Christian Church, Jacksonville, Illinois, 1832-1920* (Jacksonville, 1920), pp. [9-12]; Donnelley, *History of Morgan*, pp. 398-99.

By the middle 1850s Jacksonville boosters had reason to feel a certain sense of relief. The 1850 census reported that the town had resumed growth: its population stood at 2,745, a modest but comforting gain of 845 since 1840. Springfield, in the meantime, had far outpaced its formal rival, and now boasted more than 4,500. It was clear to most that Jacksonville no longer provided a serious economic or political challenge. Rather, the town had nurtured a distinctive image as a genteel, progressive village of colleges, churches, and modern charitable institutions. Local boosters enjoyed comparing this image of refinement with the crass political arena of Springfield, and they consoled themselves that growth was no measure of success. There were also the more tangible benefits of state revenues —some $75,000 in annual operating costs, with several hundred thousand dollars in construction costs over the years. This money fell largely to local contractors, laborers, merchants, and farmers. While Jacksonville's status as the major educational center was still up in the air, local boosters could now face the future with a "city of institutions" that would build upon the apparently firm and enlarging foundation of state support.[31]

This foundation was suddenly shaken by events of the 1850s. The first omen came on a cold winter night in 1852, when the main building at Illinois College mysteriously went up in flames. Though volunteers were able to control the blaze, President Sturtevant awoke the next morning to face "one huge indiscriminate ruin" with "three of the tall chimney stacks—standing like monuments of desolation." Worse yet, the treasurer had allowed a fire insurance policy of $4,000 to lapse, so the college, which had just begun to get back on its feet and to build an independent endowment, now faced a new financial crisis. At first optimistic, Sturtevant and the trustees planned to take the opportunity to build a more suitable structure for general use, instead of rebuilding a dormitory (which Sturtevant disdained because it kept students "remote from domestic influences"

31. Estimate made in *Institution for the Education of the Deaf and Dumb, Biennial Report, 1855-56*, in *Reports to the General Assembly, 1857*, pp. 215, 221; *Institution for the Education of the Blind, Biennial Report, 1855-56*, ibid., pp. 180-90.

provided in private homes in Jacksonville).[32] But support for rebuilding the college was slow to develop, and Sturtevant, presumably in a strategy to stimulate action, publicly threatened that the college would sell out and relocate. Even though this stirred some eighty citizens "of all sects and parties" to organize and canvass the area for subscriptions, they raised only a fraction of the $20,000 needed. Sturtevant was disappointed, and his private correspondence reveals that he began to take seriously his threat to move the college from Jacksonville.[33] The funds necessary for the rebuilding program were slowly accumulated, however, and Illinois College remained one of Jacksonville's principal institutional assets. Although it went on to build a modest endowment that drew heavily upon local resources, events of 1853 had shown that Jacksonville could not afford to take for granted one of its most important institutions.

The prosperity of Illinois College had always been uncertain, but the state institutions were coveted especially for the permanency and security they provided. This, too, was unexpectedly threatened when a scandal over nepotism and graft erupted in the State Hospital for the Insane. Following the 1852 election of Democrat Joel Matteson as governor, a faction of local Democrats led by Colonel James Dunlap began their move to seize control of Jacksonville's state institutions. Dunlap first tried to have his brother appointed hospital superintendent; failing that, he attempted to make him assistant physician. When protests arose from a majority of the seven hospital board members, led by Jonathan Baldwin Turner, the pro-Dunlap minority assumed control of the board and replaced the dissenters with their Democratic cronies. The ousted opponents used the *Morgan Journal* to publish letters and pamphlets denouncing the "evil-minded persons" who would "prostitute these trusts to their own selfish ends." Dunlap and his troupe of supporters entered the office of *Journal* editor Paul Selby following the

32. Rammelkamp, *Illinois College*, pp. 172-73; Sturtevant to Baldwin, Illinois College, Jan. 1, 1853, Sturtevant-Baldwin Letters.

33. Sturtevant to Baldwin, Illinois College, Jan. 13, 1853, Sturtevant-Baldwin Letters. Sturtevant apparently envisioned moving the college to Quincy, a largely New England settlement northwest of Jacksonville. Rammelkamp, *Illinois College*, pp. 174-75.

publication of one particularly biting anonymous letter; they drew guns and knives and then thrashed Selby for refusing to disclose the letter's source.[34]

The scandal quickly rippled through the state. Under the pretext of investigating accusations of graft in the state institutions, Governor Matteson encouraged the General Assembly to enact reforms. After a series of investigations, the legislature began by expanding the hospital's board of trustees to eight. members and replacing the current board with new appointees, including only one from Jacksonville. Under the guise of reform, however, the Democrats were making the state institutions a rich source of patronage for their own party.[35]

Predictably, the entire affair was exposed in neighboring newspapers. "The fact is," one Alton editor ranted, "Jacksonville begins to regard these Institutions . . . as her own peculiar property. . . . It is time that this very erroneous impression was corrected, and Jacksonville taught—as much as the State admires her intelligence and refinement, and rejoices in her prosperity—that she has no more interest in or right to these Institutions than the rest of the State. . . ."[36]

The issue continued to aggravate local affairs for some time. In the fall of 1853 Jonathan Baldwin Turner, who continued to speak out against abuse of local patronage, was the victim of arsonists.[37] In 1855 Governor Matteson appointed another joint legislative committee to investigate charges of corruption within all state institutions in Jacksonville; as a result of the committee's report, the General Assembly passed a law limiting local representation on all the institutions' boards of trustees.[38]

The controversy was very much alive three years later when *Morgan Journal* editor Paul Selby accused Colonel W. B. Warren (a fellow Southerner and crony of James Dunlap), then trea-

34. *Protest in Behalf of Illinois Hospital for the Insane* (Jacksonville, 1852); *Another Shawneetown Bank Affair: The Insane Hospital* (Jacksonville, 1853), both in Illinois State Historical Library; Richard Dewey, "Jacksonville State Hospital," in *Institutional Care for the Insane in the United States and Canada*, ed. Henry M. Hurd (Baltimore, 1916), II, 189.

35. Ibid., p. 201.

36. Reprinted in *Journal*, May 19, 1853.

37. Carriel, *Turner*, pp. 213-18.

38. *Report of the Joint Select Committee—to Visit Jacksonville, Appointed 1855*, in *Reports to the General Assembly, 1857*.

surer of the State Hospital for the Insane, of shaving $200 off an order to a local carpenter. Selby and Warren exchanged insults in the rival newspapers; then one afternoon Selby was walking with two friends on the public square when he encountered Colonel Warren with his son and another unidentified relative. Warren, armed with a cane and "cowhide," assaulted Selby, who retaliated by bashing Warren on the head with a revolver. The others joined in, and in the bloody fight which ensued canes, bludgeons, and horse whips were "freely used, under the most excited feeling."[39]

The accusations of graft and the dissension that followed from the Warren-Selby affray in Jacksonville brought strong official rebukes from the legislature's joint committee of investigation. "The difficulties and ill feeling which the committee regret to find existing in Jacksonville between a portion of the citizens and some of the acting members of the board, who reside there," led the committee to recommend further controls over local involvement in the state institutions. These controls limited Jacksonville's representation on the boards and endangered the local monopoly on state contracts for construction and supplies. If boosterism appealed to local unity, its victories also brought new spoils over which to battle.[40]

RAILROAD TOWN, 1853-60

While the "city of institutions" was suffering the unexpected assaults of 1853, local boosters turned toward yet another vision of the town's future, one made possible by the advent of the railroad. The faith in railroad transportation, temporarily disappointed by the Northern Cross adventure in the late 1830s, suddenly found new life in the mid-1850s. Illinois possessed only 110 miles of railroads in 1850; the figure leaped suddenly to 2,135 by 1856 and was almost 3,000 by the close of the decade.[41] This rapid increase reflected the long-overdue needs

39. *Jacksonville Constitutionist*, Nov. 2, 1853; *Sentinel*, Feb. 22, Mar. 21, 28, Apr. 18, May 16, 23, 30, June 13, 20, 1856.

40. *Report of the Joint Select Committee, 1857*, pp. 5, 238-39.

41. Joseph C. G. Kennedy, *Preliminary Report on the Eighth Census, 1860* (Washington, 1862), pp. 227-28.

of the agricultural hinterland for adequate transportation to markets; furthermore, the railroad boom fed off the rabid competitiveness of nascent frontier towns struggling to establish ascendant positions. The railroad seemed to open the race for urban prominence all over again. Towns that had been passed by in the first round of county-seat battles, internal improvement schemes, or state institutions competed with a new intensity to acquire transportation routes, the lack of which many of them saw as the only barrier to their inevitable development as great cities.[42]

A town like Jacksonville, which might have been content to rest upon its reputation as the refined home of education and state charity, was now aroused by the lust for commercial empire. Boosters wasted no time in responding to the new railroad bonanza. The dilapidated Northern Cross had been acquired by eastern capitalists in 1847 and renamed the Sangamon-Morgan Railroad. The line was entirely rehabilitated by July, 1849, and reopened, this time with more success. Local businessmen could now import goods shipped up the Mississippi and Illinois Rivers at about two-thirds the previous cost.[43]

Though it continued as a successful line, the route from Jacksonville to the Illinois River was soon circumvented by Springfield's connection to Alton on the Mississippi. The Springfield and Alton Railroad began operation in 1850, and by 1852 it had added steamship service downriver to St. Louis. The next year the line was extended northward to Normal, where it connected, via the Illinois Central and the Rock Island Line, to the bustling ports and rail depots of Chicago and from there to the rich markets of the East.[44]

Springfield managed to establish connections to the two most important ports and rail centers in the West during the same disastrous period when Illinois College burned and the state institutions came under attack. All of these events only fueled

42. Paul W. Gates, *The Illinois Central Railroad and Its Colonization Work* (1934; reprinted, New York, 1968), pp. 16, 122.

43. Hildner, *Jacksonville*, p. 5; John Moses, *Illinois Historical and Statistical* . . . (Chicago, 1889), II, 1045, gives rates of the new railroad; *Patriot*, May 11, 1833; William K. Ackerman, *Early Illinois Railroads* (Chicago, 1884), pp. 106-7.

44. Arthur Charles Cole, *The Era of the Civil War, 1848-1870*, The Centennial History of Illinois, vol. 3 (Chicago, 1919), pp. 42-43.

the boosters' energy. A furious effort was now initiated to create a network of railroad lines which would bring Jacksonville the rich harvest of cattle and grain in central Illinois. Each railroad radiating from Jacksonville connected to Chicago or St. Louis but deliberately avoided rival Springfield. (See map, p. 82.) To the north two roads would wind toward Chicago: the Jacksonville, Havana Railroad (which became part of the Illinois River Railroad) and the Tonica and Petersburg Railroad (which connected with the Illinois Central at Bloomington). The Sangamon-Morgan line was extended from Naples to Quincy, where it connected to the prosperous Chicago, Burlington, and Quincy. To the south, Jacksonville sought its own direct connection "without paying tribute to Springfield" by building the Jacksonville-Carrollton Railroad, later extended as the Jacksonville, Alton, and St. Louis Railroad.[45]

In this race to throw out transportation lines, Jacksonville could not look to the state government, which still remembered the expensive lessons of the Northern Cross. Instead, private subscriptions and bond issues at a county or town level provided funds. "No one man can build a plankroad or a railroad," James Berdan reminded a mass meeting of citizens in Jacksonville in 1853. "This must be done by a combination of all who are interested; and"—he evoked the booster's familiar equation of individual and communal destinies—"every man who owns real estate is interested."[46]

By 1855, when local railroad promoters were trying to whip up support, they pointed ominously to Springfield's gains in population and business activity. "Unless something is done soon to hurry up Old Morgan to her proper rank, it will be but a short time 'till Trade will be to us but a transient passenger, sleepily looking out the car windows on the Great Western Road, and then, wondering at our sluggishness, sinking back to sleep until it reaches—*Springfield*." Businessmen and farmers were urged to support railroad development if Jacksonville was to become "renowned not only for its educational but for its business facilities."[47]

45. *Sentinel*, Feb. 9, 1855.
46. *Journal*, May 5, 1853.
47. *Sentinel*, Dec. 7, 1855.

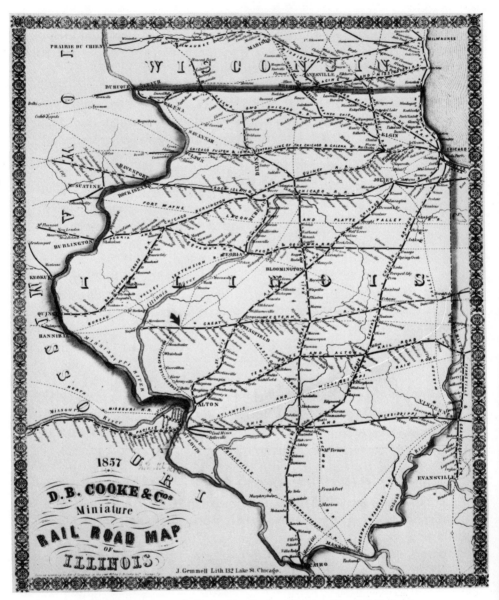

Illinois Railroads, 1857. From Newberry Library, Special Collections.

This last appeal was a gentle way of suggesting that the educational and state rehabilitative institutions were inadequate foundations for Jacksonville's future growth as a major city. In an editorial entitled "Jacksonville—her future," J. R. Baily dealt at length with the town's recent gains and the need for future development of commerce and manufacturing. "She has, it is true, thus far attained a fair start, in the race, with her sister towns in the state, but if she neglects laying a firm basis by securing those commercial advantages now within her reach, she may yet be outstripped and shorn of much future prosperity."[48] "Jacksonville," an editorial the following month reiterated, "has hitherto be[en] in advance of most of our inland towns, and the only way that she can continue her growth to [become] a city of extensive business and heavy population will be to increase her facilities inviting the accumulation of capital and labor. These by the invariable laws of trade concentrate only at such places as afford an easy and cheap transit of their supplies and productions."[49]

Worried by attacks on its state institutions and anxious about Springfield's growing advantage, Jacksonville once more raised its hopes and joined the race for urban prominence, this time as a city of commerce and industry. Local promoters watched the progress of railroad development with satisfaction; by 1860 Jacksonville had five separate rail links to the outside world. Railroads were promoted with techniques similar to those used to bring colleges and state institutions to Jacksonville. Mass meetings were called, and local capital was drawn out through warnings of ascendant rivals and promises of the abundant wealth within the community's reach. Local subscriptions flowed freely from businessmen and farmers anxious to profit from Jacksonville's development as a commercial depot. Boards of directors were carefully chosen from among prominent citizens of Jacksonville and other towns along each rail line, and local voters approved large bond issues which were floated in the East to support these ventures.[50]

48. Ibid., Feb. 9, 1855.
49. Ibid., Mar. 16, 1855.
50. Ibid., Dec. 5, 1856; *Illinois Daily Journal* (Springfield), May 27, 1856; *Illinois State*

The strong support for railroad development was in direct response to the lucrative rewards railroads brought to local businessmen and farmers. The meager volume of exports reported in the 1850 census showed Morgan County's need for agricultural market outlets. By 1856 over 30,000 bushels of wheat and nearly 1,500 head of hogs were exported by rail in the month of October alone.[51] While wheat and pork found ready markets, Morgan County's agricultural forte emerged in the 1850s in a prosperous cattle trade. The leader of the local beef industry was a colorful German named Jacob Strawn, who owned several thousand acres of land—almost half a million dollars' worth—mostly east and south of Jacksonville. He sold $96,000 in beef in 1854 and for years supplied or controlled the entire St. Louis beef market. Together with William M. Cassel, John T. and George D. Alexander, these Jacksonville "cattle kings" built their empires on the progress of railroads in Morgan County and were later to reap enormous profits from the demand for beef during the Civil War.[52] "Agriculture flourished as never before," wrote one buoyant observer of Morgan County in the railroad era; "the rich prairies around were loaded with their harvests, and thousands of fat cattle were wading knee deep in the blue grass of their pastures, and every farm yard was filled with squealing hogs and bleating sheep. Every train that whistled out of our city was loaded with rich freight, and soon returned, as heavily loaded, with the necessities and luxuries of life."[53]

Jacksonville's success in railroad building seemed to feed upon itself, and its growth as an agricultural marketing center led only to higher expectations. As one booster predicted, "Our city, in addition to her other elements of prosperity, will at no distant day become an important manufacturing point. . . .

Journal (Springfield), Nov. 26, 1857. On railroad promotion, see also *Sentinel*, Nov. 30, 1855; Mar. 10, Feb. 22, Nov. 21, Dec. 5, 1856; Apr. 13, 25, May 27, Nov. 26, 1857; June 27, Oct. 15, 1858.

51. J. D. B. DeBow, *Statistical View of the United States . . . A Compendium of the Seventh Census . . .* (Washington, 1854), pp. 222-23; *Sentinel*, Nov. 21, 1856.

52. Cole, *Civil War*, pp. 83n, 376-77. Paul W. Gates, "Cattle Kings in the Prairies," *Mississippi Valley Historical Review* 35 (1948): 383-86, 402.

53. Baily, *Gazetteer*, p. 322.

'Old fogeyism' will be routed from our midst and a new impetus will be given manufacture, commerce and trade, that will bear us forward in successful rivalry with any other section of the West."[54] Two years later another Jacksonville advocate escalated these goals: "When these roads shall have been finished, Jacksonville will be the center of a greater number of rail roads than any other inland town in Illinois." "Jacksonville," he added, "is destined to be one of the largest cities in the State."[55] Indeed, the new railroads were bringing people as well as goods and capital into the town. The state census of 1855 reported more than 6,000 inhabitants, more than double the population five years earlier.[56]

The population and prosperity that attended the coming of the railroads brought a rapid spiral of land prices. Lots around the square rose from $50-$100 in 1849 to as much as $1,500 by 1855.[57] Property within the mile-square city limits was built up with large homes (concentrated on College Hill), and a multitude of shanties and tenements (on the north end, surrounding the railroad depot). A good deal of land on the periphery was now occupied by the spacious grounds of the various academies and state institutions, further limiting the number of available sites. By November, 1856, Jacksonville promoters were advertising a "Great Sale of Lots" in the first addition outside the former town limits. A large tract of land south of town and just east of the State Hospital for the Insane was divided into large lots of two to five acres and sold at public auction for $300 to $690 per lot. Though the lots were advertised as "suitable for private residents," most buyers were looking toward Jacksonville's future growth, when the population would spread southward and bring rich rewards to those who speculated early.[58]

54. *Sentinel*, Nov. 30, 1855.

55. *Illinois State Journal* (Springfield), Nov. 26, 1857.

56. Reported in *Illinois Daily Journal* (Springfield), Aug. 17, 1855; *Sentinel*, Jan. 17, 1856.

57. Morgan County Tax Lists, 1849, 1855, Morgan County Courthouse, Jacksonville.

58. *Illinois Daily Journal* (Springfield), Oct. 25, 1856; *Sentinel*, July 25, Nov. 7, 24, 1856.

The trend was only beginning to be apparent, according to advertisements: "No one thinks strange of being asked three or four times as much for a lot of ground now as it sold three or four years ago," one ebullient editor reported. Lots around the square, another claimed, "have increased six or seven fold in value. . . . All have been touched by the magic influence of railroad connections with the principal markets." These gains would be made ten times over in the near future, one booster proclaimed, pointing to the "many advantages we enjoy commercially, socially, and especially in an educational point of view. . . . We shall soon," he prophesied, "be gathering an influx of population which will shake fogeyism to its very centre. . . ."[59] One observer noted, in 1856, that "the suburbs of our pleasant city are already dotted by the erection of new buildings, some already completed and others in progress." These, he said, were "much needed to accommodate the increasing business and population of the place. . . . A ten years onward progress at the present ratio of increase," he dreamed, "will make Jacksonville 'some' of a place."[60]

As the town grew, its promoters continued to project the image of distinctive beauty and order. "From the square, in every direction for the distance of a mile in one or two instances, they have sidewalks made of plank," wrote an envious Springfield visitor. "These walks are well shaded, and thus makes a beautiful walk."[61] Elms, which soon grew into pleasant shade trees along West State Street, were planted in other sections of town. A local editor encouraged each homeowner to plant trees and shrubs on his own lot to make "our city surpassingly beautiful."[62] With Jonathan Baldwin Turner (a college professor turned horticulturist) setting the standards, the area surrounding College Hill developed into a lovely residential section. "In no place," wrote one partial observer, "is there such uniformity of neatness and good taste. . . ."[63]

59. *Sentinel*, Nov. 7, Dec. 5, 1856.
60. Ibid., May 16, 1856.
61. *Illinois Daily Journal* (Springfield), July 15, 1851. See also ibid., Nov. 8, 1853, for a Springfield visitor's long description of Jacksonville's beauty and orderliness.
62. *Journal*, Mar. 15, 1860.
63. Baily, *Gazetteer*, p. 322.

The center of town was also improved to conform to the new dictates of taste, order, and prosperity. The ugly courthouse still offended one editor, who described it as "disgraceful to the community's character of liberality and public spirit."[64] But around the square rose a number of new brick buildings, some of them three stories high, which replaced, for the most part, the shoddy rows of frame buildings present in earlier years. Though the offensive railroad depot was removed from the square to the northern part of town in 1849, it was, of course, the rail lines which brought new prosperity to business on the square. "Our streets are becoming enlivened with the bustle of Spring business," reported one paper, "and our sturdy draymen are kept constantly engaged in transporting boxes, bales, barrels, etc. from the Depot to the square." "On Saturdays especially," the same editor wrote, "our streets are thronged with wagons and people. . . . Since her acquisition of railroad facilities, the business of Jacksonville has been rapidly increasing and her borders enlarging."[65]

The railroad boom also brought several significant changes in the character of commercial activity. New services were now in demand as Jacksonville became a major entrepôt for beef, pork, and agricultural products. In 1852 Marshall and Augustus Ayers opened a bank, the first in Jacksonville since the ill-fated state bank collapsed in 1842. The new bank was unchartered and held meager capital assets, but it provided an essential service that helped meet a growing demand from local farmers, cattle ranchers, and businessmen for ready credit. Capital had previously been available only through wealthy individuals who made high-risk loans, often with rapacious rates of interest. When R. Elliot and William Brown introduced a second local bank in 1858, customers could be more confident of borrowing at competitive rates and with less dependence on the personal ties or political loyalties that must have played an important role in the less formal lending that went on before.[66]

64. *Journal*, Mar. 15, 1860.

65. *Sentinel*, Apr. 4, 1856; Apr. 26, 1855.

66. Donnelley, *History of Morgan*, p. 354; Frederick Gerhard, *Illinois as It Is* (Chicago, 1857), p. 426; *Journal*, July 1, 1858. Both banking partnerships changed several times in subsequent years.

Other businesses were established to profit from processing the agricultural goods which were arriving in Jacksonville. Edward Lambert opened a slaughterhouse and meat-packing factory to supplement the Morgan County cattle industry; by 1860 a tannery also opened, to the enthusiastic praise of local boosters.[67] Joseph Capps, who had operated a wool-carding business in Jacksonville since 1839, expanded in 1857 by opening a "large woolen manufactory." This factory began producing a variety of items, including blankets, shirting, and women's dress goods, most of which were aimed at the retail market in Jacksonville and outlying towns.[68]

Aside from financial and processing services that built up around agricultural exports, some very noticeable developments took place in Jacksonville's retail business during the late 1850s. First, the general store and the barter system were quickly disappearing. The numerous dry goods merchants still handled a wide range of merchandise, from patent medicines to ladies' corsets, but more specialized stores were opening each year.[69] A typical list of advertisers in the 1858 *Morgan Journal* included Austin Rockwell, specializing in agricultural implements; W. Catlin and Co., musical instruments and books; Frederick Fries, wigs, toupees, and hair dressing; William M. Mayo, pianos and jewelry; John Q. Adams, news and periodicals; William M. Harlo, furniture and pianos. Though most merchants hedged by carrying more than one line of goods, these stores were marked departures from the former general store.[70]

The increasing numbers and prosperity of the surrounding population were, of course, important reasons for these changes, but the cheap railroad access to markets in Chicago, St. Louis, and the East made these new merchandising practices possible. Several of the larger merchants now went east each spring to purchase wholesale goods directly, avoiding the

67. *Sentinel*, Jan. 17, 1856; *Journal*, May 17, 1860.

68. Heinl, *Centennial: J. Capps*, pp. 5, 7. Complementing the cattle industry in Morgan County was a thriving sheep-raising business dominated by a settlement of Yorkshire immigrants outside of Jacksonville.

69. Lewis E. Atherton, *The Frontier Merchant in Mid-America* (1939; reprinted, Columbia, Mo., 1971), pp. 142-53.

70. *Journal*, July 1, 1858.

higher prices of St. Louis. They proudly advertised a wide selection of stock, personally selected and purchased by the proprietor. A growing segment of the retail market now consisted of the wealthy middle class who were anxious to adorn their homes with books, pianos, jewelry, expensive furniture, and other accoutrements of a genteel, cultured lifestyle made all the more precious by the distance from the East, where these goods originated. Many advertisements were clearly aimed at women shoppers, who were assured that the latest eastern fashions were available and that service was courteous and prompt.[71]

Along with specialization came other important changes in the methods of merchandising. The competition of Jacksonville's booming business environment and the wider readership of local newspapers produced a noticeable increase and elaboration of advertising. Where previously it was considered sufficient merely to list one's firm and general line of products in an unobtrusive two or three-line advertisement, now whole columns of the paper were devoted to elaborating on the great variety and high quality of merchandise. The relentless announcements of inventory or seasonal sales seemed to anticipate modern merchandising techniques. Even sacred holidays became vulnerable to commercial exploitation. With only four shopping days left before Christmas, a local editor looked forward to "its proverbial array of good cheer; its roast pigs, fat turkeys, and last but not least, its Santa Clause, with his endless store of nicities to gladden the hearts of happy childhood. . . . The hard cares of business are for the time discarded and forgotten and the heart expands for a brief season under the influence of a happy holiday." "Our business establishments," he added immediately and with unintended irony, "are prepared to supply the holiday wants of the public." A list of merchants and gift suggestions followed.[72]

A more significant change in business practices involved the switch to cash trade, which replaced the traditional credit sys-

---

71. See Atherton, *Frontier Merchant*, pp. 65-67; Richard C. Wade, *The Urban Frontier: The Rise of Western Cities, 1790-1830* (Chicago, 1959), pp. 129-57.

72. *Sentinel*, Dec. 21, 1855.

tem for several of the larger merchants in the late 1850s. The risk of extending credit and the problems of collecting bills were extraordinary, given the shortage of cash and the rapid turnover of the population. The newspapers in any given year were filled with both subtle appeals and angry threats by worried creditors demanding money from evasive debtors. Prices were often advertised to be lower to cash customers, but this inducement could not affect the many farmers and craftsmen who bartered produce or services and saw little cash during the year.

The flush times of the middle 1850s brought more capital into circulation, however. By 1856 Corcoran and Austin, one of the largest firms in Jacksonville, announced their switch to straight cash trade. By offering lower prices, they hoped to compete with merchants who still extended credit. This policy was followed by other merchants but apparently was not popular with farmers in the area; they still relied upon the personal ties with a local merchant in order to secure needed credit, which they then paid off at the next harvest. The *Morgan Journal* praised a compromise policy adopted by Alexander McDonald; he offered low prices to cash customers and to those who paid their bill at least once a year, instead of raising prices across the board to cover bad credit risks.[73] It is likely that other merchants also found it convenient to continue extending credit and adjusting prices to established customers, but the traditional practice of credit and barter was now significantly modified by more rigid policies of credit and bill collection.

The credit system collapsed entirely for a time following the Crash of 1857. Though many businessmen were hurt by the crash at first, its overall effect was to increase Jacksonville's commercial strength. Most of the merchants operating in small villages and crossroads in Morgan County went under entirely, enabling the larger Jacksonville merchants, who had sufficient capital reserves, to take advantage of the misfortune of their smaller competitors by carefully fostering trade with rural customers and thereby enlarging the Jacksonville market.[74]

73. Ibid., Dec. 14, 1855; *Journal*, Jan. 26, 1860.
74. Baily, *Gazetteer*, p. 322. "Weils Clothing House, Redemption [1857]," broadside B-423, Illinois State Historical Library.

By 1860 Jacksonville had staged a remarkable comeback as a booming young town. After laying an innovative foundation of state charitable institutions and elaborating upon its reputation as an educational center in the 1840s, the "Athens of the West" set out to create a somewhat incongruous but moderately successful reputation as a commercial and manufacturing center in the 1850s. Though they may have been defined differently by those on College Hill and those on the town square, and though they changed with each new prize that loomed on the horizon, the goals of material progress provided an undeniable sense of common purpose among Jacksonville's leading citizens. Boosterism could bring enemies together across political, sectarian, or regional divisions in a united effort to make their town a great city (and to make their fortunes great as well). "Every country town," Lewis Atherton explains, "had an inner circle whose own personal interests were so tightly interwoven with those of the community at large that one cannot determine where self-interest ended and public spirit began."[75] But the bonds of boosterism were both limited and tenuous—limited to the extent that they embraced only those who stood to gain from the town's future success; tenuous because the bonds of boosterism rested on the inflated hopes of anxious promoters. "Property is rising in value," exclaimed one eager booster. "Jacksonville is destined to become one of the most prosperous as well as one of the most beautiful cities in the State."[76] But from its own past experience, Jacksonville knew these hopes could be easily denied in the open and unpredictable race of mere ambitious towns striving to become great cities.

75. Lewis Atherton, *Main Street on the Middle Border* (Bloomington, Ind., 1954), pp. 23, 24-32.
76. *Sentinel*, Apr. 26, 1855.

Citizens and Strangers

Many came here with no idea of permanent stay, but as a place for outlook for a future home still further on in the wilds. They were here as in a sort of caravansary for a temporary sojourn.

—TRUMAN POST[1]

THE BOOSTERS' DREAM of urban greatness countered the contentiousness that plagued Jacksonville's formative years, but that dream did not always appear to everyone in the same form. The link between individual opportunity and community destiny was strongest among those who enjoyed some material investment in the town and who planned to linger long enough to turn a profit on that investment. This chapter will demonstrate that only a small core of Jacksonville's population had an ongoing interest in the town's future. While these citizens enjoyed rich opportunities for individual upward social mobility, most of the town's population at any given time were transient strangers.

Jacksonville newspapers frequently used traditional terms— "citizens," for permanent residents, and "strangers" for outsiders—as though they had the same meaning they once had in a more settled society. However, in a community of newcomers, churning with continual migration, it was not so easy to tell the difference. The transient quality of the frontier became a central feature of nineteenth-century American life, and it lay at the very heart of the problem of community in Jacksonville.

1. Truman Augustus Post, *Truman Marcellus Post: A Biography Personal and Literary* (Boston, 1891), p. 49.

To alarmists of the day, the migratory frontier and the teeming cities were both seen as disturbing symptoms of social disintegration. The traditional order of family and community were being surrendered to the demands of an expansive, democratic, capitalist society of self-reliant individuals, or "self-made men," according to the expression of the day.

Measured against the communal ideals of the past, these fears were partially justified; yet the new community emerging in Jacksonville designed its economic and social institutions, as well as its values, around this constant movement of the population. A hidden and largely unconscious social order was constructed amid all the movement. This chapter will explore that hidden order by examining how economic forces and the dictates of the life cycle selectively ordered the procession of migration, and how the household, family, and kinship helped organize a transient community.

MOVERS

Theoretically, almost everyone stood to gain something from Jacksonville's future growth. A rise in land values was not the only way to prosper in a booming town; laborers might also profit from more work and higher wages, landlords from higher rents, merchants and tavern-keepers from more customers. While the boosters never lost a chance to recite this theme, their purpose was to create illusions. Their image of a community united by collective material interest is almost impossible to penetrate, if we look only at their own carefully constructed imagery as it was presented in contemporary newspapers.

Other historical records allow us to look at the community from a different angle. The most fruitful sources are the federal census manuscripts, particularly those for 1850, 1860, and 1870, when complete information on every individual's age, occupation, wealth, and birthplace was collected by the census marshal as he made his rounds. These records allow the historian to follow the census-taker on his tour, and to peek into the private sphere of community life. With the aid of twentieth-century computer technology, we can summarize the data from hundreds of these individuals and families and trace them from one census to the next. The clatter of computer hardware can hardly match the flamboyant rhetoric of the town booster, but with its assistance these mute lists can speak volumes about the social context of community in Jacksonville.[2]

Walking the streets of Jacksonville today, one cannot help sensing the appearance of stability and continuity in this small community. Unravaged by the throes of industrialization and rapid growth, the old houses stand as though part of an unintended museum of nineteenth-century architecture, some showing the weather of age and neglect, others gracefully preserved by caring owners. Surely the magnificent old homes on College Hill, each with a unique design, were custom built to suit the particular tastes and needs of individual owners. In a new western town the elite made a special effort to build elaborate homes to display newly acquired wealth. The houses of Jacksonville's Southerners, with their large Doric columns in front, are interspersed among ornate Victorian houses with expansive front porches, oval windows, elaborate cupolas, and gingerbread decoration. These were dwellings built for families who planned to live out their lives, and those of generations yet to come, in the community. In the parlors of those old homes one can almost hear the buzz of gossip—of marriages, deaths, and scandals—the kind of gossip that informs and knits together an intimate community. Here must have been a midwestern town equal to the fictional settings of Sinclair Lewis and Edgar Lee Masters. Jacksonville appears in retrospect to convey all the security and intimacy, along with the parochial pride and internecine jealousies, that an urban nation now imagines to have inhered in the small-town life of a simpler past.

For the wealthy families who owned homes on College Hill, this image of community bore an undeniable relation to historical experience. In contrast, most of those who resided in Jack-

2. Norman H. Nie et al., *SPSS: Statistical Package for the Social Sciences*, 2nd ed. (New York, 1975), and Merle Curti et al., *The Making of an American Community: A Case Study of Democracy in a Frontier County* (Stanford, 1959), have both been instrumental to coding and computer processing of the census data in this chapter.

sonville a century ago lived in nondescript frame cottages or four-flat tenements, few of which have survived along with the mansions. Or they lived in the homes of the wealthy, in attics or basements or in small ten-by-ten rooms at the top of steep, narrow stairways that led from the kitchens where they worked.[3] Their rooms, like the wagons or railroad cars that brought them to Jacksonville, were little more than temporary quarters during a brief stay.

Transients were such a common part of nineteenth-century western towns that contemporary accounts adopted the term "movers" to describe this portion of the population, as though migration alone defined their social place. Often this expression referred to anyone in the process of migration to a new western home.[4] However, the movement of people through Jacksonville involved more than a fringe population of westward-bound pioneers. The turnover of the population, in fact, involved all but a small stable core; around this core flowed two contradictory currents of immigration and emigration.

For each census between 1850 and 1870 individual data were gathered for every household head, for all others who reported some gainful employment, and for any other males twenty years or older. The individuals who fell into one or more of these three categories make up what we may call the "non-dependent population." By attempting to trace these individuals from one census to the next, we learn the first demographic fact of life in nineteenth-century Jacksonville: only a minority of the population remained in the community for a decade. A little over one-quarter of those in the 1850 non-dependent population could be traced to the 1860 census. The turnover of population increased with the turmoil of the Civil War; only 21 percent could be traced from 1860 to 1870. Some of those who disappeared were women who changed their names by marriage but remained in town; others died, and still others may have been temporarily away when the census marshal came around. But

3. Special thanks to Mrs. Alma Smith and Mr. and Mrs. Ernest Hildner for personal tours of their nineteenth-century homes in Jacksonville.

4. Mitford M. Mathews, ed., *A Dictionary of Americanisms on Historical Principles* (Chicago, 1951), II, 1092.

none of these factors could have changed the persistence rates by more than a few percentage points.[5]

While this steady flow of out-migration was draining Jacksonville, far larger numbers were continually moving into the community, producing a net gain between each census. (See Appendix, Table 1.) The railroads, state institutions, and processing mills generated a booming economy with opportunities that attracted hundreds of newcomers in the 1850s and 1860s. Given the constant out-migration, a population several times larger than the net population gained had to move into Jacksonville over the course of the decade.[6] This mobility was part of a pattern in nineteenth-century America, as a rapidly growing population distributed itself across the continent. In cities, towns, and rural counties of all sizes, the rate of persistence over a decade normally hovered between 40 and 50 percent.[7] Jacksonville's persistence rates were lower, not because the town's economy was stagnant, but because the community grew within a rapidly developing region. It served as a "caravansary" (to use Truman Post's apt term) where migrants stopped briefly before choosing a nearby site for permanent settlement, or before following the perpetual lure of new opportunities in the next town, county, or state. Jacksonville experienced only a mildly exaggerated form of a more general phenomenon that

5. The non-dependent population contained about 7% women in 1850, 19% in 1860, and 24% in 1870. Persistence among males alone was 28% 1850-60 and 24% 1860-70.

6. See Stephan Thernstrom and Peter R. Knights, "Men in Motion: Some Data and Speculations about Urban Population Mobility in Nineteenth-Century America," *Journal of Interdisciplinary History* 1 (1970): 7-35, on the relation between annual and decennial population turnover.

7. The number of mobility studies has multipled in recent years. Stephan Thernstrom, *The Other Bostonians: Poverty and Progress in the American Metropolis, 1880-1970* (Cambridge, Mass., 1973), pp. 221-32, and Peter R. Knights and Richard S. Alcorn, "Most Uncommon Bostonians: A Critique of Stephan Thernstrom's *The Other Bostonians*," *Historical Methods Newsletter* 8 (1975): 101, both summarize the results of many of these studies. See also Curti, *American Community*, pp. 65-77; Howard P. Chudacoff, *Mobile Americans: Residential and Social Mobility in Omaha, 1880-1920* (New York, 1971); Peter R. Knights, *The Plain People of Boston, 1830-1860: A Study in City Growth* (New York, 1971). Richard S. Alcorn, "Leadership and Stability in Mid-Nineteenth-Century America: A Case Study of an Illinois Town," *Journal of American History* 61 (1974): 685-702. Other sources on mobility in western towns are cited in my article on "Social Theory and New Communities in Nineteenth-Century America," *Western Historical Quarterly* 8 (1977): 155-56, note 8.

reshaped community life almost everywhere in nineteenth-century America.

This central fact of mobility offers an important key to our understanding of the nineteenth-century American community; it also provides the most frustrating obstacle to the historian's task of research. No amount of diligence can overcome the unhappy fact that most transients left behind few tracks. Yet the historian's problems in knowing more about Jacksonville's inhabitants may be nothing more than an echo of the difficulty they experienced in knowing one another.

Jacksonville was more than a place where strangers passed one another. Within the dynamic flow of population a stable core persisted, of people who built businesses, homes, and careers in Jacksonville, who raised children there and watched as those children took their own places in the community. In the late 1860s, when the first generation of early pioneers began to die off, some called a meeting for all "old settlers" (defined rigorously at first as those in Morgan before the unforgettable Deep Snow of '31). The courthouse overflowed with people who came to share a common past. In the 1870s, when the first local history was published for Jacksonville and Morgan County, the inevitable list of "old settlers" included some four hundred citizens with a half-century of history in or near the community.[8]

Selective forces pulled newcomers to Jacksonville and continually pushed others away. These forces were stronger at some levels of the social structure than at others, and they left some unmoved for decades. The important variables that helped set apart Jacksonville's transient strangers from the more stable citizens were occupational status, wealth, and stage in the cycle of life.

OCCUPATION AND MOBILITY

Although the stable core of Jacksonville's population agreed that the boosters' link between individual opportunity and

---

8. Donnelley, Loyd & Co., *History of Morgan County, Illinois: Its Past and Present* (Chicago, 1878), pp. 319-30; *Sentinel*, Sept. 2, 1870. See Lewis Atherton, *Main Street on the Middle Border* (Bloomington, Ind., 1954), pp. 206-9.

community destiny was undeniable, the pursuit of individual opportunity compelled most people to migrate continually from one town to the next. In Jacksonville, and most communities of nineteenth-century America, those who worked in less-skilled jobs moved more often than those of higher status.[9] Table 2 shows that Jacksonville's growth in this period was accompanied by a significant increase in the number of unskilled laborers. This group included railroad workers, domestic servants, and a large majority who had no specific skills and were listed in the census simply as "laborers." The migration of these workers into Jacksonville was enormous compared to other occupational groups; their share of the work force went from less than one-fifth to more than one-third between 1850 and 1870. But this same group of unskilled laborers contributed most to out-migration, as Table 3 illustrates. Only 13 and 9 percent persisted for a decade or more.

So, while Jacksonville experienced a growing demand for unskilled labor due to the boom in railroads, construction, and the requirements of an increasingly prosperous middle class for servants, there was a constant stream of laborers leaving the community at the same time. This contradiction is explained largely by short-term fluctuations in demand for unskilled labor, particularly in the case of seasonal work like housing, highway, and railroad construction, that ebbed during the cold winter months. Draymen and railroad loaders, who helped transport agricultural supplies and products at the beginning and end of each growing season, were also victims of winter unemployment. Each laborer's year was probably filled with several brief jobs; for draymen and common laborers, this could mean employment from day to day. When the demand for construction crews and day labor flagged with the end of harvest and the onset of winter, Jacksonville's economy was neither large enough nor diverse enough to absorb many of these workers, and they moved on to new jobs elsewhere. Then, as the tempo of the local economy picked up in the spring, as construction was renewed and as farmers streamed into town for new supplies, Jacksonville recruited hundreds of new workers to

9. See sources in note 7, above.

satisfy the seasonal demand. This process occurred without newspapers publishing advertisements for workers and without deliberate recruitment. Those anonymous movers who responded to the unspoken call for workers in Jacksonville unfortunately left no records explaining how they understood this process.[10]

Even within this transient lower stratum of the work force there existed a small stable element, many of them domestic servants, who found more steady employment or were able to adapt to seasonal fluctuations in the job market. Some were simply too old or too burdened with family to keep up with the relentless search for new employment. All of them shared at least a small part of the economic prosperity that had drawn them to Jacksonville, but most found their stay much too brief and their stake in the community far too shallow for them to be a part of the booster's community of collective interests.

Those with special skills were significantly more stable than those below them on the occupational ladder. In the 1850s and 1860s about one-fourth of the skilled laborers could be traced through two consecutive censuses. They experienced less pressure in Jacksonville than in eastern cities, where industrialization was quickly making their skills obsolete. Some, however, did find themselves in competition with machine-made goods (like boots and shoes) imported from the East, and the presence of skilled laborers diminished significantly between 1850 and 1870 as railroads pulled the Industrial Revolution closer.[11]

The relative decline of skilled labor can also be explained by

10. The description of Jacksonville's seasonal economic cycles is drawn from dozens of newspaper accounts. See *Sentinel*, Apr. 26, 1855; Apr. 4, 1856. Stuart M. Blumin, *The Urban Threshold: Growth and Change in a Nineteenth-Century American Community* (Chicago, 1976), pp. 70-74, 86, suggests that labor migration in Kingston, N.Y., was cyclical as well as seasonal; i.e., many workers returned to the community year after year. Tamara Hareven's research on mill workers in Manchester, N.H., suggests that kinship ties were important means of communicating employment opportunities. See her article, "Family Time and Industrial Time: Family and Work in a Planned Corporation Town, 1900-1924," in her *Family and Kin in Urban Communities, 1700-1930* (New York, 1977), pp. 187-207. A combination of both processes may have operated in Jacksonville, but the paucity of historical sources on this question allows only speculation.

11. Newspaper advertisements offer the clearest signs of competition from eastern manufactured goods. By the 1860s Morgan County had its own nascent manufacturing sector in agricultural implements and woolen clothing.

99

the ambiguous nature of this category. It included blacksmiths, harness-makers, masons, and a wide array of other skilled and specialized laborers who worked with their hands. But many of these same men were proprietors of shops where they employed several workers, or perhaps sold retail goods manufactured outside their shops. It was not at all uncommon for them to retain their artisan titles even as they moved into purely mercantile occupations. A saddle-maker like Mat Stacy, for example, opened a harness shop with his son and gradually moved into the insurance business. Stacy was the perpetual town treasurer and a proud member of several prestigious lodges and associations, but he carried his title as saddle-maker with him long after he laid down his tools and took up a frock coat.[12] Their economic functions, involving both skilled manual labor and proprietory roles, do not allow easy division of this category; however, for our purposes the artisan-proprietors can be distinguished by their wealth, with $500 in real or personal property as the minimal requirement for inclusion.[13]

Once we sort out the skilled laborers who do not qualify as proprietors, it is clear that their migration behavior was similar to that of the unskilled laborers. Though they brought more skills to the marketplace, these men were also hired by others and subject to the seasonal fluctuations of work. Skilled laborers in the building trades (carpenters, masons, and plasterers) probably came and went with the ebb and flow of spring and summer construction projects. Bursts in construction occurred with the expansion of state institutions, and dozens of these workers arrived in Jacksonville for short-term projects.

Even these skilled workers could exert little leverage on the forces that determined their wages and working conditions. A few isolated attempts to organize within single trades in Jacksonville were frustrated by the fluid nature of the work force. During the construction of the new wing of the State Hospital in 1858, bricklayers protested their wages of $2.75 per day,

12. U.S. Census MSS, Morgan County, Ill., 1850, 1860.

13. Knights, *Plain People*, pp. 149-56, uses $1,000 in real and personal property to distinguish proprietors. In Jacksonville the $500 criterion corresponded fairly consistently with data on a random sample of cases listed in business directories available after 1860.

but after only a few days of unsuccessful striking the diehards moved on. One unsympathetic source reported that "the more reasonable of the strikers have become satisfied of the injustice of their demands, and have gone back to work again at the old prices. . . . But many have left, and there is a great demand for more workmen." In 1869 journeymen saddlers and harness-makers also tried to bargain collectively but were inundated with eager replacements from outside. Acts of violence against the newcomers failed, and the strikers soon gave up and left town.[14] The workers' freedom to move postponed development of the very organizational strength and wage increases that might have encouraged them to stay.

Above the skilled and unskilled laborers were significantly more stable business, professional, and artisan-proprietor groups. Taken together as a white-collar class, 47 percent persisted during the 1850s, three times greater than the combined rates for skilled and unskilled laborers. The stability of this upper stratum declined to 33 percent for the next decade because of an inexplicable drop in persistence in business and professional occupations. Still, those in white-collar occupations remained substantially more settled than those below them.

The relative stability of businessmen, professionals, and artisan-proprietors was also a function of certain economic imperatives. The very nature of their work tended to reward residential stability. Most merchants and artisans worked alone or in partnerships; they had to set up shop, accumulate inventories, purchase advertisements, borrow money, extend credit to customers, build up a clientele, and, above all, establish a reputation in the community. It might take years before this kind of enterprise began to pay off, and for those who were even moderately successful the ties of credit, customers, and a familiar market were strong. Professionals, particularly doctors and lawyers, faced many of these same problems in setting up new practices, and similar economic considerations reduced their mobility. Professional organizations like the Morgan County Medical Society and Bar Association also helped plug these men into local professional networks and thereby encour-

14. *Illinois State Journal* (Springfield), Oct. 15, 1858; *Sentinel*, Jan. 29, 1869.

aged persistence. While many in business and professional occupations never locked themselves into the local economic infrastructure (as Table 3 shows), as a group they were far more persistent than those who traded only their manual labor in the marketplace.

What kind of opportunities for social advancement did Jacksonville offer to those who used it as more than a temporary stopover? Could the historical reality ever match the flamboyant claims of unbounded upward mobility touted by boosters of the new West? Perhaps not; but Jacksonville did provide an unusually healthy climate for social mobility for those who stayed a decade or more. Tables 4 and 5 summarize the complex process of occupational mobility among persistent residents in the 1850s and 1860s.

Toward the top of the occupational ladder, most were able to maintain their positions, with some attrition into the "no occupation reported" category as older businessmen and professionals retired. The movement of artisan-proprietors into the business and professional column, particularly evident in the 1850s, suggests that many of these men were eschewing the titles of their craft and adopting labels of "merchant," "agent," or "dealer," stressing their roles as businessmen rather than as artisans.[15]

Even more upward movement occurred among skilled laborers, who entered what we have defined as the proprietor category when their acquisition of property qualified them for that higher rank. Although few unskilled laborers remained over the course of either decade, the opportunities for upward occupational mobility were sufficient to allow 30-50 percent to move up one or more rungs on the occupational ladder.

How did this pattern of occupational mobility match that of other communities in nineteenth-century America? For comparative purposes occupational categories can again be compressed into white-collar and blue-collar strata, dividing

15. U.S. Census MSS, Morgan County, Ill., 1850, 1860, 1870. Michael B. Katz, *The People of Hamilton, Canada West: Family and Class in a Mid-Nineteenth-Century City* (Cambridge, Mass., 1975), ch. 3, esp. p. 143, addresses the problems of measuring social mobility among artisans.

just below the artisan-proprietor rank. Among those who were blue-collar workers at the beginning of both decades, about 40 percent (44 and 37) reported white-collar occupations at the end of ten years. Most of this movement occurred among skilled non-proprietors who moved into the proprietor ranks. Since Stephan Thernstrom's overview of occupational mobility studies indicates the average movement from blue-collar to white-collar occupations over a decade was usually limited to 10-20 percent of the persistent blue-collar work force,[16] Jacksonville's blue-collar workers enjoyed almost twice the normal rate of upward mobility. The occupational mobility experienced by Jacksonville's more stable population under-lines the important class differences that distinguished the permanent residents from the transients: 70-80 percent of the persistent population had white-collar jobs by the end of both decades.

WEALTH AND MOBILITY

Wealth was another economic factor that conditioned the movement of population in and out of Jacksonville and defined the social status of its citizens, with wealth in land being particularly important. The census recorded the landed wealth of each person in town, and for a few select years the county tax lists yield more detailed information on land value. The boosters' claim of a community of joint interests rested most squarely upon the expectation of rising land values, so it is especially important that we examine landed wealth, its distribution among the local population, and its relationship to migration, persistence, and social mobility.

Throughout Jacksonville's early history a vigorous ethos of land speculation permeated the newspapers and private correspondence. In streetcorner conversations men must have bargained for town lots, planned a new subdivision, or talked idly of fabulous profits made from early investments in a prosperous real estate market. The town site itself was born in 1825 as part of two speculators' scheme to enrich themselves, and that

16. Thernstrom, *Other Bostonians*, p. 234.

spirit of speculation continued. By the 1860s newspapers were devoting increasing space to reports on the sale of town lots and buildings. New subdivisions were touted more for their investment potential than for their residential attractions. Public auctions of select lots or the estate of a deceased citizen attracted large crowds and stimulated an ever-present awareness of the town's promise for ventures in real estate promotion.[17]

But the intensity of this speculative fervor could not have been felt by more than a small minority of Jacksonville's residents. The census manuscripts reveal that a growing majority of the non-dependent population, more than 70 percent by 1870, owned no real property; even more owned no property inside the town itself. These residents stood to gain nothing from real estate booms that excited the newspaper editors and local boosters, and their large numbers show how limited the boosters' community of material interest actually was.

Wealth in land was highly concentrated in the hands of a small minority. As Table 6 illustrates, at least half of the total wealth was owned by 10 percent of the property-owners, or about 3 percent of the non-dependent population. Table 6 also includes a statistical measure of the distribution of wealth among owners. The Gini Index specifies the degree of inequality in distribution of wealth on a scale from 0 (perfect equality) to 1 (perfect inequality). This index, measuring only the distribution of property among *owners*, remained consistently high for all three censuses.[18]

The census reports on wealth in real property did not distinguish between land located in Jacksonville and elsewhere, and only a fraction of the reported wealth consisted of lots in the town itself. Many of Jacksonville's wealthy citizens invested in rural land surrounding Jacksonville, or in lots located in outlying towns. Still others invested in Chicago lots, or held land in their former homes outside Illinois. The interests of many

17. Examples of speculative activities pervade Jacksonville's history; see *Journal*, May 19, June 9, 1864; Feb. 2, 1865.

18. Cf. David Klingaman, "Individual Wealth in Ohio in 1860," in *Essays in Nineteenth Century Economic History: The Old Northwest*, ed. David Klingaman and Richard Vedder (Athens, Ohio, 1975), pp. 177-90; Lee Soltow, *Men and Wealth in the United States, 1850-1870* (New Haven, 1975).

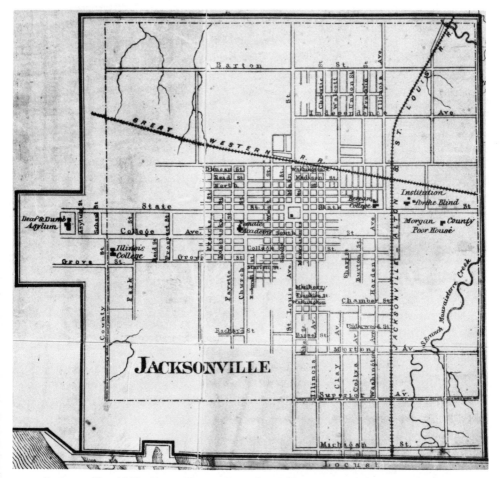

Jacksonville, 1863. From Henry Francis Walling, *Map of the State of Illinois* (Chicago: T. E. Hopkins, [1863]); in Newberry Library, Special Collections.

owners were thus diversified and not dependent solely upon the fortunes of Jacksonville. Local land-owners can be identified through tax lists compiled annually by the county, and although almost all of Morgan County's nineteenth-century tax lists have been destroyed, one for 1849 survives and allows comparison with data on landed wealth in the 1850 census.[19]

The total wealth in town lots among resident owners in 1849 amounted to less than one-fifth the total value of real property reported in the next year's census. While this ratio varied for individual land-owners, it qualifies the boosters' notion of a community of investors. Few investors had their eggs all in one basket; their interests were often spread over the county, or even the state. Furthermore, the total wealth in town lots was distributed in much the same pattern as the wealth in real property. About three-quarters of the non-dependent population in the 1850 census did not own town lots in 1849. Among resident owners of lots, the wealthiest 10 percent owned over 40 percent of the total, and the Gini Index was also high. (See Table 6.)

Moreover, about 40 percent of the town lot owners listed in 1849 were not residents of Jacksonville according to the 1850 census. Some of these missing owners may have moved out of Jacksonville only recently—like the Heslep brothers, who were seized by gold fever and went to California with the intention of bringing their newfound riches back to Jacksonville.[20] Other lot owners, like Jacob Strawn, lived outside the town limits but were in effect stable citizens of the community. This non-resident segment of owners controlled about one-quarter of the total wealth in local property. Not only was a direct economic interest in Jacksonville's rising land values limited to a minority of the residents, but a good number of those who held stock in Jacksonville's future were connected to the community only by a distant speculative interest.

For those who owned property of any kind, the land served as a firm stake in the local community and encouraged persis-

19. Morgan County Tax Lists, 1849, Morgan County Courthouse, Jacksonville.
20. Dr. Augustus M. Heslep, "The Santa Fe Trail," in *Southern Trails to California*, ed. R. B. Bieber (Glendale, Calif., 1937), pp. 353-56; *Sentinel*, Feb. 23, 1855.

tence. Table 7 divides the population into groups according to the wealth reported at the beginning of the decade and shows the different rates of persistence for each group. The pattern is strong and consistent for both decades: those with real property were two to three times more likely to stay in Jacksonville until the next census; among the propertyless, 80-90 percent left before the decade ended. Of those who owned town lots in 1849, about 40 percent departed in the 1850s; over 80 percent of those without town lots left.

The relationship between property and persistence was reciprocal—those with a "stake in the community" were inclined to stay, and those who stayed improved their chances of acquiring property. To explore the gains made by the persistent core of the community, we may compare the relative financial positions of individuals at the beginning and end of each decade. Tables 8 and 9 rank persistent property-owners into five equal wealth groups, in addition to those who owned no property. In each decade the quintile ranks were computed from data from the total population of property owners. In both decades the pattern of mobility in wealth was similar, with about 85 percent of the persistent either improving or maintaining their already favorable positions. At every level (except those already near the top) over half of the persistent cases climbed at least one quintile rank.

Those with ten or more years of residence as adults represented no more than one-eighth of the total non-dependent population in both 1860 and 1870, yet they controlled 40-50 percent of the total wealth in real property. Very few appear to have lost wealth in these two decades, though some did experience declines in their relative positions. The persistent doubled their previous wealth over the course of a decade on the average and gained a dollar amount of $5,000. This was due to more than general inflation of land values, for most of these people were rising within the community as well.

To summarize, the stable core of Jacksonville's population was distinguished by wealth and higher occupational status; long-term residents experienced significant upward mobility along both these tracks. Within this stable core were the leaders

and the principal beneficiaries of Jacksonville's economic progress during the prosperous 1850s and 1860s. Here were people
who could understand, and speak fluently, the language of
boosterism. For them the boosters' notion of a community
united by material interests was not just rhetoric; it was an undeniable part of their experience, a faith confirmed every time
they counted their assets. But if the rewards of social mobility,
measured in occupation and property, created a powerful force
that kept many rooted to the community for decades, the
range of that force was limited. Those very goals of individual
opportunity required most low-skilled and unpropertied workers to use Jacksonville as one of a series of job markets through
which they moved with the ebb and flow of seasonal work.

THE SELF-MADE MAN AND THE FAMILY CONNECTION

Those who lived in Jacksonville needed none of these statistics to tell them that individual opportunity was a central theme
in their lives. The chances for unprivileged but hard-working
young men to succeed in an open society were continually
celebrated in newspapers, literature, and political rhetoric. The
West fostered its own special version of the nineteenth-century
American cult of success. The model was a young man who left
his family and secure environment in the East in order to build a
career and fortune in a wonderfully open western society. The
life stories of those who came west and found unobstructed
paths to the highest public offices or business empires, and who
built their careers and fortunes out of nothing more than their
own talent and sheer determination, can be found in the back of
every county history, where the biographies of eminent citizens
were displayed as testimony to the dream of success.[21] Myth and
experience blend in all of these accounts, yet they tell us something important about the ideals of this society.

No one understood those ideals better than western politi-

21. See the biographical sketches in Donnelley, Loyd & Co., *History of Morgan
County*, and William F. Short, ed., *Historical Encyclopedia of Illinois . . . Morgan County*
(Chicago, 1906). Abner D. Jones, *Illinois and the West* (Boston, 1838), pp. 102-4, offers
advice to the ambitious migrant.

cians, who possessed an instinctive ability to mimic the people's cherished values. A biographical sketch of Jacksonville's Murray McConnel, published during his 1855 gubernatorial campaign, provides a classic example of the politician's art. When McConnel was but fourteen years old he left his father and stepmother on their farm in upstate New York "for reasons convincing to himself." He "set out on his life journey alone and unaided," worked on a farm in western Pennsylvania for a while, and then encountered his father, who had followed the youth to persuade him to return home. McConnel defiantly refused his father's pleas and "set out again alone without any spoken farewell." He worked in Philadelphia and then moved on to Pittsburgh; fearing that he was still "too close to home," he took a flatboat to Louisville and from there to New Orleans. McConnel ventured through the Southwest, finally coming to rest in Missouri. There he bought a farm, married, "and 'settled down' as men call it"—but not for long. Soon after the Missouri Compromise in 1820 McConnel sold his farm, picked up his family, and moved north to Morgan County, Illinois, where he bought a farm and began to carve his niche in a new society. During the long winters he read the law on his own, and he put the profits from his farm into land in the new county seat. When Jacksonville began to show promise around 1830 McConnel moved his family into town, set up a law practice, and launched the political career that led him to the offices of state legislator, colonel in the Black Hawk War, commissioner of public works, auditor of the federal treasury, and state senator. "Young McConnel," his generous biographer summarized, "found himself among strangers, with no profession or trade, destitute of money and all else save that energy of mind, which shows itself at any time of life, in the talented independent and self-denying young American, which was now called into requisition."[22] McConnel's life story was no doubt improved by his biographer for public consumption, but it was typical of dozens of equally heroic narratives sketching the lives of emi-

22. *Sentinel*, Aug. 16, 1855; cf. George Murray McConnel, "Some Reminiscences of My Father," *JISHS* 18 (1925): 89-100.

nent citizens. More familiar figures such as Stephen Douglas and Abraham Lincoln also stressed their youthful independence and achievements as self-made men.

One theme comes through clearly in every story: the young man's willingness to reject the security and comfort of life back home (indeed, to reject his father's inheritance, in McConnel's case), to risk moving West, and to keep moving in response to the shrewdly calculated opportunities offered by an expansive frontier society. These success stories gave special meaning to the expression "self-made men," for these were truly men alone, cut off from the affections as well as the material benefits of the family, kin, and community they knew as youths.[23]

The half-mythic presence of these self-made men looms large in our national past, especially in the history of the West. Data on the actual patterns of social mobility in Jacksonville suggest that the myth had some basis in historical experience. But because the myth also projects an image of western society as consisting of free-floating young men unattached to family or kin, it seriously distorts our understanding of the vital role of the family, household, and kinship in the everyday experience of most people.

Even in its rawest frontier stage the population consisted of a base of family units, not just lone individuals.[24] The memoirs of early pioneers suggest that many of the young men who struck out alone were the advance agents for family units which were eventually reconstituted on the frontier.[25] The volume of migration in western society meant that at any moment family members might be scattered across the land, but this image of apparent family disintegration belies the more important process of transplanting whole kinship networks to the new society. We must, nonetheless, try to reconstruct some of the basic

23. See Irwin G. Wyllie, *The Self Made Man in America: The Myth of Rags to Riches* (New Brunswick, N.J., 1954).

24. Jack E. Eblen, "An Analysis of Nineteenth-Century Frontier Populations," *Demography* 2 (1965): 399-413; John Modell, "Family and Fertility on the Indiana Frontier, 1820," *American Quarterly* 23 (1971): 615-34.

25. See, e.g., Charles M. Eames, *Historic Morgan and Classic Jacksonville* (Jacksonville, 1885), pp. 45-47 et passim. Robert E. Bieder, "Kinship as a Factor in Migration," *Journal of Marriage and the Family* 35 (1973): 429-39; Eblen, "Frontier Populations," and Modell, "Family and Fertility," all stress the early importance of family units in frontier society.

outlines of Jacksonville family life from census data that offer only a few snapshots of the population.

In its early frontier stage, the Morgan County population was distinguished by its extraordinary youth; in 1830 only 5 percent of the residents were forty or older. Nevertheless, the population was not dominated by single males—nearly 40 percent of the total were children under the age of ten, signifying a preponderance of young fertile marriages. The age distribution of this youthful frontier population quickly converged with the national averages after the 1830s, and by 1850 only minor discrepancies remained. The top of the age pyramid began to fill out as the first generation of settlers matured and as railroad transportation made it easier for older people to come west. Simultaneously children under ten constituted a shrinking portion of the total population.[26]

Within Jacksonville's dynamic population, older people and heads of families with children contributed heavily to the stationary core of the community. Young single men and women in blue-collar occupations made up the bulk of the transients. Among the non-dependent population, the persistence rate of those under thirty was less than half that of people thirty and older (16 versus 35 percent between 1850 and 1860; 13 versus 27 percent between 1860 and 1870).

More than age alone, marital status determined the selective pull of migration in and out of the community. By 1850 a little less than 40 percent of the adult males were single. Some of these men might have been married but temporarily separated from their wives, a situation the census marshal had no way of indicating. For example, Irish railroad workers often came west for a season of work, leaving their families back east. But most of those who appear to be single were men in their early twenties, and by nineteenth-century norms they were not yet ready for marriage.[27]

26. See Eblen, "Frontier Populations," and Modell, "Family and Fertility." Age distributions for Morgan County were derived from the published U.S. Census, volumes on population, 1830, 1840, 1850, 1860, 1870. U.S. age distributions for this period are summarized in *Historical Statistics of the United States from Colonial Times to the Present* (Washington, 1957), Table A-22.

27. Oscar Handlin, *Boston's Immigrants: A Study in Acculturation*, rev. ed. (New York,

There was no severe shortage of marriageable young women in Morgan County even in the earlier years, as Table 10 demonstrates. In fact, by 1860 Jacksonville attracted a surplus of women who came to work as house servants, teachers, seamstresses, and to perform dozens of other jobs provided by an expanding local economy. Still, this trend toward a more favorable ratio of women to men hardly affected the proportions of married and single men in the population.

The presence of this young single population contributed to the constant turnover within Jacksonville. Married men were three times more likely to stay in Jacksonville than single men; only one-tenth of the latter persisted for a decade in the 1850s and 1860s. Among the stable population more than 80 percent were already married as the decade began, and almost all were married by the end. Those with children were even more prone to persist, at least in the 1850s. None of this violates well-known rules about the selectivity of migration, but it does verify that one's stage in the life cycle influenced migration behavior, perhaps even more than economic factors of occupation and property.[28] The differences in family status between movers and long-term residents also helps explain the sharp conflicts over issues like temperance and vice that will be explored more closely in a later chapter. In these and other contests a stable population of mostly middle-class family men defended their moral world against a steady stream of young, unmarried, and largely lower-class movers who floated through town.

Before we go too far with this idea of young singles and family heads living in different social and moral worlds, we must understand that these two populations often lived in intimate physical proximity due to a widespread practice of households taking in unrelated boarders. Throughout Jacksonville's early history there was a chronic shortage of housing which no amount of building seemed to alleviate. With the coming of Irish and German railroad workers in the 1850s, several jerry-built frame tenements were thrown up on the north end of

---

1970), p. 71. See Thomas P. Monahan, *The Pattern of Age at Marriage in the United States* (Philadelphia, 1951).

28. Everett S. Lee, "A Theory of Migration," *Demography* 3 (1966): 47-57.

town. After the Civil War the newspapers badgered local capitalists to build more of these tenements to house the bulging population. "Shall we make no room for any portion of these industrious, freedom-loving people?" one editor asked in the spring of 1866. "Shall we drive them to building huts in the allies and to squatting upon the outskirts of the town?" Within two months his answer came in a report of some three hundred tenant houses under construction, but housing still remained crowded.[29] Boosters felt certain that the housing shortage was costing Jacksonville valuable additions to its population. This may have been true, but the practice had always been to pack the new population into existing households as boarders, servants, or, in a few cases, apprentices.

The patterns of boarding were fairly constant between 1850 and 1870, and the average household size of six or seven persons continued to hold, as it had since 1830. Not all of the boarding population was necessarily unrelated to the household head. There were in-laws, cousins, or female-linked kin whose last names differed from that of the household head; however, since none of the censuses before 1880 specify these relationships, we are forced to include these cases as unrelated boarders. The census manuscripts do allow us to differentiate members of the household head's immediate family from those males whose surnames were the same but whose ages make it reasonably clear that they were brothers or elderly fathers boarding with their kin.

The rest of the unrelated boarders were spread out through the families of Jacksonville, with about half of the households containing at least one unrelated lodger.[30] Some of these households were in fact boarding houses and small tenements, but even by 1870 only about twenty dwellings reported ten or more boarders. More than two-thirds of the households with

29. *Journal*, Apr. 23, June 12, 1866.
30. John Modell and Tamara K. Hareven, "Urbanization and the Malleable Household: An Examination of Boarding and Lodging in American Families," *Journal of Marriage and the Family* 35 (1973): 468, summarizes similar studies by Blumin, Glasco, and Bloomberg et al., of lodging in several communities which show a norm of about one in five families with lodgers. Like Modell and Hareven, I am using the terms "lodger" and "boarder" interchangeably.

boarders had only one or two living there. Some were servants, who by 1860 and 1870 were present in about one of every six households. Not all of these appear to be employees of the household head, but in the wealthy business and professional class a domestic servant, often a young Irish woman, was a common luxury. Among the rest of the boarders economic ties to the household head seem to have been rare; only a handful were listed as apprentices in the same occupation. There were more cases of clerks and young artisans who lived with their employers' families, and Joseph Capps, the woolen manufacturer, had four of his factory hands living with his family in 1860. But most of the unrelated lodgers appear to have had no employment ties to their landlords.

For household heads, this practice of renting space in the home provided an important source of income, especially among a growing number of single women, often widows, who might have had no other means of support. With the ever-present shortage of housing, rents remained notoriously high in Jacksonville. Newton Bateman's elderly father wrote to him in 1850: "Our town continues to be crowded. Hard getting board such as I want in retirement. . . . I find in these times tis not worth wile to stan about the price, the important thing is to get in at any rate." Mr. Bateman's landlady had just raised the rent fifty cents to take advantage of an influx of "emigrants" that spring; this meant an exhorbitant rent of two dollars per week for room and board for the old man. By 1866 rent alone was up to ten dollars a month for a small two-room apartment.[31] Newspaper appeals to local capitalists argued that generous profits from rent and land appreciation lay in wait for those who would build new rental housing. By 1870 about one-sixth of Jacksonville's boarders lived in hotels, boarding houses, and tenements with ten or more residents per dwelling. Still, the dominant pattern was one or two lodgers renting space in the back rooms, attics, and basements of families throughout the town; about two-thirds of boarders and servants continued to live in houses with no more than two unrelated lodgers.

31. Bateman to Newton Bateman, Jacksonville, May 7, 1850, Newton Bateman Papers, Illinois State Historical Library, Springfield; *Journal*, Feb. 1, 1866.

This population of individual lodgers also occupied a special place in the demographic and economic structure of the town. Table 11 compares the household heads and their unrelated boarders with respect to both their stage in the life cycle and their position in the social structure. The differences are striking on every count. The lodgers were predominantly young, unmarried, manual workers who rarely owned property and who migrated frequently. It made sense that people in these circumstances found housing as boarders in existing households, and that families in turn took advantage of the situation to increase their incomes or compensate servants. Most of the unrelated boarders needed only a room or a bed in the corner while they worked during the day and, no doubt, spent much of their spare time amid the crowds of loafing men on the town square or in the saloons and billiard halls that were considered the bane of Jacksonville by respectable families.

Despite their different age groups, different social classes, and different degrees of commitment to the community, these two subpopulations nonetheless lived in close proximity through this system of lodging. The household unit served as a central organizing force for most of the population, even for those unattached young men who drifted through town. Within these households the transient youths mingled with the more stable families in Jacksonville, and by this arrangement the potential for social disorder and anomie in a new and volatile community must have been softened. Lodgers were not mere strangers to the household head, even if they were not always full citizens of the community.[32]

THE BONDS OF KINSHIP

Very early in its history—surprisingly early, when we consider the newness and mobility of the community—a substantial portion of the community was tied together by bonds of kinship. Biographical and genealogical records give us an enticing glimpse of some of Jacksonville's more prominent families and their extended relations. The Dunlap clan, for example, was

32. See Modell and Hareven, "Malleable Household."

headed by an old Virginia patriarch, the Reverend James Dunlap, who came to Jacksonville when he was seventy-two in order to join several of his thirteen children. Dunlap served as minister of the Baptist church, later passing on the position to his son, James Dunlap III. At least six of Dunlap's children lived in Jacksonville, and all of them enjoyed positions of influence in local business and political affairs.[33] The Dunlap clan played a central role in the violent battle over nepotism and graft in the state institutions during the 1850s. As the scandal became fully exposed in the local newspapers, the extensive range of the Dunlap's kinship connections was revealed by the several in-laws and cousins implicated as recipients of James Dunlap Jr.'s patronage.[34] The Dunlap scandal illustrates only one of many ways, legitimate or otherwise, that kinship helped knit together and assist the members of a young and transient community.

Dozens of scattered references in biographical sketches and memoirs support this notion of the early importance of kinship. The enthusiastic letter of a brother, cousin, or son brought many people to Jacksonville in the first place. Kinship connections could help smooth over the initial problems of housing, employment, and credit, as well as supplying essential psychological support to migrants who were strangers to the town but not to their relatives. For a young man starting a new business, kinship connections were instrumental in acquiring credit. The credit reports of R. G. Dun & Company, collected from the 1840s forward, refer constantly to the financial backing of prospective borrowers by fathers, brothers, and in-laws living in Jacksonville.[35]

No surviving records can give a full picture of Jacksonville's kinship networks, but we can at least see one part of that network from the census manuscripts. By examining surnames,

33. Short, *Historical Encyclopedia*, pp. 814-15.
34. See pp. 77-78.
35. R. G. Dun & Company, Credit Ledgers, Morgan County, 3 vols., Baker Library, Harvard University. Thanks to Dun & Bradstreet, Inc., and to Robert Lovett of the Baker Library for allowing me to microfilm these records. See Sally and Clyde Griffen, "Family and Business in a Small City: Poughkeepsie, New York, 1850-1880," in Tamara K. Hareven, ed., *Family and Kin in Urban Communities, 1700-1930* (New York, 1977), pp. 144-63.

along with ages and birthplaces, we can identify many of the adult brothers and the father-son relationships. Most lived within the same household or next door to one another, making kinship linkages easy to infer. For those with common surnames, and those not living together, linkage was frequently impossible to discern. For some well-established families, published biographical sketches were available to substantiate relationships. Uncertain linkages were eliminated, leaving only those which were clearly related. This crude index is limited to adult male-linked kinship, and to relations that can be easily identified. Although it measures no more than the tip of the iceberg, it does give an indication of the importance of kinship within this young and transient community.

Table 12 summarizes the study of kinship in Jacksonville for 1850 and 1860. (The 1870 population was far too large to handle by this tedious method.) The results are striking, especially when the limitations of the data are appreciated. More than one-quarter of the adult males present in 1850 had at least one other adult male relative (father, son, or brother) living in Jacksonville. Better than one-third of the adult male population could make this claim a decade later. Most of these kinship ties were between fathers and their adult sons, and many existed within the same household. The method is surely biased toward underestimating the number of adult sons living elsewhere in the community; brothers living apart are also probably undercounted. But the important point is that so much of this young and restless population could be identified as kin. Most of these linkages at first involved no more than two adult males, but by 1860 far more had four and five members.

Kinship was not confined to any one segment of Jacksonville's population, in contrast to the way that marital status and boarding set apart one level of the community from another. Among blue-collar and white-collar workers the bonds of kinship were about equally prevalent. Those under thirty, who seem so alone when considered only by their marital status, appear less isolated when these ties are examined. Almost one-third of the people in this age group had an adult male relative in Jacksonville, usually a father with whom they were living.

117

Nor were these bonds the special property of the more stable element within the population. In both censuses those with adult kin in Jacksonville were slightly more inclined to persist over the decade, but kinship alone was less of an impediment to those leaving Jacksonville than factors such as marital status, occupation, and property. Mobility would, in many cases, sever the ties between brothers, fathers, and sons, yet this was perhaps a sign of the strength of kinship in a mobile society. Many groups broken by migration would again be reunited, just as new kinship networks were constantly being reconstituted by newcomers to Jacksonville.[36]

The flexibility of kinship bonds reflects one of the central features of the community itself—always breaking down and reorganizing, always in process, never fixed. The unconscious forces that pulled the movers in and out of Jacksonville and structured the community around the household and family had their own logic, even though the hidden order they shaped was not always appreciated by everyone caught up in the process. Some saw the transience of the West as an unmistakable sign of social chaos. Their quest for stability and order within Jacksonville became manifest in a series of institutional reforms that went beyond the realm of the family in attempts to invest order in a new community made up of both citizens and strangers.

36. See Bieder, "Kinship as a Factor in Migration."

Jacksonville, Illinois, about 1861. This, and the following nine illustrations, are from the *Journal of the Illinois State Historical Society* (April, 1925).

Morgan County's second court house, erected in the Jacksonville public square in 1830, razed in 1869.

Illinois College in 1833, three years after it opened.

Jacksonville Female Academy, opened in 1833.

Illinois Conference Female College in 1854 (established in 1846).

Deaf and Dumb Asylum in 1846 (established in 1843).

Illinois Institution for the Education of the Blind in 1853 (established in 1848).

Illinois State Hospital for the Insane in 1851 (established in 1845).

Experimental School for the instruction and training of idiots and feeble-minded children, 1868–78.

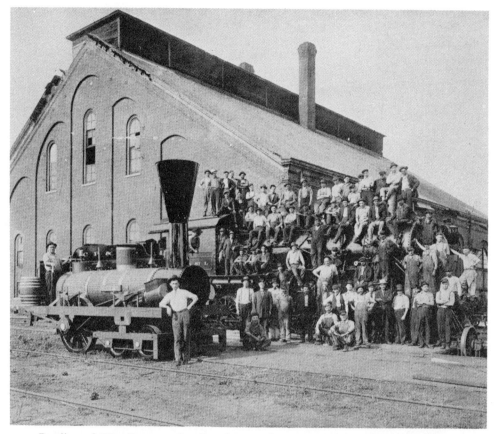

Replica of The Rogers, the first locomotive operated in Illinois. Original engine was placed on the Northern Cross Railroad at Meredosia on November 8, 1838.

George Graff, dealer in lumber and building supplies; one of many enterprises that flourished with the coming of railroads. Opposite freight depot of T. W. & W. Railway. This, and the following illustration, are from *Morgan County Atlas* (Chicago, 1872).

View of the lumber yard of J. S. and G. S. Russel, Lafayette and North Main Streets, near "Madeira" and the Irish "Patch."

The Boundaries of Culture

> When foreigners come to our country . . . they should
> become Americanized as soon as possible and this
> can never be done if they are located in isolated
> communities.
>
> —*Illinois Journal*[1]

WHATEVER HIDDEN ORDER ruled Jacksonville's restless
population as it shifted in response to economic opportunity and the life cycle, the constant flood of strangers presented one of the most obvious challenges to the construction of
a new community. The early presence of families and the practice of absorbing movers into households as lodgers helped
integrate this footloose population. The steady flow of transient
strangers was only part of the problem, however; migration also
brought to the community people who faced each other as
cultural strangers. The divisions between Yankees and Southerners, natives and foreigners, whites and blacks, fragmented
the community into separate social components, the boundaries
of which were staked out by residential clusters, churches, and
clubs. Across these boundaries political parties reached out to
pull in the disparate elements of the community. A common
ethos of individual opportunity and a group discipline also
permeated each cultural unit, revealing a deeper level of
community existing beyond divisive residential and institutional boundaries.

1. *Illinois Journal* (Springfield), Aug. 7, 1849, quoted in George Rawlings Poage,
"The Coming of the Portuguese," *JISHS* 18 (1925): 125.

YANKEES AND SOUTHERNERS

New England clergymen and educators remained the most articulate and worried critics in western society. There was no question in the minds of the Yale Band: the proper model for Jacksonville and the West to emulate was New England, which they described as an unchanging society of tight-knit villages, each with its schoolhouse and church embodying the collective values of the community. These institutions, along with a good share of New England's population, were transplanted to the West where their presence was intended to invest moral order and purpose in western society. "Let him adhere to the economical, industrious habits to which he has been trained," Abner Jones advised his fellow Yankees in Illinois. "Let him mingle freely and unsuspiciously with his neighbors, and . . . strive to bring up their habits, by a successful example, to the New England standard."[2] Julian Sturtevant, one of the more ardent champions of the New England mission in the West, had an even grander messianic vision of the Yankee's destiny: "I believe that the great conception of a Christian society, which was in the minds of the Pilgrims of the Mayflower, is yet to prevail in glorious reality, from the Atlantic to the Pacific and from the frozen north to the Southern gulf; that it is to displace and blot out the foul strain of African slavery, with all its heaven-offending enormities; that before its onward march our vast and heterogeneous foreign population is either to be subdued and won to its principles and its blessings or to give place to the seed of the righteous. . . ."[3]

Not all New Englanders shared Jones and Sturtevant's

2. Abner D. Jones, *Illinois and the West* (Boston, 1838), p. 157. See also Carrie P. Kofoid, "Puritan Influence in the Formative Years of Illinois History," Illinois State Historical Society *Transactions* 10 (1905): 264-338.

3. Julian M. Sturtevant, *An Address in Behalf of the Society for the Promotion of Theological Education at the West* (New York, 1853), p. 7. See also Travis Keene Hedrick, "Julian Monson Sturtevant and the Moral Machinery of Society: The New England Struggle against Pluralism in the Old Northwest, 1829-1877" (Ph.D. dissertation, Brown University, 1974); Lois K. Mathews, *The Expansion of New England* (Boston, 1909); Stewart H. Holbrook, *The Yankee Exodus: An Account of Migration from New England* (New York, 1950); and Page Smith, *As a City upon a Hill: The Town in American History* (New York, 1966).

sense of mission, but they still suffered the understandable resentment which Illinoisans expressed toward their would-be saviors. "Many persons who emigrate from older to younger states," one admonished, "set out with the spirit of reformers; and aware of the superior advantages which they have enjoyed, and of the high degree of civilization and improvement to which they have been accustomed, fondly imagine that they can easily transplant these to their new places of residence."[4] Indeed, Yankees did bring with them a chauvinistic confidence in "the New England way."[5] But their very determination to mold the West in the New England image at first sharpened cultural boundaries that kept Yankees apart from other Westerners.

In Jacksonville by 1833 New England regional identify found refuge in the new Congregational church. Its founding, as we have seen, all but destroyed the experiment in interdenominational cooperation with mostly non-Yankee Presbyterians. The Congregational church remained a nucleus of Jacksonville's New England community. Yankee cultural identity was also cultivated outside the church by certain individuals' prominence in reform associations, the antislavery and public education movements in particular, and by their dominance on the faculty of Illinois College.[6]

Early in Jacksonville's history Yankees were resented for their moral righteousness and exclusiveness. When William Thomas came from Kentucky as early as 1826, he "soon found two classes in society. Those from the North and East were called 'Yankees' and those from the South and West 'White people.'"[7] The very term "Yankee," another early resident recounted, was "one of reproach, and the unfortunate person who bore it, was watched with suspicion, and deemed hardly fit for association

4. [James Hall,] "Emigration," *Illinois Monthly Magazine* 1 (1831): 420.

5. Richard L. Power, *Planting Corn-Belt Culture: The Impress of the Upland Southerner and Yankee in the Old Northwest* (Indianapolis, 1953).

6. Julian M. Sturtevant, *Origins of Western Congregationalism* (Jacksonville, 1884), in Tanner Library, Illinois College, Jacksonville. "Church Record, Organization, etc., 1833-1878," MSS in Congregational Church, Jacksonville, includes a list of members and their nativity ca. 1833.

7. Charles M. Eames, *Historic Morgan and Classic Jacksonville* (Jacksonville, 1885), p. 47.

with those who thought themselves in some sort the rightful proprietors of the country."[8] The friction between Yankees and Southerners later became a central theme in Jacksonville's local histories. One New Englander recalled the situation as a Civil War in microcosm: "a collision between two antagonistic civilizations, one born directly or indirectly of slavery and the other of freedom."[9]

This view clearly exaggerated both the degree and the consciousness of sectional conflict within Jacksonville, and it ignored the historical evolution of that conflict. Despite their important influence in the local colleges and state institutions, New Englanders never made up a very large portion of the town's population (about 7 percent). Nor were all Southerners in Jacksonville the champions of slave society. Most came from border states, especially Kentucky and Tennessee, where slavery was least entrenched; many claimed they left the South to be rid of the peculiar institution and the planter class whose power derived from it.[10] Furthermore, the heavy flow of migrants from Middle Atlantic states (constituting 15 percent of the population in 1860) blurred the sectional dichotomy which some were determined to see in Jacksonville's early history.

After the Civil War the same local histories that perpetuated the idea of irrepressible conflict within the community waxed eloquent about the cultural hybridization that joined "the energy and enterprise of the Yankee" to "the generosity and hospitality of the Southerner."[11] The contradictions of these local legends suggest the evolution of regional antagonisms within Jacksonville, for by the 1850s a certain melding had blurred the cultural boundaries between Yankees and Southern-

8. Robert Wilson Patterson, *Early Society in Southern Illinois* (Chicago, 1881), p. 105.

9. Truman Augustus Post, *Truman Marcellus Post: A Biography Personal and Literary* (Boston, 1891), p. 91.

10. Nativity estimates are based on the non-dependent population (defined in the preceding chapter) in the U.S. Census MSS, Morgan County, Ill., 1850, 1860, 1870. On southern migration to Illinois, see John Barnhart, "The Southern Influence in the Formation of Illinois," *JISHS* 32 (1939): 358-78; William O. Lynch, "The Westward Flow of Southern Colonists before 1861," *Journal of Southern History* 9 (1943): 303-27; Fabian Linden, "Economic Democracy in the Slave South: An Appraisal of Some Recent Views," *Journal of Negro History* 31 (1946): 140-89.

11. Eames, *Historic Morgan*, p. 14.

ers. Earlier resentment toward the imperious Yankees burst out in occasional assaults upon the college and on antislavery activists, but by the late 1840s and 1850s sectional antagonisms were checked by a number of countervailing forces.

The most important integrative force was the unifying influence of boosterism. Southerners in Jacksonville took eagerly to the business of town boosting. If this meant supporting a "Yankee college," many wealthy Southerners, like Kentuckian John J. Hardin, gave generously to its endowment. Or if Jacksonville's growth depended on new state charitable institutions imported from the Northeast, Southerners like Hardin and William Thomas led the lobby effort in Springfield, and others willingly gave of their money and energy. When Jacksonville's good name was tarnished by drunkenness and debauchery, Southerners joined the "Puritan" crusade for temperance and moral order. Finally, the taboo that boosterism placed on open discussion of internal conflict helped subdue sectional friction by eliminating any public forum for discussing it.[12]

A second integrative force was political. Local party alliances cut across sectional divisions, at least among Jacksonville's party spokesmen, sufficiently to render the issue of regional origin politically dangerous. Even as the slavery question took center stage in political debate in the 1850s, the regional origin of political leaders was almost never used publicly in appealing to Jacksonville voters. The Democratic leadership drew heavily from southern migrants, and Republicans relied on Northeasterners for their spokesmen; nevertheless, there was enough crossing of these lines among party leaders, and presumably among voters, to defuse regional origin as an explicit local political issue. Even on the state level the confusion of regional origin among party leadership allowed Stephen Douglas, a Vermonter, to speak for the largely southern-born Democratic

12. The fourth chapter details the joint efforts of local boosters; the eighth chapter demonstrates southern support for prohibition on Jacksonville's town board. According to Robert R. Dykstra, *The Cattle Towns* (New York, 1968), pp. 361-67, the "taboo on divisiveness" was only a veil behind which conflict raged; however, I believe that the suppression of hostile public rhetoric was in itself an effective way of controlling, if not eliminating, internal conflict.

stronghold of downstate Illinois against Abraham Lincoln, a Kentuckian, who became the champion of antislavery forces in northern Illinois, where the native population came largely from the Northeast.[13]

Persistent sectional hostility in Jacksonville erupted occasionally under the strain of the Civil War. Yankee exclusiveness remained evident also in the pattern of limited intermarriage with Southerners, as the census manuscripts reveal.[14] But by the 1860s enough stitches had been sewn between the rival regional cultures to close the wounds, even if they were not altogether healed.

THE DREAM OF HOMOGENEITY

The distance still separating Yankees and Southerners seemed to shrink after 1850, when native American Protestants of all regions watched from across a broad cultural chasm as the town swelled with a stream of Portuguese, German, Irish, and black immigrants. Yet when the first contingent of aliens came into Jacksonville, the initial instinct of natives was not to draw

13. The regional origins of local party leaders were determined by locating in the census manuscripts the names of men listed as speakers, delegates, and candidates in newspaper accounts of party events. On the gingerly treatment of sectional origin in the Lincoln-Douglas debates, see Robert W. Johannsen, ed., *The Lincoln-Douglas Debates of 1858* (New York, 1965), pp. 157-58.

I am leaving room here for the plausible argument that broadly recognized sectional divisiveness did not always *need* to be articulated by politicians; it could have persisted on a subliminal level. But we would need to know more about voter behavior to conclude that these divisions were still important in the 1850s and 1860s. Unfortunately, poll books are not available after 1848, and state-level correlations between regional origin and party identity only beg the question of what happened within the heterogeneous local context of central Illinois. John Michael Rozett, "The Social Bases of Party Conflict in the Age of Jackson: Individual Voting Behavior in Greene County, Illinois, 1838-1848" (Ph.D. dissertation, University of Michigan, 1974), pp. 143-98, argues for the early importance of regional identity in a county just south of Morgan. William G. Shade, *Banks or No Banks: The Money Issue in Western Politics, 1832-1865* (Detroit, 1972), makes the case for sectionalism on the basis of statewide analysis. I am grateful to Professor Shade for sending me an unpublished paper on the bank question in Illinois.

14. In 1860, 64% of New England–born husbands were married to New England–born women; 45% of Mid-Atlantic and 65% of southern-born husbands married within their own groups (N = 67, 122, 212). Only 10% of New England-born husbands had southern wives, and 10% of southern-born husbands had wives from New England; U.S. Census MSS, Morgan County, Ill., 1860.

124

boundaries excluding them; rather, they attempted to en-
compass the newcomers within the enduring dream of a homogeneous community.

The Portuguese who came to Jacksonville in the winter of
1849 were peculiarly well-suited subjects for this generous experiment in assimilation. They were actually from the island
of Madeira, where a Scottish Presbyterian missionary named
Robert Kalley had landed quite by accident in 1838. Kalley
stayed on in Madeira, opened a hospital, and began converting
his patients to the Protestant faith. Within a few years he built
up a sizeable following, large enough at least to excite the
Catholic leaders of the island to repress any further growth of
Protestantism. Persecutions intensified and Kalley's Protestants
fled to Trinidad. After an unhappy year of exile, the Madeira
refugees eagerly accepted an offer from the American Hemp
Company to colonize a small agricultural community east of
Jacksonville. There, it was promised, they would be employed at
fair wages and given ten acres of land for homes and gardens.
The company reneged on this offer after the exiles were already
en route, but Presbyterians in Jacksonville and Springfield rallied behind a plan to bring the Portuguese into their communities. "We *never* approved of that plan," wrote one editor,
renouncing the American Hemp Company's proposed colony.
"When foreigners come to our country, in our opinion, they
should become Americanized as soon as possible and this can
never be done if they are located in isolated communities."
A joint committee from Protestant churches in Jacksonville
quickly organized and sent a letter urging the exiled Portuguese
to come to Jacksonville, where "all of them could find the means
of living with comfort from the rewards of their industry."[15]

The welcome mat was almost withdrawn by worried Jacksonville citizens when they learned that some refugees had been
struck by the cholera epidemic then sweeping through the East.
Serving as spokesman for the local churches, Julian Sturtevant
urged the Portuguese, then in New York City, not to begin their
journey to Illinois because of the "great sensitiveness about the

15. *Illinois Journal* (Springfield), Aug. 7, 1849, quoted in Poage, "Portuguese,"
p. 124.

propagation of the disease by infection from Cholera patients."
"These apprehensions," Sturtevant thought, "are excessive, but
they are real, and would be likely to stand in the way of that
kindness and hospitality which would otherwise be extended to
these persecuted disciples."[16]

After the cholera passed and the Madeira exiles were on their
way to Illinois, religious leaders began a campaign appealing to
the charity and missionary spirit of local Protestants. "Hundreds of them can have situations secured in families in the
towns of Jacksonville and Springfield," an eager editor announced. "They would thus learn our manners, our habits (we
hope our good ones only), and our way of doing business of all
kinds—and become useful to themselves, and in time amalga-
mated with us." Much was made of the desire of these Protestant
refugees to work for their keep, and plans to bring them under
the influence of American domestic life apparently entailed
more than a missionary goal to assimilate them. "The labor of
these exiles is much wanted," wrote one editor in an appeal to
potential employers of the Portuguese. "They will not understand our manner of doing work and it will take them some time
to learn 'our ways.' We do not suppose they will expect wages
until they can become useful."[17] Whether they expected or
received wages is unknown, but many Madeira refugees were
indeed brought to work in the homes of prosperous families.
Others withdrew to outlying farms to work as tenants or
farmhands.[18]

In these capacities the Madeira refugees served the practical
needs of Jacksonville's wealthy families for cheap and relatively
stable domestic labor, as well as the spiritual needs of the Protestant community to extend its charity to victims of Catholic
persecution. The Portuguese came to occupy a very special
place in Jacksonville's half-mythical local history. With missionary pride they were held up as conclusive evidence of the open

16. Ibid., p. 121.

17. *Illinois Journal* (Springfield), Aug. 7, 1849, quoted in Poage, "Portuguese,"
pp. 125, 127.

18. U.S. Census MSS, Morgan County, Ill., 1850, 1860, 1870. Ruby Stovall, "The
Geographical Study of Jacksonville, Illinois," p. 16, typescript, 1961, in Morgan County
Historical Society Collections, Jacksonville Public Library.

paths to social advancement, and as testimony to the dream of cultural consensus. "As a class they are industrious, frugal, upright, peaceful, law-abiding citizens and may be found in all trades and professions, to which they readily adapt themselves. . . . Their boys are bright and active, quick to learn and many of them will make good thrifty business men."[19]

Before the 1850s this kind of tolerance was extended generously, albeit from a distance, to other aliens as well. German immigrants settled in Arenzville, a few miles northwest of Jacksonville, in the 1840s. When the Arenzville Band played for the Illinois College commencement in 1843, they were embraced by one editor not as exotic visitors but as models for American youth: "Let us have more of these German emmigrants. They are just what we want. They are true republicans in their very bones whatever their creed may be. And if their appearance, simplicity, courtesy, industry and modesty should be copied by all our youth, happy would be our land. . . . Cousin Germans, welcome to our shores."[20]

These same gestures could even extend to those beyond the pale of Protestantism. When plans were announced in 1843 for a colony of Irish Catholics in Illinois, Jonathan Baldwin Turner accepted it with calm confidence: "However formidable it may look we have got to meet it with courage. So long as the Roman Catholic emigrants *become dispersed* among us, I have no sort of fear, if Protestant Christians do their duty." Their duty was, of course, to penetrate the darkness of Catholic belief with evangelical Protestant light, a mission Turner thought possible even within a compact, isolated Irish colony in Illinois. "Even when grouped together upon the plan proposed, it is not likely that in a country like ours, where everything is in motion, they can be kept long together." For Turner the transient character of American life became, paradoxically, a force for social harmony. Once Catholics left the cloistered colony and became exposed to Protestant life—its business ways, its schools, and its culture of sober discipline—they would imitate and blend into a homogeneous American culture. Few among the Protestant

19. Eames, *Historic Morgan*, pp. 127-28.
20. *Illinois Statesman*, July 3, 1843.

clergy were as confident as Turner on this matter, yet the long campaign of anti-Catholicism in America had always been premised on the argument that it was the Catholic ecclesiastical hierarchy who kept their innocent subjects in darkness. It was up to Protestants to oppose the works of the Catholic church, but at the same time to open their hearts to its victims and "win them to the truth."[21]

The dream of homogeneity was rarely voiced once the actual presence of the foreigners was fully comprehended. By 1870 nearly 40 percent of Jacksonville's population was foreign-born; most were from Ireland, Britain, and Germany. (See Table 13.) They came with the railroads and the expanding economic opportunities offered by Jacksonville's booming economy during the 1850s and 1860s. The success of boosterism ironically brought a host of internal social problems that challenged the boosters' illusion of social harmony, moral order, and common purpose. The rhetoric of assimilation was quietly subdued, as each subculture rallied around the institutions and values it understood to be its own. Churches, voluntary associations, political parties, and places of residence all helped stake out the boundaries within which each group nurtured its own culture. The lines drawn in the 1850s defined cultural distinctions that had been blindly denied only a few years earlier. Cultural boundaries for the Portuguese, Germans, Irish, and blacks continued to set them apart from the rest of the community well into the twentieth century.

MADEIRA

The Portuguese exiles who came to Jacksonville in 1849 at first found themselves nearly engulfed by gracious Protestants who brought them into their homes as servants and laborers. Yet the Portuguese quickly withdrew to build their own community, and the Portuguese Presbyterian church, established in the spring of 1850, came to form its center. At first the

21. Ibid., Nov. 27, 1843. See also Turner, *Mormonism in All Ages* (New York, 1842); Mary Turner Carriel, *The Life of Jonathan Baldwin Turner* (1911; reprinted, Urbana, 1961), pp. 228-30.

Madeiran congregation used the natives' Presbyterian church, but within three years they were able to build their own house of worship. A schism split the church by 1858, but both sides thrived, each with its own church building. The two congregations claimed some four hundred members between them by 1870. The Portuguese Presbyterian churches allowed the Madeirans to worship in their own language, and they served as the centers for dozens of social events and organizations.[22]

Both churches were planted in what became a Portuguese residential enclave on the north side of town, commonly known as "Madeira." This cluster, and another outside town known as "Portuguese Hill," never contained all of the scattered members of this community. Nonetheless, Madeira did comprise a distinct ethnic turf within the town. Trespassers could be startled by the tribal intensity with which Madeira's residents defended its boundaries. In 1862 Constable Fry entered Madeira with a posse of six men in order to recover a horse allegedly stolen by Abiga Vasconcellas. He and a few policemen soon found themselves surrounded by Portuguese one hundred strong, "armed with every conceivable kind of weapons, guns, sticks, spades, hoes, axes." The Madeirans "commenced battle . . . with loud cries of vengeance," and Fry's men retreated with bloody heads and a new respect for the "belligerent Portuguese." Fry later returned with a whole mob of citizens "eager to clean the Portuguese out," and the Madeirans, in turn, "rallied with loud cries to meet them." The "Battle of Madeira" ended without further bloodshed, but with both sides possessing a keener appreciation of the boundaries that separated them.[23]

The autonomy of the Portuguese churches and residential community was never equalled in the economic realm. During the week most Madeirans worked for American natives, the women as house servants and laundresses, the men as general laborers and gardeners who maintained the yards of the rich on

22. *Northminster Presbyterian Church: Celebration of the One Hundredth Anniversary of the Organization of the Church* (Jacksonville, 1950), in Illinois State Historical Library, Springfield; Donnelley, Loyd & Co., *History of Morgan County, Illinois: Its Past and Present* (Chicago, 1878), p. 371. A Portuguese school was also founded sometime before 1865. See *Journal*, Nov. 30, 1865.

23. *Sentinel*, May 16, 1862.

College Hill. Several women also found employment in J. J. Capps' woolen mill as seamstresses. Some of the Portuguese worked into positions as small proprietors, small grocers and dry goods merchants. Others moved into the building trades as carpenters, painters, plasterers, and masons. (See Table 14.) The upward social mobility of the Madeirans never fully matched the optimistic claims of the natives, who used them as models of immigrant aspiration. "They came here poor, many of them almost destitute," wrote one patronizing Democratic editor, "but by untiring industry and unusual frugality, nearly all of them have acquired comfortable homes, and a number have become wealthy."[24]

The generous descriptions of Madeiran achievements may have exaggerated the truth, but these laudatory accounts tell something more important. The flattery bestowed upon the Portuguese had an obvious political purpose, whether it came from Republican or Democratic sources, and it suggests that the Portuguese vote was both significant and well organized. By the Democrats' account, the Portuguese were slavishly Republican; this they attributed to the early influence of Presbyterian sponsors, who bound their Madeiran co-religionists to the emergent Republican coalition. "This class of citizens," one Democrat complained of the Portuguese in 1868, "has for several years held the balance of political power in this city." This too was an exaggeration, but the Portuguese were eventually able to demand some rewards for their loyalty to the Republican majority, and by 1868 one of them was given a place in the city police department.[25]

The political ties of the Portuguese to the locally dominant party, and the efforts by Democrats to lure them away, contributed to the generally favorable public image the Portuguese enjoyed in Jacksonville newspapers and local histories. The public plaudits for hard work, sobriety, and success were occasionally betrayed by incidents like the 1862 "Battle of Madeira," which revealed deeper animosities between the Portuguese and natives. Reports of drunkenness, bootlegging, street fighting,

24. Ibid., Apr. 24, 1868.
25. Ibid.

and other minor crimes were also reported on occasion, with the clear purpose of bringing shame on all Madeirans. "The Portuguese nation must be on a general spree this week," a Republican editor chided after a series of crime reports. But these reproofs were usually balanced by other accounts which described them "as a class" to be "characterized by civil behavior, industry, sobriety, and thrift—distinguishing marks of good citizenship."[26] Still, this admiration, however sincere, was offered at a certain distance, one defined and protected in different ways by both natives and Portuguese.

COUSIN GERMANS

The German inhabitants of Jacksonville were not colonized the way the Portuguese were. Most arrived during the 1850s and 1860s, when the tide of German immigration rose following the abortive revolution of 1848. In the early 1840s many came to work beside the Irish on the new railroads that crossed Illinois. Yet from the beginning an impressive proportion of Germans, about half, were in skilled occupations, and by 1870 one in five could claim a position in business or the professions. (See Table 14.) Compared to all other foreign-born residents of Jacksonville, the Germans enjoyed a distinctly favored position in the local economic structure. Like the Portuguese, they frequently won praise for their industry, thrift, and discipline, but they also quickly created a set of churches, schools, and clubs which set them apart from the rest of the community.

The German subcommunity also revolved around its churches. The German Methodist Episcopal Church, founded in 1856, was established to preserve cultural autonomy from the other two large Methodist congregations. Within a year of their founding the German Methodists purchased the old Baptist church west of the square, and by the 1870s they could claim a congregation of about forty members. The major German church in Jacksonville was the Salem Evangelical Lutheran Church, founded in 1858. Within five years the Lutherans were able to erect their own church building a few blocks southeast of

26. *Journal*, Dec. 8, 1864; *Sentinel*, Apr. 24, 1868; Eames, *Historic Morgan*, pp. 127-28.

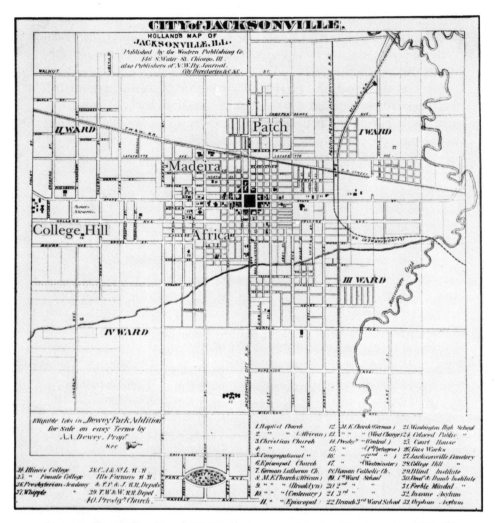

Jacksonville, 1871. From *Holland's Jacksonville City Directory for 1871–72* (Chicago, 1871); in Illinois State Historical Society Library.

the square; soon they gathered a congregation of about a hundred members.[27]

As more families joined the German community, the Lutherans led a movement to found a separate "German public school." They wisely opened the school to children of "other confessions" and designed the curriculum to perpetuate German language and culture. Still, the Lutherans were equally concerned that their children receive proper religious instruction, and they warned all parents that "confirmation instruction, Bible History and religious instruction and catechism shall be given exclusively for the children of the congregation on special days and at specified hours." To these precautions the Lutherans added: "Methodists, Catholics and Jews and the like shall not be absolutely forbidden to take part in the instruction in the Evangelical faith."[28] Throughout the 1860s the enrollment remained at about thirty students, only a small fraction of the German school-age children. Theological disagreements may have presented one limitation, but the cost of schooling was perhaps equally important. Lutheran parents were required to send their children to the German school, yet many were too poor, and by 1871 the church agreed to "grant these parents such support that [they] are not dependent on the earnings of their children so that the children may attend the school of the congregation."[29] Enrollments increased substantially thereafter, and the school continued to pass on German language and culture for several generations. Not until the turn of the century did the Lutherans, under heavy pressure, abandon their native tongue in the school and the church.[30]

Outside the churches, Germans came together in secular associations. The most visible of these was the Turnverein, a fraternity derived from nationalist societies in Germany and

27. Donnelley, *History of Morgan*, pp. 371-72; Arthur A. Hallerberg, "The Germans in Early Morgan County and the Early History of Salem Lutheran Church," typescript, 1958, in Illinois State Historical Library, Springfield; "Statistical Records, Salem Congregation," MSS in Salem Lutheran Church, Jacksonville.

28. "Minutes of the German Evangelical Salem Congregation," Mar. 7, 1864, p. 8, translated typescript of MSS in Salem Lutheran Church, Jacksonville.

29. Ibid., Jan. 8, 1871, p. 50.

30. Hallerberg, "Germans in Early Morgan," p. 9.

organized around gymnastic displays, mutual aid, and social festivities. Jacksonville's Turners founded their lodge in 1858 with only seven members. After the Civil War membership grew, and by 1870 they were able to build a new Turners' Hall on North Main at a cost of nearly $10,000. There they met on the first Sunday of each month to socialize and plan their next gymnastic display, holiday beer fest, masquerade ball, or children's fair.[31] The Turners, along with the locally famous German Brass Band, also served as ambassadors to the rest of Jacksonville by participating in festivities on the Fourth of July and Washington's Birthday. They received praise in the newspapers for their efforts and demonstrated to skeptical natives a public loyalty to their adopted nation.[32]

As the Turners and the German community grew, their parades more often led away from town. Beginning about 1862 the Turners organized an annual May festival; it usually began with a grand parade around the square and then, to the cadence of the "oom-pah-pah" band, marchers proceeded to one of the picnic grounds outside town. At the same time, national holidays like the Fourth of July became occasions for separate German celebrations. One cause for German withdrawal was the growing pressure to enforce strict prohibition ordinances in town—after a sweeping victory of teetotalers in the town elections of April, 1862, the Germans began marching out of town to enjoy their beer. Soon thereafter two enterprising Germans opened the Jacksonville Brewery just beyond the one-mile legal limit north of town. The brewery was surrounded by a shady grove and picnic grounds to which the Turners frequently repaired to pass the day in "innocent hilarity and social enjoyment." Other "Suburban Refreshment Gardens" cropped up to cater to thirsty Germans; one was just south of the mile limit in Mr. Motschman's Reservoir Grove, and another, west of town.[33]

31. William F. Short, ed., *Historical Encyclopedia of Illinois . . . Morgan County* (Chicago, 1906), p. 746; *Sentinel*, June 6, Sept. 12, Oct. 3, 1867; Feb. 4, 1870.

32. *Journal*, July 1, 1858; *Sentinel*, Mar. 1, 1861. The German school also made a special point of observing American national holidays; see "Minutes, Salem Congregation," Mar. 22, 1864, p. 9.

33. *Sentinel*, May 20, 1864; May 12, Aug. 11, 1865; June 6, 1867; "Minutes, Town Board" (title varies), May 12, 1866, MSS in City Clerk's Vault, Jacksonville Municipal Building (now available on microfilm, Illinois State Historical Library).

German affection for beer and native middle-class commitment to strict temperance produced social and political strains that continually threatened to weaken the partisan bridge between the Germans and the Republican leaders of Jacksonville. Ever since the formation of the Republican coalition in 1854, the Germans formed an increasingly important component of the party; they were tied to it by their antipathy to slavery, their evangelical Protestantism, and their moderately favorable position in the social structure of Jacksonville. Their loyalty to the Republicans was admitted by spokesmen for both parties, but this loyalty was tested by the recurring strains of the local temperance question. During the Civil War Republicans renewed their efforts to enact more stringent temperance legislation. The prohibition movement did not cramp the German's love for beer until June, 1862, when the town board passed a broader ordinance prohibiting sale of "any Spiritous, vinous, Malt, Fermented, Mixed or Intoxicating Liquors" and levied a fine of twenty-five dollars for each offense.[34]

Though Republicans were dominant in Jacksonville, they shrewdly advanced the cause of temperance as a purely nonpartisan local issue. The Democratic party, nonetheless, eagerly pounced on temperance to expose its Republican advocates and lure the German (and Portuguese) voters away. Democrats worked fervently after 1862 to make temperance a partisan issue. The Democratic editor of the *Sentinel* defended German cultural traditions and denounced prohibition, albeit without ever denying the virtues of temperance. The tactic was to oppose prohibition not as undesirable, but as unenforceable so long as a "large minority" rejected total abstinence as a moral ideal.[35]

The Republican newspaper, anxious about the upcoming elections in November, 1862, refused to defend prohibition as a

34. Arthur C. Cole, *The Era of the Civil War, 1848-1870*, The Centennial History of Illinois, vol. 3 (Springfield, 1919), pp. 343-44; "Minutes, Town Board," June 10, 1862. Paul Kleppner, *The Cross of Culture: A Social Analysis of Midwestern Politics, 1850-1900* (New York, 1970), pp. 37-51, explains that most Germans, particularly Catholics and "Old Lutherans," voted Democratic. In Jacksonville, however, the Germans were predominantly Evangelical Lutherans and Methodists; these religious ties, as he argues, would have bound them to the Republican party.

35. *Sentinel*, Apr. 4, 11, 1862.

party goal and tried again to support it as a local matter which deserved the support of "respectable gentlemen" of both parties. Some Republicans seemed willing to abandon the issue altogether if it meant endangering Portuguese and German support. In the meantime, the strategy was to soothe the Germans and accept a distinction between hard liquor and beer. "Our very best German citizens are beer drinkers," one Republican editorial argued, "and though we are by no manner the advocate . . . of beer drinking, we do not propose any political quarrel with them on account of their habits in this respect." In a shrewd maneuver, the Republican editor distinguished a small band of Germans "who ignore the habits of their countrymen, and have taken to the stronger cup." These whiskey-drinking Germans and their bootlegger compatriots had indeed found a welcome home in the Democratic "whiskey party"; the editor concluded that they were no great loss to his own party. Throughout the 1860s the Republican party in Jacksonville could be seen, as the Democrats accused, "drawing in its prohibitory horns" before national and state elections to keep from alienating the German and Portuguese vote in Morgan County.[36]

Democratic politicians worked equally hard to seduce the Germans away from their rivals. Representatives from both parties beat a well-worn path to the Turners' Hall to pay homage to the Germans of Jacksonville and to proclaim their liberal tolerance for the cultural traditions of the German people.[37] The Germans were able to use their political leverage to extract tangible gains as well as puffy rhetoric from local politicians. The lot for the new German school was leased to the Lutherans for five years, gratis, by the town board in November, 1862, just two days before state and congressional elections. In September, 1866, this generous lease was extended for another five years by the predominantly Republican board of trustees. By 1869 Germans also won a place on the city council: Leopold Weigand was elected alderman of the heavily foreign-born First

36. *Journal*, Nov. 16, 23, 1865; *Sentinel*, Oct. 3, 1867.
37. *Journal*, Nov. 23, 1865; *Sentinel*, June 6, Oct. 3, 1867; *Daily Journal* (Springfield), July 26, 1860.

Ward.[38] These prizes were not so much signs of assimilation as offerings given to placate a minority whose institutions and culture made it a distinctive and, at the same time, an integral part of the larger community.

THE PATCH

If the presence of Portuguese and Germans created new cultural boundaries in the 1850s, they were divisions bridged by a common faith in Protestantism and a fairly constant loyalty to the dominant Republican party. The coming of the Irish created not just a vague line of demarcation but a yawning chasm, one which their Catholic religion and their adamant loyalty to the Democratic party helped to widen. The Irish came with the railroads; they dug the roadbeds and laid the tracks for these symbols of progress that brought new trade and wealth to Jacksonville's door. Most of these Irishmen were in their twenties, and most were either single or had left their wives back East as they worked for a season on the roads. They were distinguished even among the foreign-born for their poverty, their lack of job skills, and their low level of persistence in the community. (See Table 14.)

Road gangs found cheap housing in the cluster of frame shacks and tenant apartments that popped up around the railroad depot in the 1850s, and as their numbers grew "the Patch," as it came to be known, became the residential nucleus of the Irish community. Census manuscripts indicate that Irish laborers and servants boarded with families in every part of town, but the Patch became the institutional center of their community, the home of the Irish church, as well as of many saloons and brothels which offered various pleasures to young, hard-working, lonely men.[39]

New England missionaries had come west to found Illinois College as part of a grand design, outlined in Lyman Beecher's *Plea for the West*, to save the disordered frontier from what they

38. "Minutes, Town Board," June 10, Nov. 4, 1862; Sept. 7, 1866; Donnelley, *History of Morgan*, p. 360.
39. U.S. Census MSS, Morgan County, Ill., 1860, 1870.

saw as a despotic Catholic conspiracy to undermine the American republic. Now from high on College Hill the Protestant elite could look down upon the Patch and witness the Catholic menace intruding, not as a stealthy conspiracy of the priesthood, but as a rowdy band of Irish railroad laborers—rough young men who drank too much, and who gambled and wenched in the back-alley dens that now pocked the genteel face of the "Athens of the West." The ungoverned Irish came to epitomize the antithesis of middle-class Protestant self-discipline.

If the Irish lacked temperance, there were those willing to impose moral restraints upon them. In the summer of 1853, the first season of heavy railroad construction in Morgan County, the town board passed a strict prohibition ordinance and created a full-time police department of ten men to replace the town constable. The ordinance allowed for controlled sales of liquor to "respectable" citizens for "sacramental, chemical, mechanical, or medicinal purposes," and forbade it to the intemperate. A broader ordinance was passed in February, 1855, to repress gambling, prostitution, and a variety of other sporting sins thought to be natural allies of intemperance.[40]

Predictably, the prohibition laws only drove underground a flourishing realm of business. These enterprises catered not to the Irish alone, but to a large population of men who drifted through town and were eager to leave their crowded rooms for some cheap excitement in saloons and gambling dens. The illegal liquor trade persisted despite the town board's sincere efforts to repress it. Some outraged citizens were willing to bypass legal authorities to enforce their standards of moral discipline. An open letter to the Republican *Journal* denounced Bazaleel Gillett, a prominent Democrat, whose tenement apartments in the Patch were allegedly rented to Irish bootleggers:

> We have used all exersions in our power to do away with this nuisance and all to noe effect. . . . These low Irish that is in the habit of trespassing on the laws of our Constitution we are fully

40. "Minutes, Town Board," June 13, July 12, 1853; Dec. 25, 1854. See the eighth chapter for a fuller discussion of prohibition and law enforcement in Jacksonville.

resolved we can get no other good of them [than] to burn them down to the lowest pit of hell. You my Dear Sir, can get respectable tenants for your houses. . . . And in case you shan't recognize our aggreevance, we shall leave you without house or tenants. . . .[41]

Gillett could only respond that "the Irish all over town both drink and sell whiskey," and he urged his attackers to appeal to legitimate law enforcement to repress this practice. "Now if they cannot prevent the traffic," he continued, "I don't think it incumbent upon me to run about Town and smell of every Irishman's breath to find out whether he has been drinking whiskey or not. . . ." "Are we," he asked in conclusion, "to burn all the houses in which the Irish live because they sell whiskey?"[42] Some citizens may have been prepared to answer this last question affirmatively, but most were willing to leave enforcement of morals to the police. The *Journal* kept up a steady stream of reports on incidents of drunkenness and violence among the Irish, adding a spate of jokes and ethnic slurs to reinforce the image of Irish degradation.

The Irish found refuge in a community of their own. While saloons and impromptu "tippling houses" continued to serve an important service by offering fellowship and entertainment as well as hard drink to these despised transients, the church formed the most visible and coherent basis of the Irish community. Protestants who came to Illinois to save the West from papist conspiracy must have witnessed with horror the first mass held in Jacksonville in 1851. As the numbers of Irish Catholics grew in the early 1850s, the congregation began to meet regularly, first in private homes and then in the county courthouse. They raised money to build a church of their own, and Murray McConnel, a shrewd Democratic politician, wisely donated a lot on North Sandy Street near the western border of the Patch. There a small brick building housed Jacksonville's Catholic Church of Our Savior until after the Civil War.[43]

By the 1860s the transient Irish railroad laborers were bal-

41. *Journal*, Feb. 2, 1860.
42. Ibid.
43. Short, *Historical Encyclopedia*, p. 728.

anced by a growing number of Irish women and families who brought a certain permanence and stability to the Patch. Now the Irish struggled desperately to live up to Protestant moral standards and project a reformed image of sober discipline. The Hibernian Temperance and Benevolent Society, formed around 1860, held a festival in Union Hall; after listening to several temperance speeches they "paraded our streets in full regalia and led by a brass band playing martial airs." "The procession," a Republican editor reported, "was quite creditable both in number and in general appearance." The *Journal* could not refrain, though, from adding a barb to the report: "We are informed that this society is strictly a *temperance* society as opposed to *total* abstinence. The fraternity do not absolutely abstain, but indulge temperately as their health demands, in moderate quantities, say from a gallon to a quart per day, according to the amount of strychnine in the whiskey."[44]

The Catholic Men's Association, founded by Father Mangan in 1862 as a lay society, superseded the Hibernians and enforced a strict code of total abstinence. They purchased a small subscription library of Catholic newspapers and books on temperance, self-improvement, and Irish history. At weekly meetings after mass they gathered to collect dues, admit new members, and administer fines and expulsions to backsliding members guilty of drunkenness, gambling, and other scandalous behavior. The accused were required to stand before the brethren and defend themselves or make full public confession of their sins.[45]

The Catholic Association also made a conscious effort to demonstrate moral discipline to doubting Protestants and to the Irish community around them. St. Patrick's Day became the unlikely occasion for displaying Irish temperance. In 1862 the Catholic Association carefully planned a full day of ceremonies, beginning with morning mass. The members assembled in the

44. *Journal*, Feb. 23, 1860; cf. Joan Bland, *The Hibernian Crusade: The Story of the Catholic Total Abstinence Union of America* (Washington, 1951).
45. "Records of the Catholic Association of Jacksonville, Illinois," MSS in rectory, Church of Our Savior, Jacksonville.

schoolhouse and were supplied with long green ribbon badges to be worn over their left breasts; they then "formed in ranks two by two" and, "preceded by a small banner," marched into the church to the tune of "Saint Patrick's Day in the Morning," played on violin and melodeon by two of the members. After mass a choir of schoolgirls sang "Hibernia's Champion Saint all Hail," "the melodious echoes of which no doubt ascended to the throng of the glorious St. Patrick, and caused him to smile on the dear children of Ireland." Then the Catholic Men's Association, "having formed in order," marched again out of the church.

That evening the Irish packed the schoolhouse for an "evening Soiree." With "gentlemen seated on the south side of the schoolroom and the ladies on the north side" (an arrangement that "materially contributed to the decorum" of the evening), the audience was treated to an elaborate program of music, singing, and long orations on English persecution of the Irish and the value of education. Each event was punctuated with refreshments of cakes, apples, and lemonade. (A faction within the Association had unsuccessfully advocated substituting beer.) "Not the least remarkable feature of the evening," the secretary of the Catholic Men's Association recorded with obvious satisfaction, "was the tone of morality that ruled the proceedings and the strict decorum that was observed . . . (with however a few well known exceptions)."[46]

These meticulously organized St. Patrick's Day celebrations became annual exhibitions of Irish self-discipline, and they were reported favorably to the community at large in the Democratic press.[47] The Catholic Men's Association also translated national holidays into celebrations of Irish identity. Even the Fourth of July, usually an occasion for blurring the community's internal factions, by 1862 served to clearly define cultural boundaries no one could ignore. The Catholic Association members, with green silk scarves around their necks, sponsored the Irish procession and barbecue at the fairgrounds

46. Ibid.
47. *Sentinel*, Mar. 18, 1864; Mar. 27, 1868.

while the Germans and native Protestants held their own separate celebrations at a distance.[48] The leadership of Catholic
temperance groups suggests that the purpose of these separate
Irish celebrations was not to evade the natives' moral regula-
tions; on the contrary, the Irish turned these occasions into
public displays of temperance. In 1867 the Irish Fourth of July
procession was arranged by the Catholic Total Abstinence Society, successors to the Men's Association. Led by the recently
formed Catholic Brass Band, the procession marched through
the town and out to the fairgrounds. Catholic schoolchildren
were prominent participants in these celebrations. At the
Fourth of July procession in 1870, one hundred members of
the "Daughters of Mary" dressed in white with blue ribbon
badges, the embodiment of the purity these events were designed to evoke.[49]

By the middle 1860s the Irish in Jacksonville had outgrown
their small church in the Patch. Coincident with the new consciousness of self-improvement manifest in the founding of the
Catholic Men's Association, they began raising funds for a new
church "in a more desirable part of the town." The Catholics
appealed directly to the Protestant community for support of a
fund-raising supper and fair. "This new building," the Democratic editor remarked of the proposed Catholic church, "will be
an ornament to the city and our citizens should lend a liberal
hand in the aid of this enterprise." The supper and fair were
held in Strawn Hall, usually reserved for major public meetings
and concerts attended by the Protestant middle class. Afterward
Father O'Halloran proclaimed its success and issued thanks to
the citizens "of all denominations" for their "generous liberality." Within a year the Irish, with help from their Protestant
benefactors, were able to begin building a large new brick
church just east of the square at a cost of $65,000.[50]

A new rectory and school went up beside the church, and in
the fall of 1869 the dedication ceremony for the new buildings

48. *Sentinel*, June 27, July 4, 1862; "Records, Catholic Association," May 31, 1863;
Journal, July 2, 9, 1863.

49. *Sentinel*, July 11, 1867; July 8, 1870.

50. Ibid., Feb. 24, Mar. 3, 1865; *Journal*, Feb. 23, Mar. 2, 1865; Donnelley, *History of Morgan*, p. 372.

became yet another public occasion to display Irish aspirations toward respectability. A procession of two hundred Catholic school girls, dressed in white with veils, sang Latin chants as they marched around the square and then to the church.[51]

These efforts toward social uplift helped to counter the prevailing negative view of the Irish as a violent, intemperate, religiously enslaved people, an image fed by the nearly constant stream of newspaper reports on Irish involvement in bootlegging, street brawls, and drunken sprees. In a predominantly Republican town the Irish suffered special abuse for their rigid loyalty to the Democratic party—"voting cattle," the Republicans disdainfully called them.[52] Republicans vented their disapproval of the Irish in a way that they dared not with the Portuguese or Germans, for fear of losing valuable votes.

But this political situation was altered around 1865, with the rise of the Fenian movement in Jacksonville. The Fenians were an Irish nationalist society that began during the Civil War, when soldiers formed "Fenian circles" committed to the military liberation of their homeland. In June, 1866, a Fenian army actually invaded Canada, but their plans to spark an anti-British revolt were quickly squelched by U.S. military intervention. In Jacksonville Fenianism was a young man's movement that revolved around weekly meetings and social picnics. The Catholic church officially disapproved of the Fenians, and the Democratic party cautiously avoided it as a potentially divisive independent political force.[53] When Democrat Murray McConnel, a long-time friend of the Irish in Jacksonville, spoke before the Catholic Fourth of July celebration in 1866, he was forced to defend President Andrew Johnson's intervention in the Fenian invasion of Canada and was roundly denounced by angry Fenians in the audience.[54] The Republicans eagerly worked their own political wedge between the Fenians and the Catholic-Democratic coalition. Colonel George Smith, editor of the

51. *Sentinel*, Sept. 3, 1869.

52. Ibid., Oct. 4, 1866.

53. Carl Wittke, *The Irish in America* (Baton Rouge, 1951), pp. 150-60; Cole, *Era of the Civil War*, pp. 344-46, 403; Thomas N. Brown, *Irish-American Nationalism, 1870-1890* (Philadelphia, 1966), pp. 38-41.

54. *Journal*, July 12, 16, 1866.

Republican *Journal*, actively courted the Fenians before the judicial elections of 1867 by helping to sponsor meetings with Fenian speakers from Chicago. The *Journal* now also carried favorable reports on Irish efforts to build a new church, and, for a time at least, dropped the usual list of Irish arrests and derisive ethnic jokes.[55]

By 1867 the Irish were able to use their increasing political leverage to elect one of their own, James Redmond, as alderman of the First Ward; his brother, Daniel Redmond, was elected in 1870. The new ward system introduced in 1867 allowed the Irish to consolidate their strength in the Patch, thus carrying the First Ward for the Redmond brothers. Along with the Germans and Portuguese, the Irish now enjoyed at least token recognition within the official power structure. But as the local Fenian movement fizzled out after 1867, Republican efforts to woo the Irish vote subsided, and the cultural divisions of temperance and religion emerged with new intensity.

The Democrats, at the same time, worked hard to remind the Irish of these cultural boundaries by publicizing the fervent prejudice of Republican politicians and their evangelical Protestant clergymen. A convenient opportunity came when Father Joseph La Costa (an Italian Carmelite) took over as priest of Our Savior in 1860, and the interdenominational Ministerial Association of Jacksonville extended to him an unprecedented invitation to join. When La Costa refused on principle, a verbal torrent of anti-Catholic abuse followed, all reported thoroughly in the Democratic press.[56] A series of anti-Catholic sermons issued from Protestant pulpits, and the same sentiments were expressed in an interdenominational meeting in Strawn Hall. Up on College Hill a student literary society met to debate the question: "Resolved: Catholicism should be abolished by law." La Costa demanded equal time and offered his own lecture "in defense of Catholicism" before a large audience. By this time the communication across cultural boundaries served only to

55. *Sentinel*, Oct. 4, 1866; May 23, July 4, Aug. 8, 1867; *Journal*, Feb. 23, 1865; June 5, 1866.

56. *Sentinel*, Dec. 6, 1866; Jan. 10, 1867.

remind both sides of how fixed and unbridgeable their differences seemed to be.[57]

AFRICA

A small black population also formed a discrete social entity within a society which, in their case, never pretended to want anything but separation. Still, blacks found existence within Jacksonville reasonably congenial, so long as their numbers were few and their demands mild.

Jacksonville, in fact, enjoyed a legendary reputation as one of Illinois' several benign havens for freedmen and runaway slaves, an island within a hostile state controlled by enlightened antislavery Yankees who offered shelter and a certain level of dignity to long-suffering blacks. After the Civil War local historians enshrined the legend with a series of firsthand interviews of benevolent whites who risked their lives helping blacks pass through Jacksonville on the Underground Railroad.[58] The legend distorts the blacks' true situation in Jacksonville, but it also underlines the peculiar ambivalence of so many whites toward this most distinctive element within the community.

The laws of antebellum Illinois clearly defined the Negro as *persona non grata*. An 1824 decision to ban slavery in Illinois owed as much to white hatred for blacks as it did to moral objections to the extension of slavery. Subsequent laws denied Illinois blacks the basic rights of citizenship; they were excluded from the poll booths, juries, state militia, and public schools. In 1848 the white voters of Illinois took their racial antipathy further by voting overwhelmingly in favor of future legislation to prohibit continued migration of blacks into the state. (Only a few of Jacksonville's supposedly enlightened voters registered their objection to this measure.) Legislation passed in 1853 enforced this popular mandate by imposing fines of $100 to $500 against illegal black immigrants; the labor of those unable to pay was sold at public auction.[59]

57. Ibid., Dec. 16, 1866.
58. Eames, *Historic Morgan*, pp. 136-43.
59. Norman D. Harris, *History of Negro Servitude in Illinois* (Chicago, 1906), pp.

A handful of blacks had migrated to Morgan County with the first wave of settlers, and most concentrated within Jacksonville. By 1850 almost a hundred black residents made up less than 4 percent of the town's population. The Black Codes of 1853 had their effect on the local scene; Jacksonville's black community grew to only 156 by 1860, by then less than 3 percent of the total population. Except for a few who were clergymen and farmers, blacks served in menial positions as servants, unskilled laborers, or in personal services as barbers and waiters. (See Table 14.) In 1850 40 percent of blacks in the non-dependent population reported no occupation to the census-taker; they appear to have been living off one another by taking in black boarders. Within the next ten years the small black population gained a firm, if lowly, foothold in the local economy. Over one-third were able to report skilled occupations, and the portion reporting no gainful occupation was reduced from 40 to less than 20 percent. Only a few rose above the level of skilled labor, most either as clergymen or petty shopkeepers serving the black community. Property ownership among blacks was far below that of whites throughout this period, yet there were signs of modest prosperity within the black community.[60]

Blacks could be found living in nearly every part of town as servants or boarders, but by the early 1840s a dense miniature ghetto formed just southwest of the square. "Africa," as it was commonly known, was the institutional center of Jacksonville's black community. Here the two black churches were built, and in Africa a separate black society fostered its own saloons and "flesh pots," schools and social clubs. Mount Emory Baptist Church was founded with just seven members in 1837. Within a decade the slowly growing congregation was able to move out of rented quarters to their own church on Anna Street. The Rev-

235-36; "Poll Books, Morgan County, 1848 Presidential Election and Constitutional Referendum," microfilm, Illinois State Archives, Springfield. Charles N. Zucker, "The Free Negro Question: Race Relations in Antebellum Illinois" (Ph.D. dissertation, Northwestern University, 1973), offers an insightful analysis of race relations for this period. See also V. Jacque Voegeli, *Free but Not Equal: The Midwest and the Negro during the Civil War* (Chicago, 1967), for the political ramifications of the race question.

60. Zucker, "The Free Negro Question," ch. 4, has similar data on blacks in various other Illinois communities.

erend Andrew W. Jackson, a local barber, took over as pastor of Mount Emory Baptist in the late 1840s; by virtue of his position he became the principal spokesman for black Jacksonville. The Reverend Mr. Jackson graciously helped found a second black church in 1846, the African Methodist Episcopal. A handful of members held services in the new Mount Emory Baptist Church until 1850, when they were able to move into their own A.M.E. church, also constructed in the heart of Africa.[61]

These black churches were dependent to some degree on the financial aid and good will of wealthy whites. Judge William Brown and other white patrons sponsored the building of the new A.M.E. church in 1850; again ten years later the same church thanked the "gentlemen and ladies of Jacksonville for their generous and liberal patronage" at a fund-raising supper.[62] Indeed, Jacksonville, with its self-image as an enlightened community with strong New England influence, seemed to take a certain paternalistic pride in the progress of freedmen in Africa. Not only did white congregations lend a hand in building new black churches; several, including Congregationalists, Christians, and Methodists, had at least one black member as a token of their tolerance. Before the Civil War occasional racial slurs appeared in the newspapers of both parties, and there were a few recorded assaults on blacks by whites chasing runaway slaves. But there is little evidence to suggest any systematic policy of intimidation or degradation of Jacksonville's blacks.[63]

The Civil War altered this pattern of race relations by opening the whole debate over blacks' place in America, and by simultaneously opening a new flow of black migration

61. Short, *Historical Encyclopedia*, pp. 731-32.
62. *Journal*, Apr. 12, 1860.
63. Sturtevant, *Origins of Western Congregationalism*, p. 60, lists former slave Emily Logan, who was befriended by the church in 1843. "Church Book, Records, Minutes and Proceedings of the Church of Jesus Christ in Jacksonville," Box 1, Central Christian Church Records, Disciples of Christ Historical Society, Nashville, Tenn.; see entry for Lucinda Lee, "colored woman," Nov., 1843. *150th Anniversary of Centenary Methodist Church* (Jacksonville, 1971), p. 5. Samuel Willard, "My First Adventure with a Fugitive Slave . . . ," p. 6, Willard Papers, Illinois State Historical Library, Springfield.

into Jacksonville and Illinois. The unspoken rules that allowed an amiable if unequal coexistence of blacks and whites were now debated heatedly. But whites dominated this debate, and they disagreed only over how to maintain the social distance that separated the races, not on whether that distance should be obliterated.

When contraband slaves were brought into Illinois for resettlement beginning in 1862, Democrats quickly seized the race issue and used it with vengeance against their Republican foes. The Democratic strategy was to identify Republicans as champions of the Negro, and then to polarize the issue by arguing that there was no middle ground between total degradation of blacks and total amalgamation with whites. They exploited white fears by raising the spectre of black competition in the job market and—more frightening still—in the marriage market. "Racial amalgamation" seemed to threaten one of the clearest social boundaries in a loosely formed social structure, and the Democrats adroitly played on this threat. As Lincoln prepared to sign the Emancipation Proclamation in 1863, Jacksonville's Democratic *Sentinel* bitterly anticipated the coming "nightmare" of racial equality and the flood of "low niggers" into the community.[64]

New laws excluding black migration into Illinois had been put before the people in 1862 as part of a state constitutional referendum. The constitutional convention itself was rejected, but the separate Negro exclusion section, and one other to prevent blacks from holding office, were approved by staggering majorities that clearly cut across party lines. Even the most notably liberal Republicans realized there was no politic defense of black equality, and they quickly back-pedaled, defending the war against slavery, assuring Illinois whites that freedmen would stay in the South, and defending blacks not as equals, but as deserving Christians.

Republican intellectuals had to devise a racial policy that admitted the notion of black inferiority while calling for protection of blacks against white exploitation. To this task Jack-

64. *Sentinel*, Oct. 31, 1862; *Journal*, Dec. 31, 1863; Voegeli, *Free but Not Equal*, pp. 6-7, 13-29, passim.

sonville's Jonathan Baldwin Turner, a liberal proponent of antislavery, universal education, and a state industrial university, brought his considerable talents. His book, *The Three Great Races of Men*, published at the outset of the war on the basis of lectures and papers he had written earlier, staked out the position of the midwestern Republican compromise on race. Turner's analysis of race rested on a climatological theory which defined the white, yellow, and black races by ingrained characteristics, each the environmental product of a distinct climate, polar, tropical, or equatorial. Focusing on fundamental differences between polar whites and equatorial blacks, Turner constructed a dichotomy of rational and romantic personalities: "the great mission of the polar man is to analyze and to conquer, that of the equatorial man is to enjoy and adore . . . as one is of a being of intellect, of the head—the other of sentiment of the heart." While blacks lived with whites, they would remain subservient, given their inherent traits. "The two races," he concluded, "cannot dwell together . . . *first* because God never designed that they should. . . . and *second*, because each race is still essentially barbarian in the only line where the other has begun to be civilized—the one in the head, the other in the heart. . . ." Devoted blacks, like Uncle Tom, "would choose to remain where they are"; however, the moral health of white civilization required that slavery be forcibly ended and blacks colonized in the equatorial climate of Brazil or Haiti (with, he added, heartfelt thanks for their services to America).[65] After the Emancipation Proclamation, new efforts were made to revive the colonization society in Jacksonville "after years of comparative obscurity." Only colonization of freedmen, argued the Republican *Journal* in 1864, "offers an answer to the ever-present question: What shall be done with the Negro?"[66]

Other Republican theorists defined the future position of

65. Turner, *The Three Great Races of Men: Their Origin, Character and Destiny with Special Regard to the Present Conditions and Future Destiny of the Black Race in the United States* (Springfield, 1861), pp. 1-71 passim. See George M. Fredrickson, *The Black Image in the White Mind: The Debate on Afro-American Character and Destiny, 1817-1914* (New York, 1971), pp. 97-129, for a discussion of "romantic racialism," which describes the school of thought to which Turner belonged.

66. *Journal*, Nov. 10, 1864.

blacks in American society in more draconian terms. Julian Sturtevant, president of Illinois College and emissary for Lincoln's administration in England during the war, stated the distinction between political and racial equality in his 1863 essay, "The Destiny of the African Race in the United States." His argument rested upon a confident assumption of the inherent inferiority of blacks. Once the artificial barrier (and protective shield) of slavery was abolished, blacks would compete in a free and open marketplace, and they would then rise or fall to the level of their innate racial capacity for achievement. Once "the negro is made a free laborer he is brought into direct competition with the white man; that competition he is unable to endure; and he soon finds his place in that lower stratum. . . . [There he will] struggle in vain against the laws of nature, and his children will, many of them at least, die in infancy." There was no need to artificially oppress the black man, or to carry him off to another land. Natural forces would determine his future: eventual extinction. "The negro does not aspire to political or social equality with the white man. . . . He appeals not to our fears, but to our compassion. He asks not to rule us: he only craves of us leave to toil; to hew our wood and draw our water, for such miserable pittance of compensation as the competition of free labor will award him—a grave."[67]

This confident assertion was the Republicans' way of assuring whites that the breakdown of artificial legal barriers oppressing blacks would in no way dissolve more permanent and natural obstacles to racial equality and amalgamation. The Republican stress on racial limitations allowed them to advocate the extension of basic rights of citizenship to blacks, while at the same time denying the goal of racial equality or amalgamation.[68]

Whatever the unlikely long-term prospects of colonization or

67. Sturtevant, "The Destiny of the African Race," *Continental Monthly* 2 (1863): 600-610; Fredrickson, *Black Image*, pp. 158-59. See also Fredrickson, "A Man but Not a Brother: Abraham Lincoln and Racial Equality," *Journal of Southern History* 41 (1975): 39-58.

68. No clear consensus existed among local Republicans on the free Negro question. Governor Richard Yates of Jacksonville and the *Journal* both came out in favor of black suffrage in the summer of 1865, but conservative Republicans managed to nominate their own slate in the 1866 elections. See the incisive report on local politics by a *Chicago Tribune* correspondent in *Journal*, Nov. 16, 1865.

gradual extinction of blacks, their actual population in Jacksonville was rapidly increasing. The black community which had numbered 156 before the war now swelled to over 400—nearly 500, with those blacks living on the periphery of the town limits. Although they still constituted less than 5 percent of the town population, they were now more visibly concentrated within the expanding boundaries of Africa. The influx of freedmen during and after the war gave new life to black institutions in Africa. In 1866 the Reverend Andrew W. Jackson led a $7,000 fundraising drive to build a new two-story brick church for his rapidly growing Mount Emory Baptist congregation. Jackson became a major force for black uplift through the church and Sunday school movement, and his efforts in behalf of these goals won hearty praise from Republicans throughout the state. Even the Democratic editor recognized Jackson's vital role as "the true Moses of the colored people of this city."[69]

The growth of the black community during the Civil War was also manifest in the flurry of social events that now took place in Africa. Like other ethnic groups, blacks defined their separate identity in a series of public celebrations on occasions unique to black tradition: a picnic each August to observe the emancipation of Haiti, a festival in January to celebrate their own emancipation, and a grand reception and dinner to welcome Jacksonville's "colored soldiers" home from the war.[70] The Republican paper noted with approval the "respectable appearance and highly creditable" behavior of blacks on these occasions. It also welcomed a visit by Frederick Douglass, a "self-made and talented man," and admonished those "who have no faith in the negro" to "be present on this occasion and judge for themselves." Some whites in Jacksonville encouraged black churches as agencies for black self-help, supporting building programs and encouraging black efforts in missionary work and Sunday schools.[71]

69. *Journal*, Oct. 5, 1865; Apr. 10, 1866; *Sentinel*, Apr. 8, 1870; Short, *Historical Encyclopedia*, p. 731. Population data on blacks based on Francis A. Walker, *A Compendium of the Ninth Census* (Washington, 1872), p. 160.

70. *Journal*, Aug. 4, 1864; Dec. 14, 1865; *Sentinel*, Jan. 6, 1865; Aug. 8, 1867; Sept. 10, 1869.

71. *Journal*, Aug. 4, 1864; Oct. 5, Dec. 14, 1865; Feb. 22, Apr. 10, 1866; *Sentinel*, Sept. 6, 1866.

Under the leadership of the Reverend Mr. Jackson, blacks also enlisted the aid of "liberal white citizens" to build a free public "colored school" in 1865. The Republican editor urged white support: "Whatever may be the future status of the colored man . . . no one can now . . . deny to the colored children the right to demand of the community in which they live, the means of a common school education."[72] The old Mount Emory church building in Africa was sold to the school board in 1866 for use as the new "colored school." For the first time blacks were officially granted the right to free public education in Jacksonville, albeit within a segregated institution. The hypocrisy of this reform was not lost on Democratic critics, who ridiculed their rivals' painful contortions over the free Negro question. For three months running the Democratic newspaper gleefully published an angry letter by Thomas Rountree, a black resident who objected to a segregated school. "Now we are citizens in common with other men," Rountree proclaimed. If black children were going to attend a special school in Africa (where fewer than half of the black children lived), then logically whites should also install separate polls at elections, separate railroad cars, and separate facilities of every kind. Rountree's alternative of total segregation, which he of course intended to seem absurd, was to become the standard for American race relations by the end of the century. He was simply arguing that racial equality had to be all or nothing.[73] The Democrats who published Rountree's letter agreed with this analysis (though they would have preferred that nothing be granted to blacks), and they used his indignant letter as proof that the Republican compromise of extending minimal civil rights, coupled with a firm faith in natural racial limitations, would never maintain the social distance which members of both parties thought was necessary between the races.

The Republicans held fast to their compromise position and defended the extension of voting rights to blacks after the Civil

72. *Journal*, Apr. 6, 1865.
73. Short, *Historical Encyclopedia*, p. 731; *Sentinel*, July 8, 1865. Rountree's letter was mercilessly reprinted in every *Sentinel* issue through September under the editorial headline, "An Appeal to Radical Sincerity."

War. Jonathan Baldwin Turner, who only a few years earlier had argued for colonization, now pleaded for black suffrage by arguing that restriction on account of race could logically be applied to Irish and Germans on account of language or nativity.[74] The Fifteenth Amendment guarantee of voting rights for blacks reinforced the black alliance with the Republican elite of Jacksonville, for now blacks could return a solid bloc of votes for favors from their white allies. These political bonds were solemnized at a large public meeting in Strawn Hall to celebrate passage of the constitutional amendment in 1870. Long speeches by Turner and Jackson made clear the mutually helpful arrangement of local race relations.[75] Implicitly, the residents of Africa had become defined as simply another ethnic group with an equal claim to fundamental rights of citizenship. Yet the extension of rights to education and the vote were in no way intended to elevate blacks to the level of whites; rather, they created a floor of minimal status above which, in the Republican view, natural racial capacities would preserve clear boundaries.

The divisions between blacks and whites, justified by a notion of immutable racial inequality, were only the sharpest of several boundaries that crossed the face of this deceptively complex community. Within this small, constantly moving population the boundaries of culture came to define a certain social order and continuity by providing easily identifiable categories into which newcomers could quickly be sorted.

This process of social sorting was reflected in the residential patterns that allowed Jacksonville's citizens to refer to Madeira, the Patch, and Africa as recognizable neighborhoods. Actually, the distribution of each of these subpopulations betrays the idea of homogeneous residential enclaves. Table 15 (see Appendix) compares the residential concentrations of each minority in 1870; an index of dissimilarity measures the percentage of each population that would have to change neighborhoods in order to effect perfect distribution throughout the town. The small

74. *Journal*, Nov. 30, 1865.
75. *Sentinel*, Apr. 8, 1870. The *Sentinel* criticized the *Journal* for slighting Jackson's contribution to the meeting.

Portuguese population, concentrated in the northwest quad-
rant, was the most segregated; among the other minorities, only
about one in five would have had to move to another ward in
order to equalize their representation with that of native whites
in each ward.[76]

The pattern of rapid growth, the shortage of dwellings, the
widespread practice of lodging, and the use of immigrants and
blacks as live-in domestic servants all militated against absolute
physical segregation for any of these groups. Even with a certain
amount of residential concentration, the scale of the town simply would not allow any social group to insulate itself completely. There must have been constant face-to-face contact
among segments of the community at the town square, the poll
booth, and political rallies. Although there were efforts to
minimize these contacts with separate churches and public
celebrations, clear limits imposed by the compact scale of the
town constantly forced strangers upon one another.

The boundaries that separated Portuguese, Germans, Irish,
and blacks were defined not so much by spatial arrangements as
by a set of formal institutions which protected distinct cultures
defined by language, religion, race, and historic tradition.
These separate churches, voluntary associations, and celebrations were demonstrative and enduring expressions of the
fragmented nature of the community. Yet even as each segment
of the community institutionalized its separate cultural identity,
it did so in ways that betrayed a deeper level of community.
Yankees, Portuguese, Germans, Irish, and blacks all found their
central identity as a group through religious organizations;
the theological differences between Congregationalism and
Catholicism, for example, should not obscure the obvious similarities in the social functions of each church within the local
context. Common forms also emerged in the organization
of voluntary associations, from the German Turners to the
Catholic Men's Association to the Colored Washingtonian So-

76. See Nathan Kantrowitz, "The Index of Dissimilarity: A Measurement of Residential Segregation for Historical Analysis," *Historical Methods Newsletter* 7 (1974):
285-89; Kathleen Neils Conzen, *Immigrant Milwaukee, 1836-1860: Accommodation and
Community in a Frontier City* (Cambridge, Mass., 1976), esp. ch. 6.

ciety, all part of a larger pattern within the community. The formal organization of religious and social institutions pervaded each segment of the community; furthermore, an ethos of temperance, personal discipline, and self-improvement evident in nearly all these associations belies the very cultural uniqueness they were designed to preserve. The sober Irish marching two by two on their way to mass on St. Patrick's Day; the Turners and their magnificent brass band strutting around the square en route to their suburban beer gardens; the new citizens of Africa in buggies and on foot proceeding in "admirable order" to their picnic celebrating the emancipation of Haiti—each marched in different directions toward a particular cultural identity. Yet all seemed to imitate a model of social organization and personal discipline that existed beyond the boundaries of culture.

This was a key paradox in the definition of community that emerged in Jacksonville: a people fragmented by religion, ethnicity, and race could, at the same time, share common forms of social organization and similar values of self-improvement. The formal associations within each segment of the community revolved around another paradox: they were designed to serve individual opportunity, yet demanded submission to a regimen of group discipline. This model of organization descended from the dominant native white middle class, and it is within these social boundaries that the following chapter will explore more fully the intertwining roles of voluntarism, individual opportunity, and social control embodied in the community's formal associations.

The Voluntary Community

Society is not . . . dissolving; but is merely taking to itself forms in which it can live and act in its new mode of being.

—JONATHAN BALDWIN TURNER[1]

A S JACKSONVILLE'S MINORITIES clustered in separate but similar religious and secular associations, they followed a powerful drive to organize formal social institutions within the dominant native middle class. The vaunted individualism of the early West competed with an equally vigorous claim for social organization, and both ends were served through churches, political parties, clubs, and reform societies that sprang up in multitudes in towns like Jacksonville. The apparent contradiction between the pursuit of individual opportunity and the need for community order was resolved, for a portion of the population at least, through the principle of voluntarism.

At the heart of the new community was the idea of voluntary commitment to that community and its institutions. Involuntary social groups define their members by the accidental fact that they happen to be born, for example, into a particular family, culture, or religion. In contrast, individuals *choose* to join the voluntary community, according to their assessment of how well the community, or a single institution within it, serves their specific needs; they withdraw when those needs are no longer satisfied. One's commitment to the voluntary community is determined more by carefully calculated personal goals, such as

1. *Illinois Statesman*, Mar. 18, 1844.

156

social mobility, than by deep primordial bonds to kinship and place. A corollary to this principle of voluntarism is the central role of formally organized institutions. They allowed the voluntary community to shuffle members in and out with ease, and, at the same time, provided this mobile, diverse, and seemingly disorderly swirl of individuals with a cohesive and constant form of social order.

This chapter will explore three institutional components of the voluntary community. The first two, the churches and political parties, evolved in ways that helped organize and regulate conflict that had torn apart the community in its early years. On one hand, the churches attempted to reduce sectarian divisiveness by stressing personal piety over theological doctrine; on the other, the political parties translated parochial battles between personalities into national contests of ideology. The third, and most important, institutional component of the voluntary community was the voluntary association, which bridged the chasms of sect and party by stressing the unifying values its members shared as community leaders. Pervading all three sets of institutions were the paradoxical needs of the voluntary community for individual opportunity and social discipline. To the extent that those needs were served, the problem of community was at least partially resolved.

THE VOLUNTARY CHURCH

The church provided one of the most potent instruments for organizing the diverse and fluid population of the new community. The evangelical Protestant churches in particular soon learned to reduce sectarian conflict and internal schisms by stressing piety and fellowship over rigid doctrinal orthodoxy. They opened their doors to newcomers, assisted transient members, and brought to the West a sorely needed mechanism for social discipline.

One of the recurring problems in early Jacksonville was the divisiveness of sectarian squabbles. By the 1860s about half of Jacksonville's population belonged to eighteen different congregations spread among eight separate denominations. The "confusion and religious anarchy" which Julian Sturtevant de-cried stemmed from the cultural heterogeneity of the new community and the inevitable jealousies among "unfortunate personalities."[2] Of course, Jacksonville's religious divisions were part of larger national forces that shattered Protestant America into dozens of competing sects. Yet, beneath all the rabid denominational competition and theological debates, the churches were broadening their popular base and, in so doing, lowering the standards for admission. They stressed personal pietism over doctrinal orthodoxy, and they welcomed newcom-ers at revivals or accepted letters of transfer with relative ease. Like the town boosters, evangelical preachers measured success in numbers. The doors to the church opened wide in the competition for new converts; this was no time to enforce the fine points of theological orthodoxy. As a result, Protestant churches became like voluntary associations, excluding few but requiring submission to a pietistic code of personal discipline.[3]

The history of Jacksonville's Church of Christ reveals the havoc that doctrinal issues could bring to an essentially pietistic fellowship. The Christians, or Disciples of Christ, began as an evangelical "New Light" offshoot of Presbyterianism. Im-pressed with the possibilities for Protestant unity by his experi-ence at the famous Cane Ridge revival of 1801, Barton Stone and his followers were convinced that the only way to avoid denominational divisions was to abandon doctrinal inventions of man and build a reformed Christian church based solely on the Bible. Stone came to Jacksonville in 1832; there he published *The Christian Messenger* and retired before his death in 1844. Stone successfully united two separate congregations of "Christians" and "Disciples" (the latter followers of Alex-ander Campbell), and the new "Church of Christ in Jackson-ville" grew as the center of a thriving religious movement in

2. *Julian M. Sturtevant, An Autobiography*, ed. J. M. Sturtevant, Jr. (New York, 1896), pp. 160-61; Charles M. Eames, *Historic Morgan and Classic Jacksonville* (Jacksonville, 1885), p. 173.

3. Sidney Mead, *The Lively Experiment: The Shaping of Christianity in America* (New York, 1963).

central Illinois. By 1854 the Christian church opened Berean College in Jacksonville to train its own ministers.[4]

Despite their vision of Christian unity and their freedom from rigid creed, the Christians of Jacksonville fell prey to the same divisive sectarian spirit that afflicted other churches. In 1857 they hired a new pastor and president of Berean College, Walter S. Russell, a bright young scholar. Russell's published articles and sermons soon made it clear to a faction within the congregation that his "ultra views" on "inner light" and baptism by sprinkling countered the spirit of Barton Stone's "Reformation." When it came time to reelect Russell as pastor, the church, founded on the principle that man-made creed was an artificial source of division, fell into a bitter sectarian feud. "Father against children. Elders against Elders, family against family. Brother against brother," rebuked an outside witness to the Russell controversy. "And the curious among our sectarian friends looking on to see the practical working of these people whose religion is founded upon the Bible alone—and will return from this house singing the Song—you cannot get along without a creed . . . we told you so. We told you so."[5]

But the truth was that Jacksonville's Christians could get along quite comfortably *only without* a clearly defined creed. The anti-Russellites lost the election two years straight, issuing formal protests to the congregation before each poll was taken. In 1859 they bolted the church and set up their own "true Church of Christ" in rented space in the courthouse. Later they brought suit against the majority and claimed to be the only rightful heirs of the church founded by Barton Stone.

The majority, who still held the church building on North Main Street, denounced the anti-Russellites as poor losers and stood their ground. Soon Russell left his feuding congregation for a more peaceful existence as an army chaplain; he was killed in the Civil War in November, 1863. The main body of the

4. *History of the Christian Church, Jacksonville, Illinois, 1832-1920* (Jacksonville, 1920), pp. 6-8.

5. "Church Book, Records, Minutes and Proceedings of the Church of Jesus Christ in Jacksonville," Aug. 23, 1858, Box 1, Central Christian Church Records, Disciples of Christ Historical Society, Nashville, Tenn.

church, weakened by the split and startled by the refusal of the Christian church to appoint a new minister to their congregation due to the protest of the anti-Russellite faction, now began to consider a pragmatic merger with the Baptists.

With Russell gone, however, others felt that the church might be reunited, and cautious feelers were put out to the anti-Russellite minority. A "joyous reunion" was finally consummated in the spring of 1866, with a formal ceremony and "mutual confessions from the Chief Actors in past scenes." They buried "all past dissentions in oblivion" and threw their energy into a fund-raising campaign for a new church building. The reunion ultimately depended on the ability of both factions to submerge theological doctrine, to "ignore all teachings of men," to "trust alone in the Bible," and to decide all other details by tactful rule of the majority. Doctrines only divided; fund-raising drives for a new church building provided a much better adhesive for the voluntary church.[6]

In place of divisive doctrine, the voluntary church offered fellowship. Newcomers were immediately plugged into a whole circuit of potential friendships and business contacts.[7] Throughout the week the churches provided ample opportunity for social intimacy among their members; in addition, all offered two services on Sunday, one at eleven in the morning, the second, usually a prayer meeting, at seven in the evening. This was supplemented by a midweek prayer meeting on Wednesday night, and the hearty souls of the First Presbyterian Church added a Friday evening lecture.[8] Beyond this were dozens of sectarian voluntary associations, the maternal societies, social circles, and committees galore, which kept an active member in almost constant interaction with the brethren.

The diary of Elizabeth Duncan, a member of the First Presbyterian, suggests how closely some lives revolved around the church—particularly the lives of middle-class women, who found in religious activities one of the few socially approved

6. Ibid., June 12, 19, 1864; May 20, 1866.
7. T. Scott Miyakawa, *Protestants and Pioneers: Individualism and Conformity on the American Frontier* (Chicago, 1964), pp. 130-31.
8. C. S. Williams, comp., *Williams' Jacksonville Directory and Business Mirror for 1860-61* (Jacksonville, 1860), pp. 25-27.

outlets from the domestic circle. Mrs. Duncan's journal faith-fully records the subject of each sermon she heard and each prayer meeting or Bible class she attended. Her Sundays were normally occupied with morning and evening services, and more than once after morning worship she hurried down to the Congregational church to attend yet another service. The heresy trials and sectional antagonism that forced the Con-gregationalists to split off from the Presbyterians did not keep Mrs. Duncan from hearing another good sermon. Between services her time was absorbed by a steady round of maternal society meetings, formal visiting, afternoon teas, and dinner parties among the well-to-do on College Hill. Her social con-tacts, though not confined to fellow Presbyterians, seemed to center on the church and its multitude of formally arranged activities.[9]

Increasingly the church's function in providing fellowship was openly acknowledged in the planning of blatantly non-religious functions. The oyster supper given by the "Ladies of the Baptist Church" at the Mansion House Hotel in 1860 was only one of dozens of similar affairs announced in the local papers and reported later as occasions of joyous celebration.[10] Some of these festive events were ostensibly fund-raising affairs of high-minded purpose, designed to support a new church building or perhaps a missionary program; nevertheless, the more immediate social function was undeniable. Many fund-raising church socials were open to all denominations, a practice which contributed to the secular tone of the festivities. Some ministers may have worried over the gaiety and frivolity that attended these gatherings, but the western clergy were gener-ally willing to accede to the social needs and expectations of their congregations. If oyster suppers and ice cream socials would help expand their churches' influence, few were pre-pared to challenge the propriety of such affairs.[11]

Revivalism also diluted doctrinal divisions and allowed a

9. Elizabeth Duncan Putnam, ed., "Diary of Mrs. Joseph Duncan (Elizabeth Cald-well Smith)," *JISHS* 21 (1928): 1-92.

10. *Journal*, Feb. 16, Apr. 12, 1860.

11. Cf. Miyakawa, *Protestants and Pioneers*, pp. 200-201; Mead, *Lively Experiment*, pp. 113-15, 121-27.

common religious enthusiasm to cross sectarian boundaries. A series of revivals shook Jacksonville's spiritual foundations before 1870, arousing church members and producing hundreds of conversions among those outside the fold. By 1848 Julian Sturtevant could recall six different revivals that swept through Illinois College alone; three of these were connected to revivals in town.[12] A year earlier, Sturtevant had written in discouragement to a friend back east: "I could never have predicted such a state of religious society as now exists in Jacksonville. . . . The spirit of sect has taken the place of the Spirit of Christ. . . . I see no hope of a revival in the village till the ice of a long and dreary winter is melted."[13] Yet in the winter of 1848 Jacksonville's religious spirit suddenly thawed, and the townspeople and college students entered a prolonged revival. Led by the Methodist church, whose itinerant preachers had perfected the technique of revivals (the "net of the church," as Peter Cartwright called them), it quickly spread to the other denominations. By March, Sturtevant reported that meetings were being held nightly in most churches. The doors were opened to all who would come, and dozens of converts were claimed by the various congregations. The Methodist church alone claimed some 600 conversions, including "some of the most prominent citizens."[14]

Though varying from one denomination to the next in the level and character of enthusiasm, the revival experience generally involved "protracted meetings," which continued nightly for almost two months in the winter of 1848. Preachers warned their audience of the wages of sin, and those who felt moved by the spirit came forward to the "mourners' bench" to be readied for the conversion experience. Often converts were won spontaneously, and it was not uncommon, in the Methodist revivals at least, for them to suddenly stand and loudly proclaim their newfound faith by howling like dogs or let their bodies be

12. Sturtevant to Theron Baldwin, Illinois College, Nov. 6, 1848, Sturtevant-Baldwin Letters, Tanner Library, Illinois College.

13. Sturtevant to Theron Baldwin, Illinois College, Feb. 19, 1847, ibid.

14. Sturtevant to Theron Baldwin, Illinois College, Mar. 13, 1848, ibid.; "Ideal Church Record for the Methodist Episcopal Church," MSS in Centenary Methodist Church, Jacksonville, n.p., n.d.

convulsed by "the jerks." William Herndon, a former Jackson-ville resident, remembered people at revivals "hugging each other and singing in ecstasy that was half religious, half sexual."[15] These excesses were probably not common in all denominations, for the more restrained and educated ministry of the Presbyterian and Congregational churches were less open to these spontaneous physical displays of religious en-thusiasm. The conservative attitude of Chauncey Eddy, pastor of the First Presbyterian Church (New School), caused his more enthusiastic congregation to unite in open opposition to him during the 1848 revival, a controversy that led to his departure.[16]

The differences in revival techniques caused much disagree-ment among western clergy and were a special source of friction between Yankee and southern preachers. Kentuckian Peter Cartwright had a revival in full swing in 1837 when a "new school" Yankee minister, an agent of the American Home Mis-sionary Society, insisted on helping him. The "fresh, green, live Yankee" was allowed to stand before the rustic audience and read his carefully prepared sermon, during which "the congregation paid a heavy penance and became restive." Cartwright rescued the meeting with a fast, fire-and-brimstone harangue and sent the "little hot-house reader" out into the audience to "exhort sinners." When an enormous man stood up and bellowed aloud his newfound faith, the diminutive Yankee urged him to "be composed." Cartwright rushed to the rear of the meetinghouse and yelled at the man: "Pray on brother; pray on, brother; there's no composure in hell or damnation." Be-fore Cartwright could lead him to the mourner's bench, the convert cried, "'Glory to God,' and in the ecstasy of his joy . . . he wheeled round and caught my little preacher in his arms and lifted him up from the floor; and . . . jumped from bench to bench, knocking the people against one another on the right and left, front and rear, holding up in his arms the little

15. Quoted in Miyakawa, *Protestants and Pioneers*, pp. 164-65.
16. Sturtevant to Theron Baldwin, Illinois College, Mar. 13, 1848, Sturtevant-Baldwin Letters.

preacher." Cartwright thought of warning the terrified Yankee to "be composed," but "as soon as the little hot-bed parson could make his escape he was missing."[17]

This spontaneous quality of the conversion experience and of the revival in general lent an atmosphere of equality and intense community to these meetings. Underlying revivalism was the assumption that individuals could become Christians immediately, whatever their former sins and doctrinal loyalties. Some denominations may have been less selective than others regarding converts, but the revival generally opened membership to those who sought it in all the evangelical Protestant churches. During Jacksonville's revivals the denominations were less integrated than at a rural camp meeting, where preachers usually addressed people as one large audience. But the evidence that revivals took place simultaneously in most Jacksonville churches suggests some erosion, temporarily at least, of sectarian boundaries.[18]

During the Civil War an annual series of winter revivals began. Almost all of them started at the East Charge Methodist Church, where the Reverend Levi C. Pitner, son-in-law of the famed Peter Cartwright, began in 1862 to stir "one of the greatest religious awakenings ever experienced by Jacksonville Methodism."[19] The spirit of religious enthusiasm rippled through the community again in 1863, 1864, 1865, and 1867, each time emanating from the Methodist East Charge. By February, 1867, a local editor reported with nonchalance: "the usual season for religious revivals being at hand, protracted meetings are now being held at several of the churches with promising results."[20] Perhaps for very practical reasons involving interdenominational competition, the other churches quickly followed the Methodist cue. Even the Catholics joined in with a protracted meeting of their own in 1862.[21] Though

17. Peter Cartwright, *Autobiography*, ed. W. P. Strickland (New York, 1847), pp. 370-73.

18. Mead, *Lively Experiment*, pp. 121-27; William G. McLoughlin, *Modern Revivalism: From Charles Grandison Finney to Billy Graham* (New York, 1959).

19. *150th Anniversary of Centenary United Methodist Church* (Jacksonville, 1971), p. 7.

20. *Sentinel*, Feb. 7, 1867.

21. *Centenary*, p. 7. Accounts of revivals are in *Sentinel*, Mar. 7, 1862; Jan. 30, Feb. 20, 1863; Mar. 11, 1864; Jan. 20, 1865; Feb. 7, 1867; *Journal*, Feb. 19, 1863.

stimulated by sectarian rivalry, revivalism reduced the role of doctrine and stressed the personal experience of religion as the sole criterion for admission to the church.

The revivals also provided an intense, though fleeting, experience of community. That this catharsis of religious enthusiasm usually took place during the interminable months of a lonely midwestern winter suggests that the revival impulse sprang as much from a desire for communion with each other as from a desire for communion with God.

The voluntary church was designed not only to accept spontaneous conversions, but also to welcome a steady stream of newcomers from outside the community. This required a looser definition of orthodoxy which was certified primarily by proof of prior membership in another congregation, rather than by rigid conformity to doctrine. Members were exchanged between communities by a letter or certificate of transfer, which was standardized within each denomination and used routinely to allow transient members to carry their religious affiliation with them as they moved.

Jacksonville's Presbyterian church printed up reams of these transfer forms to expedite the constant issuing of letters to departing brethren: "This may certify that [member's name] is a member of the Presbyterian Church of Jacksonville, in good and regular standing; as such [he or she] at [his or her] own request is affectionately recommended to the Fellowship of the [name] Church, or of any other Church of Jesus Christ with whom God in his providence, may appoint [his or her] residence; . . ."[22] One fascinating feature of these letters of transfer was the explicit allowance for transfer to a church of another denomination. The Christians, who theoretically recognized no sectarian boundaries, were even more open that the Presbyterians. Their letters stated simply that the bearer was "entitled to the Christian friendship and affection of those among whom his lot may be cast."[23] This flexibility was due in part to migrating members' uncertainty about their destination, as to where they were going or whether their new home would

22. In Jacksonville Presbyterian Church, "Records, Membership," Illinois State Historical Library, Springfield.
23. In back of "Church Book," Central Christian Church Records.

have a church of the same denomination. But several cases in the church records show that members transferred "by letter" to another church within Jacksonville itself. Some of these were late followers of local schisms, like those who went from the East Charge to the West Charge Methodist; others were transferring across denominational lines altogether, and this speaks for a certain tolerance of sectarian divisions.[24] As long as mobile members sought "Christian Friendship and affection," tests of doctrinal orthodoxy took second priority.

Newcomers were accepted "by letter" routinely by all the churches. The Presbyterians were stricter than most in that they required an "examination" as well as a transfer certificate.[25] The records of other churches indicate that, almost without exception, those with letters were accepted into full membership with no questions asked.[26]

In every church there were members who left "without letter," some perhaps out of haste or negligence, others who were explicitly denied recommendation. When Robert Shields asked to leave the Congregational church to join Westminster Presbyterian in 1864, his letter explained that he had "ceased to walk in the fellowship of the Church" for two years previous.[27] John S. Denny was banished from fellowship of the Church of Christ for drunkenness, and his wife was issued a letter recommending only her.[28] This final sanction of denying letters to unworthy brethren extended the social control of the church beyond local congregational boundaries.

The certificates of transfer helped to construct a vital network of ties within and between the large denominations. Its

24. See "Names of the Methodist Episcopal Church in the Jacksonville East Charge, Conference Year 1850 & 1851," MSS in Centenary United Methodist Church, Jacksonville.

25. Franklin D. Scott, ed., "Minutes of the Session of the First Presbyterian Church of Morgan County, 1827-1830," *JISHS* 18 (1925): 142-58.

26. "List of Members, Conference Year 1858-59," MSS in Centenary United Methodist Church, Jacksonville; "List of Members, 1857-1865," MSS in Grace United Methodist Church, Jacksonville; Julian M. Sturtevant, *Origins of Western Congregationalism* (Jacksonville, 1884), appendix includes membership list; "Church Records, Organization etc., 1833-78," MSS in Congregational Church, Jacksonville.

27. Ibid., Apr. 20, 1864.

28. "Church Book," Jan. 18, 1840, Central Christian Church Records.

development through constant use in the mobile society of nineteenth-century America suggests one important clue to the social continuity and order that could exist amid all the movement of this period. Newcomers who arrived with certificates of transfer carried a guarantee of quick acceptance into a church in their new community, with all the social and economic benfits church membership could bring. They were in a very real sense "card-carrying" Christians who had passed an implicitly standard test of character. Those who came without certification might not be assumed to have failed that test, but they would have to be examined anew within the local congregation.

The test of Christian character relied less upon one's adherence to denominational doctrine than upon conformity to a more general code of moral behavior. Cryptic notes in most church membership rolls are the only evidence of how church discipline was actually enforced, but the Christian church of Jacksonville left full records of the disciplinary procedures followed by elders in more than seventy cases between 1840 and 1865.[29] Most of the backsliding members were accused of a combination of moral offenses. Only one case involved the question of doctrinal orthodoxy (Brother Brassell was found guilty of "visiting groceries, keeping immoral and wicked company and also propagating the opinions of Universalisms"). Another wayward member was rebuked for "attending the meetings of others," but his principal offense was more his absence from the Christian services. By far the most frequent sin was intemperance, often complicated by gambling, "profane swearing," and "refusing to make the acknowledgement required by the Christians' discipline" before the elders or the entire congregation. Brother John Fisher enjoyed the distinction of having the longest list of charges, including "attending the Theatre," "playing at cards and other Games," manifesting "a spirit of malice and revenge" toward the brethren, and "disrespect for the Elders of the Church." Before his trial Fisher

29. Ibid. See Miyakawa, *Protestants and Pioneers*, p. 3 et passim; Paul H. Boase, "Moral Policemen on the Ohio Frontier," *Ohio Historical Quarterly* 68 (1959): 38-53; William W. Sweet, "The Churches as Moral Courts of the Frontier," *Church History* 2 (1933): 3-21.

"drank to excess . . . in order to enable him to have enough courage to defend himself"; and after being expelled, he "threatened to shoot or horsewhip" one of the accusing brethren, "thus manifesting the spirit of Satan." Fisher's obstreperous behavior was exceptional, though many like him were considered "beyond hope of reformation" and the church "withdrew fellowship" from them after an interview.[30]

The Christian elders also intervened regularly to resolve personal conflicts and, if necessary, punish those guilty of "un-Christian conduct." An ongoing feud between Brother Humphrey and Brother Russell came before the elders in 1865. Both men were admonished for their conduct, Russell for "refusing to speak to Bro. Humphrey in passing him on the street," and "refusing to receive the elements of the Lord's supper from the hands of Bro. Humphrey." Humphrey was rebuked for "leaving the meeting house when Russell was called upon to preside at the table." Each "confessed his wrongs" before the elders and the feud was patched.[31]

The Christians may have been especially strenuous in their enforcement of Christian morality, but variations among churches were more of degree than of fundamental policy. Even the Catholics embraced a pietistic ethos that could have been found in any evangelical Protestant church. The Catholic Men's Association enforced a strict code of discipline against intemperance, gambling, and bootlegging. Those found guilty were required to make a full confession of their sins before the Association Board. The first several meetings were totally occupied with the trials of backsliding brethren. Thomas Mulready and Mathew Rogers, members of the board, failed to attend the first monthly meeting; "the board being convinced they had been drunk" expelled both. Jeremiah Clancy, another absent board member who had been seen passing the day in a saloon, was brought before a special meeting and forced to acknowledge his sins: "having confessed that he had sometimes, when urged to play cards in saloons, declined on the ground, that being a member of the board of Catholic Association he

30. "Church Book," Mar. 11, 1840, Central Christian Church Records.
31. Ibid., Dec. 31, 1865.

could not play cards, but had promised to pay for the losses of a person whom he put in his place." Since "it seemed to the board that such a proceeding was contrary to the spirit of the constitution," Clancy was admonished and, after a second offense, expelled from the fellowship.[32]

Paradoxically, at the heart of this seemingly repressive regimen of personal discipline, among Protestants, was a repudiation of strict Calvinism and a liberating notion of sin as the voluntary choice of individuals. Voluntary choice was also the essence of revivalism, and it justified the growing emphasis on pietism over doctrine.[33] But voluntarism and evangelical enthusiasm were combined with the equally important concept of individual responsibility. An explicit set of rules and hierarchy of authority bound each individual to the discipline of the fellowship within each church. It was through this combination of individual voluntarism and group discipline that the church became so important to the social order of the nineteenth-century community.

THE POLITICS OF ORGANIZATION

Political parties also served as effective means of social organization in the new community. Like the churches, they opened their ranks to almost all adult males. The legendary vigor of western politics probably owed more to the need for social integration in new communities than to any egalitarian devotion to democratic principles. Still, eastern observers were often startled by the intensity of western democracy, whatever its cause.

Edmund Flagg, a starchy New England visitor to Jacksonville, was appalled by the scene he witnessed in the market house in 1836. Standing on top of a butcher's block, a candidate for the state senate was addressing the crowd: "He was a broad-faced, farmer-like personage with features imbrowned by exposure, and hands hardened by honourable toil; with a huge rent,

---

32. "Records of the Catholic Association of Jacksonville, Illinois," Jan. 1862, pp. 8, 14, MSS in rectory, Church of Our Savior, Jacksonville.

33. Mead, *Lively Experiment*, pp. 113-15, 123-24.

169

moreover, athwart his left shoulder-blade—a badge of democracy, I presume, and either neglected or produced there for the occasion . . . to demonstrate . . . his affection for the *sans-culottes*." The candidate, and his opponent in turn, "made manifest what great things they had done for the people in times past, and promised to do greater things, should the dear people . . . be pleased to let their choice fall upon him."[34]

Politics in Jacksonville was more than a means of designating government officials; it was an all-consuming part of community life. The rhythm of politics was more intense during the campaign season, but it constantly reverberated through the newspapers and through daily gossip on the courthouse steps. The spectacle that Edmund Flagg observed in the market house was simply another ritual of a voluntary community where, within certain boundaries of race, sex, and age, almost anyone could participate. Politics became a vital mechanism not only for defining the local structure of leadership, but also for integrating a diverse and transient community.

In a new community politics provided one of the most accessible ladders ambitious men could climb, and candidates scrambled furiously for an open rung. Stephen Douglas, not yet twenty-one years old, came to Jacksonville in 1833 with five dollars in his pocket and a burning desire to become a politician. Murray McConnel loaned Douglas some books to "read law," and, after a brief stint teaching school in nearby Winchester, Douglas became McConnel's partner. Douglas was rarely found at his desk, though; he was drawn to the courthouse steps, where he joined "the boys" in the constant chatter of politics. Along with his unquenchable ambition, Douglas brought to Jacksonville a fervent zeal for Andrew Jackson and the Democratic party. In 1834 he made his political debut in a rousing defense of Jackson in the courthouse, and afterward his new admirers carried him out and around the square on their shoulders. The "Little Giant," as he was known from that day forward, immediately took a leading role in the Democratic party in Illinois' most populous county.[35]

34. Edmund T. Flagg, *The Far West*, ed. Rueben Gold Thwaites (1838; reprinted, Cleveland, 1906), pp. 312-13.

35. Robert W. Johannsen, *Stephen A. Douglas* (New York, 1973), pp. 19-25.

Before Douglas arrived, the party system in Morgan County and throughout the state was a vague and shifting contest of factions based largely on personal ties. When Joseph Duncan wrote from Washington to a crony back home in Jacksonville about the wisdom of switching parties, he was informed: "It's difficult to catch the hang of parties here, for although there is considerable party feeling there is very little party organization."[36] This unstructured arrangement changed rapidly in the late 1830s as the Democrats, under Douglas's leadership, instituted the convention system and urged strong local organization. The Whigs at first denounced the convention as undemocratic, but before the presidential campaign of 1840 they, too, recognized the organizational imperative and approved "a Convention of Young Men to be holden at Springfield."[37]

By that time a coherent and durable party structure had emerged. Jacksonville's "solvent merchants," who opposed Jackson's attack on banks and feared the state's overcommitment to internal improvements, joined New Englanders (who brought their region's antipathy toward Jackson with them) to form the core of a large Whig majority in the town. The Democrats won almost every rural precinct in election after election, straight through the Civil War.[38]

The stability of the party system is suggested in the uncanny constancy of voting patterns. Between 1836 and 1872 the county Democratic vote in presidential elections ranged between 46 and 52 percent; only twice did it vary by more than 3 percent between elections.[39] Regardless of the shifts in issues and candidates, the voting patterns remained steady. The consistency of the town and county vote is all the more remarkable when we consider all the forces of growth, turnover, and ethnic diversification that continually transformed the electorate.

36. Quoted ibid., p. 27.
37. Theodore Calvin Pease, *The Frontier State, 1818-1848*, The Centennial History of Illinois, vol. 2 (Springfield, 1918), p. 259n; *Illinoian*, Jan. 13, Mar. 17, 24, 1838; Nov. 9, 1839; Feb. 21, 1840.
38. William Thomas to Henry Eddy, Jan. 4, 1838, quoted in Pease, *Frontier State*, pp. 256-57.
39. Walter Dean Burnham, *Presidential Ballots, 1836-1892* (Baltimore, 1955), pp. 382-83. See Ronald P. Formisano, *The Birth of Mass Political Parties: Michigan, 1827-1861* (Princeton, N.J., 1971).

Even as the voters shuffled in and out of Jacksonville, and with the Irish, German, Portuguese, and black populations complicating the cultural context of politics, the rival parties were able to reach out to the most transient and alien elements of the community and pull them into the political process. Very early the politicians were concerned about the role of transient voters. The Whigs protested the Democrats' use of itinerant Irish railroad and canal laborers in the state elections of 1839, arguing that they were not permanent citizens of Illinois.[40] The state constitution of 1818 required six months' residence before voting, and the 1848 constitution extended it to one full year. But in a rapidly growing region the distinction between residents and transients could hardly be defined with certainty, and the fervid competition between the parties forced both sides to ignore residency requirements. Besides, with the emergence of mass political parties the aim was to enlarge the party following, not to exclude the opponent's supporters. As a result, in state and national elections, where party identification was stressed and party organization mobilized most effectively, estimated turnout rates in Morgan County ranged between 75 and 85 percent of all adult males; in Jacksonville they were often over 90 percent.[41]

With the organization of the Republican party in 1854 the mass political party, with its ability to integrate a large and diverse electorate, came into full maturity in Jacksonville. The emergence of the convention system under the Democrats, later imitated by the Whigs during the 1830s and 1840s, put a premium on party loyalty and encouraged politicians to stress national issues over personalities and local interests. The focus on issues did not prevent party leaders from a regular exchange of personal insults and vicious rhetoric, but the emphasis was increasingly upon party rather than on personal loyalty. Before the emergence of the Republican party, politicians relied mostly upon rabidly partisan newspapers to inform their constituencies on issues and mobilize the voters; campaign speeches and

40. *Illinoian*, Sept. 14, 1839; Pease, *Frontier State*, p. 260.
41. Voter turnouts derived from various post-election newspaper reports and extrapolations from census data were used to estimate the population eligible to vote.

party rallies held in the courthouse or on the public square were also used to arouse the electorate. But party organization quickly evaporated after the election, and little more than the weekly newspaper editorials reminded voters of their party identification.

After 1854 the Republicans took the lead in organizational innovations as new techniques of voter mobilization were introduced. Coalescing around a loosely defined set of issues that centered on opposition to the extension of slavery and incorporated nativism and temperance, the Republican coalition that emerged in Jacksonville was among the first in the state. Since the Republicans were forced to build a new political coalition upon the ruins of a Whig party and were also torn by internal disagreements over ideological priorities, they were compelled to adopt new techniques of mass political organization. On one level they sought to create a sustained institutional basis for political identity through local grass-roots organizations. A Young Men's Republican Club met every Saturday evening preceding elections and even remained intact between campaigns. The club reinforced party identity, informed its eager supporters on issues, and served as a mechanism for recruitment of new members. During the 1860 election the club constructed a wigwam on the square to symbolize the Republican spirit, and it raised money to distribute five hundred copies of *Uncle Tom's Cabin* to voters as yet unaware of the evils of slavery. "Work! Work!" the Republican newspaper exhorted its readers during the 1860 campaign, "organize clubs and get up neighborhood discussions. Get together evenings and let a reader be appointed, who will read some solid speech." By 1864 a Republican Reading Room with newspapers, pamphlets, and other party literature was opened (nearly a year before the presidential election) in space above the post office, a convenient location for anyone who had a few minutes to drop by and read or, more likely, talk politics with fellow Republicans.[42]

42. *Journal*, Mar. 22, May 24, 1860; Frank J. Heinl, "Jacksonville and Morgan County, An Historical Review," *JISHS* 18 (1925): 27; Lewis Scott Gard, "Centennial History of Jacksonville, 1825-1925," p. 41, typescript in Morgan County Historical Society Collections, Jacksonville Public Library.

With the coming of the Civil War local Republicans, following a national strategy, hastened to broaden their support by exploiting anti-Confederate sentiment. They appealed to bipartisan allegiance with a "Union" ticket (a Republican "disguise," the Democrats accused) and extended their organizational strength through a Union League. An ostensibly nonpartisan organization, the Union League, met weekly after its founding in 1862 and gave a new organizational dimension to Republican party identity. This quasi-political association was supplemented by a women's auxiliary, the Ladies Loyal League, in 1863. Organized to aid distressed families of soldiers during the war, the Ladies Loyal League also signified the growing presence of women in the community's political life that accompanied the rise of the Republican party.[43]

All of these organizations represented efforts to instill Republican party identification through grass-roots institutional structures that allowed sustained political organization, instead of the sporadic activities that took place during campaigns. In addition to these institutional innovations, the new Republican party was promoted through the shrewd exploitation of massive political demonstrations. Public meetings of the party faithful were hardly new to Jacksonville in the mid-1850s, but they now took far grander form and assumed new importance as mechanisms for mobilizing the electorate. Previously political rallies had been casual affairs attended mostly by local party leaders; they were held in the courthouse, where speeches were made and resolutions passed endorsing the party position prior to state conventions. On Saturdays during the election season hopeful candidates delivered stump speeches to farmers and townspeople who milled about the public square, attracted as often by free-flowing corn whiskey as by political rhetoric.

The Republicans made the political rally a major social event combining elements of a camp meeting revival and a Fourth of July celebration. Enormous demonstrations were carefully prepared, with a series of prominent state political leaders

43. Arthur Charles Cole, *The Era of the Civil War, 1848-1870*, The Centennial History of Illinois, vol. 3 (Springfield, 1919), pp. 309-10; *Journal*, Dec. 17, 1863; Jan. 28, Apr. 7, Sept. 8, July 21, 1864.

scheduled to speak, marching bands and entertainment, and railroad transportation arranged for the party faithful in neighboring towns and outlying rural districts. These rallies absorbed the entire day and attracted thousands of men, women, and children who came by rail, wagon, or foot to witness and participate in a celebration of community that went beyond mere politics.[44]

The militaristic tenor of these political extravaganzas was revealed in full glory during the Civil War. A "Union Mass Meeting" before the 1864 presidential election drew some twelve thousand "patriots" to Jacksonville, with many coming in special trains from Whitehall, Petersburg, Quincy, and Springfield. Two marching bands accompanied an enormous three-mile-long procession. Republican politicians and army generals led the parade, followed by a series of displays symbolic of the Republican war effort: a twelve-foot obelisk to memorialize dead Union soldiers, a carriage filled with mourning widows and their children, a company of veterans on horseback, and eighty-six wagons loaded with firewood and provisions for the distressed families of soldiers. Among the various precinct delegations, the Portuguese from Jacksonville and Springfield formed their own separate unit; they had a carriage for their glee club and a line of thirty-five ladies on horseback to represent the states of the Union, followed by two hundred horsemen in double file "marching in splendid order." The entire procession marched from one end of town to the other and then several times around the square, where they assembled to hear a series of speeches.[45]

The Democrats were quick to adopt the new forms of political organization to meet the Republican challenge. "Why is it we can't have a young men's Democratic Association organized in Jacksonville?" complained a Democratic editor in 1856. "The time for action has arrived, and the young democrats of Jacksonville could not devote their fresh energies to a nobler cause."

---

44. *Illinois Daily Journal* (Springfield), Sept. 8, 29, Nov. 3, 1856. See Michael H. Frisch, *Town into City: Springfield, Massachusetts, and the Meaning of Community, 1840-1880* (Cambridge, Mass., 1972), pp. 38-42.

45. *Journal*, Oct. 27, 1864; Frisch, *Town into City*, pp. 59-60.

The Morgan County Democratic Union Club was organized in time to mobilize voters for a narrow victory in 1856. The club sponsored a series of "mass meetings" in the courthouse, where local leaders urged their supporters to meet the organizational challenge of the emerging Republican coalition. By 1863 the Democratic Club was established, well in advance of the upcoming presidential election; it met regularly on Saturday evenings to hear speakers and, like the Republicans, sponsored a Democratic Reading Room throughout the week. Three years later the Jacksonville Democrats were urging a thorough grass-roots organization "by reviving in working order a club in every precinct." "There is strength only in unity of action which can be effected only by organization," the *Sentinel* editor instructed. "See to it that your clubs are well organized, with prompt and ready officers, and that the meetings be frequent and well attended." Jacksonville's Democracy led the way by renting a club room over Hatch's Drug Store on the square, "where our Country friends are invited to make themselves at home." By January, 1868, the Democratic Club was established formally as a "permanent organization," complete with constitution, bylaws, and annual elections of officers.[46]

The Democrats quickly followed the Republican model in political rallies as well. Just before the election in 1864 the party put together a demonstration every bit as elaborate and regimented as the best Republican rallies. Trains brought delegations from outlying precincts into town, where they gathered some seven to ten thousand strong. Two marching bands gave zest to a procession led by a "triumphal car, tastefully ornamented, representing the temple of liberty," filled with "34 young ladies tastefully attired, representing the states." Women of both parties now contributed in an important way to the rallies by serving as symbols of purity and temperance; by their calculated presence, they lent a tone of refined sociability to these political events. Several delegations of women on horseback ("each attended by a gentleman") followed the triumphal

46. *Sentinel*, July 11, 1856; Mar. 4, 1863; Jan. 22, Aug. 22, 1864; Sept. 20, 1866; Jan. 30, 1868.

car. Wagons filled with "the sturdy voting farmers" of Morgan County came next, and then a long procession of wagons filled with wood and flour—the Democrats' own symbolic gifts to the families of Union soldiers. Banners held aloft by participants identified the multitude of precincts represented and denounced the "tyranny, corruption, and misrule" of the Lincoln administration. One wagon carried a large mechanical likeness of Lincoln with axe in hand, splitting a log representing the Union "to the infinite amusement of the crowd."[47]

Whatever their ideological differences, the political parties developed similar organizational forms and functioned as social institutions capable of integrating a transient population into coherent and durable political constituencies. The very massiveness of the political rallies seemed consciously arranged to impress upon participants the fact that they were part of something far larger than a mere neighborhood, ethnic group, or community; they were voluntary members of a vast national network of local associations. While the rallies dramatized the vertical links between Jacksonville and the larger society, they also brought people together in an intense demonstration of local community. To import partisans from neighboring towns seemed only to heighten the parochial pride evident in the banners, floats, and brass bands that proclaimed each unit's local identity as it took its place in the procession. The tremendous energy of western politics no doubt owed much to a simple yearning for sociability that the parties gladly satisfied. The incorporation of women and children into the rallies beginning in the late 1850s seemed deliberately designed to control and refine what were previously rough masculine affairs of hard drinking and occasional violence. Various newspaper accounts also make it clear that the rallies attracted many visitors from the opposing party. They may have come as converts or as jeering critics (both were claimed in the party newspapers), but more likely they came to enjoy a celebration of community, one they could join voluntarily with or without lasting commitment.

47. *Sentinel*, Nov. 11, 1864; see also Sept. 19, 25, 1856. Apparently the Democrats did not recognize the thirty-fifth state, West Virginia, which joined the Union in 1863.

THE VOLUNTARY ASSOCIATION

Both the churches and political parties evolved in ways that helped control internal community conflict. The churches contributed to social order by diluting doctrine in favor of pietism and sharing revival techniques. The parties, on the other hand, controlled internal conflict by constructing durable grass-roots organizations that stressed party loyalty and distant national issues, rather than battling solely over local personalities. If the churches and political parties shared common forms of organization and style with their respective rivals, they nonetheless institutionalized divisions of faith and ideology within the community. These divisions were mitigated by a third institutional component of the new community, the voluntary association. Most prevalent among the leadership of Jacksonville, these non-sectarian, non-partisan, and non-profit organizations popped up by the dozens in the form of fraternal lodges, reform societies, literary clubs, and fire companies. Whatever their explicit mission, all of these voluntary associations performed very special covert roles by integrating community leaders, enhancing individual opportunity, safeguarding the middle-class family, and serving as schools that taught organizational skills and group discipline.

In Jacksonville the boundaries separating regional, sectarian, or political rivals cut through all levels of local society, creating a continual threat of factional discord among community leaders. Voluntary associations helped stitch together these discordant factions by facilitating interpersonal contact within groups that, as a rule, deliberately avoided divisive issues involving religious doctrine or politics. This process of integration occurred mainly among the native white propertied middle class. Other organizations, like the Colored Washingtonian Society, the German Turners, and the Hibernian Temperance Society, only further defined the segregated status of Jacksonville's minorities.[48]

One measure of the integrative function of voluntary associa-

48. The ensuing discussion of voluntary associations is based on the analysis of officers and prominent members mentioned in newspapers and city directories. These sources excluded the ethnic and women's associations in Jacksonville. This section summarizes my article, "The Social Functions of Voluntary Associations in a Nineteenth-Century Town," *Social Science History* 1 (1977): 333-56.

tions appears in the multiple memberships of prominent citizens. Over 70 percent of association officers identified in pre-1860 newspapers and 35 percent of the officers listed in the post-1860 city directories were officers of two or more associations, and several were officers of three and four different groups. These men may have been unusually active joiners, but surviving membership lists show that multiple affiliations were common among the rank and file as well.[49]

Within each association the pattern of integration seems clear. The regional loyalties of northern and southern migrants, which persisted as a source of tension throughout this period, did not prevent people from all regions from joining the same lodges and associations. Southerners tended to be more active in fraternal lodges, while New Englanders were overrepresented in reform societies; however, few associations lacked officers and members from all regions, and several had foreign-born leaders (most of them British).[50] (See Appendix, Table 16.)

This pattern of integration also crossed denominational boundaries. Episcopalians and Methodists, Presbyterians and Christians mingled, even across local or national schisms within their own denomination. The sectarian jealousies that divided these men as church members did not inhibit their interaction as Masons, Odd Fellows, or members of other associations.[51] Nor did partisan rivalries prevent Whigs, Democrats, and

49. For example, at least 14 of the 54 members and initiates of the Masonic Harmony Lodge in 1852 were also active members of the Odd Fellows Illini Lodge. *Proceedings of the Grand Lodge of the Ancient Free and Accepted Masons of the State of Illinois . . . 1852* (Peoria, 1852), p. 58; "IOOF Illini Lodge No. 4, Record Book 1847-1851," IOOF Lodge, Jacksonville.

50. The Odd Fellows Illini Lodge, for example, included a member born in New England, 13 from Middle Atlantic states, 7 from the Southeast, 17 from southern states west of the Appalachians, 7 from the Midwest, and 5 who were foreign born. Ibid.

51. Data on church membership is scattered and incomplete, but the religious affiliation of more than half the leaders has been determined, and the pattern of integration among Protestant denominations, and congregations within denominations, appears prevalent. Lodges like the Odd Fellows and Masons were proud of their ecumenical character. The Masonic Harmony Lodge could claim strong representation from Episcopalians, Christians, Methodists, and Old School Presbyterians; there were also a few Congregationalists, New School Presbyterians, and Baptists. Frank J. Heinl, *Harmony Lodge, No. 3, A. F. and A. Masons, Centennial Commemorations . . .* (Jacksonville, 1937), p. 7.

(later) Republicans from mixing to promote the specific non-partisan causes these associations espoused. A case in point was the prestigious Masonic Harmony Lodge, which in the thick of the Civil War could boast as its two most acclaimed members Richard Yates, the antislavery governor of Illinois, and Colonel W. B. Warren, a staunch Democrat from Kentucky who was offered a commission in the Confederate Army by Jefferson Davis.[52]

For men of "public spirit" in Jacksonville, the "voluntary principle" was a way of deliberately uniting enlightened Christians to promote social improvement on a local and national level. As sect and party fragmented American society, voluntary organization seemed to promise an alternative means for cooperative reform efforts. "The only real bonds of society in these days," wrote Jonathan Baldwin Turner, one of Jacksonville's more ardent reformers, "is UNION OF INTEREST, and UNION OF MORAL PRINCIPLE. . . . While the difference about forms and rites and dogmas among men is hopelessly widening every year and every day, the union of interest, and real moral principle is hourly becoming compact, uniform and intense. Society is not therefore dissolving; but is merely taking to itself forms in which it can live and act in its new mode of being."[53]

For Turner, the voluntary association allowed cooperation among right-minded men who shared a commitment to specific reform goals, but a far more common sentiment admired the voluntary association precisely because it avoided controversial principles. Fraternal lodges were especially keen on rejecting tests of religion or political doctrine, and they repudiated social

52. Ibid., pp. 1-2, 6. Partial data on party affiliation can be gleaned from newspaper accounts of party candidates, delegations, and rallies. Also useful were "Poll Books, Morgan County, Jacksonville Precincts, No. 1, No. 2, Presidential Election, 1848," Illinois State Archives, microfilm. Much of the social science literature on voluntary associations stresses their integrative functions. See James S. Coleman, *Community Conflict* (New York, 1957), pp. 22-23; Herbert Gans, *The Levittowners: Ways of Life and Politics in a New Suburban Community* (New York, 1967); and William H. Form, "Stratification in a Planned Community," *American Sociological Review* 10 (1945): 605-13, reprinted in William A. Glaser and David L. Sills, eds., *The Government of Associations: Selections from the Behavioral Sciences* (Totowa, N.J., 1966), pp. 63-67.

53. *Illinois Statesman*, Mar. 18, 1844.

goals beyond the circle of the brotherhood. Churches and political parties, B. F. Bristow explained to Jacksonville's Odd Fellows, were inherently narrow: "from the very nature and being
of these organizations, a platform cannot be made broad
enough and wide enough upon which all men can stand." But
the principles of Odd Fellowship, Bristow went on, "are as high
as the heavens, as broad as the world and as vast as eternity."[54]

By serving as bridges across the troubled waters that separated local leaders of rival sects and parties, voluntary associations acted to narrow these chasms. This function of social
integration seemed to be clearly understood by one of Jacksonville's lodge members: "Were the prominent citizens, the
heads of families, and young men in *entire communities* to
mingle occasionally; to perform kind offices mutually; to agree
on some points, notwithstanding their differences on others,
the effect we humbly conceive would be most happy. They
would lose opinionative habits and dictatorial manners, they
would harmonize conflicting interests sometimes, and often
prevent feuds and soften the condition of society at large."[55]
Feuds did not miraculously disappear, but deep social conflict
was restrained by the network of associational ties that spanned,
even if they did not entirely close, the divisions between community factions. Whatever separated these men as Yankees or
Southerners, Congregationalists or Methodists, Republicans
or Democrats, they also shared certain interests as businessmen,
property owners, town promoters, family men, and community
leaders. This blending of interests was reinforced by the weekly
meetings of lodges, literary clubs, and reform societies that
brought men of diverse religious or political views together to
discuss things they could agree upon. This "power of meeting,"

54. Untitled speech by B. F. Bristow, reprinted in *Journal*, Feb. 23, 1865. Leonard L.
Richards, *"Gentlemen of Property and Standing": Anti-Abolition Mobs in Jacksonian America*
(New York, 1970), pp. 168-69, deals with an exception that proves the rule. The
American Anti-Slavery Society, Richards argues, disrupted local communities in the
1830s by going around traditional elites and agitating people with direct appeals and
mass propaganda. The Society's retrenchment after 1837 and the delegation of authority to local agents rapidly defused antislavery as an issue that incited mob violence
(pp. 157-60).

55. Reverend Alexander Van Court, *An Address Delivered before the Members of the
Illini Lodge No. 4, IOOF* (Jacksonville, 1848), p. 7.

as Alexis de Tocqueville put it, the frequent face-to-face contact between men, allowed them to communicate, to identify, and to serve the interests they shared as leaders of local society.[56]

Those who joined were no doubt far less interested in (or even conscious of) the abstract social function of community integration than they were in the more immediate personal benefits of membership. One of these benefits was the enhanced opportunity for upward social mobility. Here again, the goals of social order were fitted to the pursuit of individual opportunity. Joining a lodge or a literary or reform society was in itself an act signifying social ambition, a theme the Good Templars shrewdly employed in their recruitment plea: "Strangers seek in the lodge room worthy acquaintances . . . and others with aspirations after a higher life leave the card tables and billiard saloons, and unite with the Order."[57]

Membership in certain lodges, of course, carried more prestige. As a rule, the older the association or the more exclusive its membership, the more status it warranted in the community. Membership in the fraternal lodges required near unanimous approval by the brotherhood, and literary societies, like The Club, the Plato Club, and the Literary Union, were even more exclusive, since membership was strictly limited to twenty.[58] Admission to any of these societies might be understood as recognition of social status already achieved, but membership, particularly in the fraternal lodges, also improved the opportunities for further upward mobility.

The advantage of associational activity is visible in the marked success of officers and members identified in contemporary sources. For some, particularly skilled artisans, social mobility was reflected in new occupational titles. Over the course of a decade from one-third to half of these men moved from skilled labor into business or professional occupations, a rate signifi-

56. Alexis de Tocqueville, *Democracy in America*, ed. Phillips Bradley (1832; reprint, New York, 1945), I, 192.

57. *Journal*, Apr. 27, 1866.

58. Ensley Moore, "The Club," *JISHS* 18 (1925): 201-4; "Minutes of the Club, 1861-1883," MSS in Illinois History Collection, Tanner Library, Illinois College, Jacksonville; William Dustin Wood, "The Literary Union," *JISHS* 18 (1925): 205-8; Paul Russell Anderson, "Hiram K. Jones and Philosophy in Jacksonville," *JISHS* 33 (1940): 478-520.

cantly higher than that of all persistent artisans. Many of these skilled laborers were already prosperous businessmen who only reported a new occupational title to the inquisitive census-taker. That so many chose the more prestigious labels of "merchant" or "dealer" in preference to the once proudly born craft titles is in itself indicative of their social ambition.[59]

Improvement in wealth offers a more precise measure of the social mobility enjoyed by voluntary association officers. These men were comfortable to begin with, and as a group they were extraordinarily successful in augmenting their material fortunes. Among those who stayed in Jacksonville from 1850 to 1860, the average gain in real property was about one and a half times greater than the average for all persistent residents. (See Table 17.) These association officers may have been particularly successful men, but a roughly similar pattern of upward social mobility was shared by the members at large, if we may judge from a few available membership lists.[60]

To understand the advantages of the active joiner in the struggle for upward mobility, we must recall some of the general conditions for success in nineteenth-century Jacksonville. Here was an economy of dozens of small businesses run by partnerships or individuals who rarely hired more than one or two clerks or mechanics. These small shops and firms catered to the immediate local market in rural Morgan County and Jacksonville; they pursued profits in a competitive and risky economic climate, all of which placed a high premium upon building an established network of personal contacts for clientele and for credit.[61] In this context a merchant, artisan, or lawyer stood upon his personal reputation and his willingness to

59. U.S. Census MSS, Morgan County, Illinois, 1850, 1860, 1870; cf. data on social mobility in the fifth chapter.

60. For example, of the skilled laborers active in the Odd Fellows Illini Lodge in 1850, about 30% of the persistent moved into business occupations by 1860, and the average gain in real property for all persistent members was about $6,000. Derived from "IOOF Illini Lodge No. 4, Record Book, 1847-51," and U.S. Census MSS, Morgan County, Illinois, 1850, 1860.

61. Newspaper advertisements and business guides in the city directories give the most vivid picture of business organization and practices in Jacksonville. See also U.S. Census Office, 8th Census, 1860, *Manufacturers of the United States in 1860* . . . (Washington, 1865), p. 100; Francis A. Walker, comp., *A Compendium of the Ninth Census, 1870* (Washington, 1872), p. 819.

extend credit to customers. Competitive pricing, formal training, or business and professional skills alone were never as essential as personal connections in this economic environment.[62]
Merchants, artisans, and lawyers were overrepresented in
voluntary associations, not just because of their social standing, but because their occupations required participation for
several reasons.

First, membership immediately enlarged the sheer number
of personal and business contacts. In a community where so
many of the businessmen and customers were likely to be newcomers, this kind of formal organization allowed instant access
to large networks of potential customers, partners, creditors, or
borrowers. Participation not only increased the number of potential business contacts; these introductions took place within a
setting that encouraged economic interaction by imposing ethi-
cal restraints upon the members in their business dealings. In
some cases, like the fraternal lodges, explicit rules against cheat-
ing, breach of contract, or other predatory business practices
were written into constitutions. The Masons, for example, made
"Justice" one of their four cardinal virtues and required the
brethren to "preserve an upright position in all dealings with
mankind."[63] Expulsions and suspension of members for "dis-
honesty and falsehood," "malicious falsehood," "lying, cheat-
ing," "attempt to defraud partner in business," "swindling,"
"defrauding creditors," or "leaving the place clandestinely
without paying his just debts," all testify to the importance of
these societies as policemen of the marketplace. Expulsions and
suspensions, though hardly commonplace in Jacksonville's
lodges, were frequent enough to remind members of their
duty.[64] Those who submitted to this group discipline benefitted
from the favorable climate for business interaction, because
lodge membership publicly certified good character, ambition,

62. See Lewis E. Atherton, *The Frontier Merchant in Mid-America* (1939; reprinted,
Columbia, Mo., 1971), pp. 142-53 et passim.

63. Albert G. Mackey, *A Lexicon of Free Masonry*, 13th ed. (Philadelphia, 1869),
p. 234.

64. In their annual Grand Lodge reports Masons and Odd Fellows recorded the
names of all those expelled or suspended, along with the reasons for dismissal. Most
cases involved failure to pay dues or attend meetings, but a variety of moral offenses

and honesty, which no doubt improved business relations with the community at large.

The fraternal societies also enhanced opportunities for upward social mobility by enforcing a broad moral discipline affecting personal behavior in general and temperance in particular, matters closely tied to the all-important problem of obtaining credit. In this small and volatile economy businessmen in need of credit were judged not just upon their business record, nor solely upon their financial debts and assets, but according to a careful assessment of personal character. Character was measured by reputation and by the appearance of ambition and respectability. The credit reports which R. G. Dun & Company received from their hired agents in Jacksonville give an inside view of the criteria used to judge local businessmen. The good credit risk was invariably described as "a man of steady habits," "industrious," "prompt," "attentive to his business"; repeatedly the code "temperate" was used to signify not just abstemious drinking habits, but a whole ethos of self-discipline. Those identified as poor credit risks were frequently reported to be insolvent, dishonest, or unknown in town; their shaky financial status was commonly explained in moral terms, with references to "intemperate habits," "fondness for strong spirits," or other veiled allusions to "low morals." (There were also a few cases, obviously disturbing to the R. G. Dun agents, of a prospering businessman who "drinks too much but still makes money."[65])

These judgments of personal character were more than idle moralistic commentary. Rather, they were rational assessments made within an economic context where the prospects of a business were determined by the strength of individual businessmen. To be "temperate" and have "steady habits"

---

included fraud, breach of contract, or some other violation of business ethics. See the annual Grand Lodge reports: *Proceedings of the Grand Lodge of the Ancient Free and Accepted Masons of the State of Illinois* and *Journal of the Right Worthy Grand Lodge of the State of Illinois Independent Order of Odd Fellows*, both in the Illinois State Historical Library, Springfield.

65. R. G. Dun & Co., Credit Ledgers, Morgan County, 3 vols., Dun & Bradstreet Collection, Baker Library, Graduate School of Business Administration, Harvard University, microfilm copy. James H. Madison, "The Credit Reports of R. G. Dun & Co. as Historical Sources," *Historical Methods Newsletter* 8 (1975).

meant to be responsible, financially reliable, and upwardly mobile. This equation of personal morality and economic success, whether empirically valid or not, was a self-fulfilling prophecy.[66]

Temperance and moral discipline were central goals not just of the Sons of Temperance and the Washingtonians, but also of the Masons, Odd Fellows, Mechanics Institute, and others, all of which included specific rules on temperance as a condition for joining. Membership in these societies served as certification of good moral character and personal discipline, and this was, in effect, an endorsement as a good credit risk. The credit reports of R. G. Dun & Company were not required to provide details on the associational activities of their subjects, but it was common to describe a good credit risk as "active in community affairs," or as one who "enjoys the confidence of the community." Most important was one's local reputation for temperance and honesty, which the affiliation with voluntary associations certified.[67]

If voluntary associations aided those moving upward within local society, they also assisted many of those moving laterally in or out of the community. They supplied a vital need by allowing individuals to transfer their membership, and all the social and economic benefits attached to it, from one community to the next. Lodges like the Masons and Odd Fellows were, of course, part of national organizations that devised uniform procedures for transferral of members, much like the churches. The *Odd Fellows Manual* from 1860, for example, published standard forms for those withdrawing "by card." Transient members were normally given a year to reestablish membership, and all local lodges were expected to honor these transfer cards as a matter of routine. These standardized mechanisms for integrating mobile lodge members provide yet another clue to the sources of stability and continuity amid all the movement of the nineteenth century, for the lodges connected their mem-

66. R. G. Dun & Co., Credit Ledgers, Morgan County; see also Joseph R. Gusfield, *Symbolic Crusade: Status Politics and the American Temperance Movement* (Urbana, 1963).
67. E.g., R. G. Dun & Co., Credit Ledgers, Morgan County, "J.H.B.," I, 295.

bers to a national system of brotherhood as well as to the local community.[68]

For the transient member, a transfer card from the Odd Fellows or Masons was more than a ticket of readmission to another lodge. It was also portable certification of the status and reputation he had established in his former community, and it gave him access to a whole new network of business and social contacts.

Voluntary associations served to integrate the individual into the community and boost his upward mobility; in addition, they supplemented the member's private role as head of a family. Some of the associations in Jacksonville, like the Sons of Temperance, were deliberately designed for young single men, but most lodges, literary clubs, and reform societies drew their members from among middle-aged (25 to 45 years) married men with children.[69] (See Table 17.) Men at this stage of the life cycle were most in need of the business and credit benefits attached to association membership; furthermore, membership meant greater security for the family and a socially approved outlet away from the family circle.

All fraternal lodges collected annual dues that went toward sickness or death benefits for members or their survivors. The Mechanics Union allotted twenty dollars toward a member's funeral and another twenty dollars for the surviving widow and

68. See Reverend Aaron B. Grosh, *The Odd Fellows Manual* (Philadelphia, 1860), p. 338, for model forms for visiting members, transfer of membership, and visiting wives or widows of members. Out-migration rates among lodge members were about 7% annually. Persistence was high among association officers (90% 1850-60; 75% 1860-70). *Proceedings, Grand Lodge, Masons, 1852*, p. 58; *Proceedings, Grand Lodge, Masons, 1860*, p. 76; *Journal, IOOF, 1854*, p. 90; U.S. Census MSS, Morgan County, Illinois, 1850, 1860, 1870.

69. Similar data on all members in the Illini Lodge did not differ from those on leaders; three-fourths were between 25 and 45, three-fourths were married, two-thirds had children, and the fathers averaged three children each. "IOOF Illini Record Book, 1847-51," and Census MSS, Morgan County, Illinois, 1850. The correlations between stage in life and participation in voluntary associations have been well established by modern studies in the social sciences. See Charles R. Wright and Herbert H. Hyman, "Voluntary Association Membership of American Adults," *American Sociological Review* 23 (1958): 284-94; Wendell Bell and Maryanne T. Force, "Urban Neighborhood Types and Participation in Formal Associations," *American Sociological Review* 21 (1956): 25-34, both reprinted in Glaser and Sills, eds., *Government of Associations*, pp. 31-37, 45-51.

children. The Odd Fellows' Urania Lodge dispensed some $14,000 during its first twenty-five years of existence; about half of this went toward support of sick and disabled members, and the rest went toward funeral expenses and to "the weeping widow (she is in a very dear sense the widow of the lodge) [and] the guardian protection of the orphan children."[70]

These mutual benefit associations were the predecessors of modern life insurance agencies. They filled a crucial transitional service in the nineteenth century by supporting the nuclear family at a time when the demands of geographic mobility, among other forces, required that traditional ties of kinship be stretched and sometimes severed, particularly in a young western town like Jacksonville. Membership in these societies reduced what must have been one of the deepest anxieties of a mobile people—the fear of dying among "strangers in a strange land," with no one to look after the surviving family. In Jacksonville the death of every lodge member was observed by the publication of solemn resolutions of mourning and public commitments to the family of the deceased. These eulogies appeared in the local newspapers and were followed by public displays of mourning—the lodge hall draped in black crepe, badges worn by the members for thirty days. These rituals of bereavement were a continual reminder to the surviving brotherhood that their annual dues purchased the invaluable security of knowing that their survivors would be cared for by the artificial "family" of the fellowship.[71]

Voluntary associations also provided a sanctioned haven away from the family. The weekly or biweekly meetings of most associations were held in the evening for two to three hours. An active joiner who participated in several associations, along with a church and a political party, might be out three or four evenings each week. These were usually formal business meetings or lectures, but they were not without their social and recreational functions. Neighbors walked to and from meetings

70. *Journal*, Feb. 23, 1865.
71. *Sentinel*, Apr. 12, 1861; Jan. 24, 1864, include two typical examples of resolutions of bereavement by the Odd Fellows and Masons. The analogy of the family was used in many of the fraternal societies. See, e.g., Grosh, *Odd Fellows Manual*, pp. 59, 64.

together and, before the proceedings began, enjoyed casual conversation on business and local affairs.

Because these nineteenth-century associations were also temperate and purified, they provided approved outlets away from family life. This need for structured social contacts was one aspect of a trend toward the withdrawal and isolation of the modern family from society, and a growing formalization of relations between the family and community.[72] One measure of this process was the increasing stress upon formal visiting and entertainment among Jacksonville's better sort. Mrs. Elizabeth Duncan's private diary and the Duncan scrapbook of calling cards and party invitations have survived as testimony to the rituals that governed visiting among polite society in a community striving toward social refinement. In Mrs. Duncan's circle, calling cards were presented, formal invitations were issued, and even neighborly visits were arranged well in advance; all social contacts were planned and controlled.[73]

Within the middle class, voluntary associations provided yet another way to structure interaction between the family and community. For the men and especially the women who participated, the periodic organization meetings offered what must have been a very welcome relief from the confinement of the family circle. At the same time, these meetings were fully compatible with middle-class ideals: they stressed temperance and self-improvement and were, with few exceptions, sexually segregated. Both as insurance agencies and as social outlets, voluntary associations acted to reinforce, rather than to supplant, the family as a social institution. They also supplemented the extended kinship networks that supported the nuclear fam-

72. Phillipe Ariés, *Centuries of Childhood: A Social History of Family Life*, trans. Robert Baldick (New York, 1962), pp. 365-407; Richard Sennett, *Families against the City* (Cambridge, Mass., 1964).

73. Elizabeth Duncan Putnam, ed., "Diary of Mrs. Joseph Duncan (Elizabeth Caldwell Smith)," *JISHS* 21 (1928): 1-92; also "Duncan Family Calling Card Scrapbook, 1852-1873," and Julia Duncan, "Album of Friendship, 1853-1873," both in Duncan-Kirby Family Collection, Illinois State Historical Library, Springfield. See also Sallie Ellen Evalyn Hammond, "Happenings at No. 1 West College Street: A History of the Aaron Hammond Family, 1600-1946," 3 vols., Illinois State Historical Library; Frank J. Heinl, *Centennial: J. Capps & Sons, Ltd.* (Jacksonville, 1939), pp. 18-19; *Journal*, Feb. 2, 1860.

ily and its members during a period of extraordinary mobility and change.[74]

Voluntary associations also served as schools to teach new skills, values, and the new social discipline demanded by modern society. Much of this unconscious curriculum was directed toward imparting organizational skills to potential business, social, and political leaders. The very process of creating new lodges, literary clubs, reform societies, or fire companies gave men firsthand experience in drafting constitutions, recruiting members, presiding over meetings, public speaking, and resolving conflicts. The multiplication of associations, coupled with continual turnover of officers, meant that dozens of men could be given training even in a very small community.[75] For businessmen, municipal officials, and especially politicians, these organizational skills were used beyond the circle of any particular association. It was no accident that Jacksonville's Masonic Harmony Lodge produced three Illinois governors. Most local officials also made their political debuts after belonging to Jacksonville's voluntary associations. Associational activities not only enhanced a politician's social standing; they also imparted valuable training in group leadership and public speaking.[76]

Beyond lessons in creating and leading formal organizations, most of these associations taught personal and group discipline. Temperance was symbolic of a whole code of self-restraint. The Jacksonville Mechanics Union, for example, admitted only those of "good moral character"; they expelled "habitual drunkards" and denied benefit payments to any whose disabilities arose from "drunkenness, horse racing, boxing, voluntary fighting; or any other vicious, improper, or immoral act." The

74. Cf. Louis Wirth, "Urbanism as a Way of Life," *American Journal of Sociology* 44 (1938): 1-24.

75. David L. Sills, "Voluntary Associations: Sociological Aspects," *International Encyclopedia of the Social Sciences* (New York, 1968), XVI, 373-74; Nicholas Babchuk and John N. Edwards, "Voluntary Associations and the Integration Hypothesis," *Sociological Inquiry* 35 (1965): 149-62; Kenneth Little, *West African Urbanization: A Study of Voluntary Associations in Social Change* (Cambridge, England, 1965), pp. 103-17.

76. Heinl, *Harmony Lodge*, p. 6. Cf. Immanuel Wallerstein, "Voluntary Associations," in James S. Coleman and Carl G. Rosberg, Jr., eds., *Political Parties and National Integration in Tropical Africa* (Berkeley, 1964), pp. 318-39.

Lyceum, Young Men's Literary Association, Odeon Club, and other literary societies were devoted to educational goals, but they also upheld rigorous standards regarding personal discipline, hard study, and self-improvement. Even the fire companies took as much pride in their members' morality as they did in their fire-fighting skills.[77]

The virtues of personal discipline and the sanctions that enforced them were transmitted to members in a succession of weekly temperance lectures, patriotic speeches, educational lectures, and debates sponsored by the various lodges and societies. The expulsion or suspension of a recalcitrant brother, the fines and humiliation of other wayward brethren, and the constant surveillance of members by one another helped keep most on the straight and narrow path. The Odd Fellows, as one righteous lodge member explained, "watch over our brethren not only in the lodge room but in our intercourse with the world at large."[78]

Another kind of discipline taught by voluntary associations affected their behavior as groups, rather than as individuals. This was evident in the remarkable capacity of very diverse and in many ways unfamiliar people to come together in "orderly assemblies." By the 1840s there emerged an impressive pattern of group discipline in Jacksonville's public meetings, even when the gatherings involved issues that were leading toward massive violence on the national scene. Whether it was a political party caucus, a public lecture to debate Catholicism or the Civil War, or perhaps a town meeting to propose a new waterworks bond or public library, these public gatherings followed a consistent, orderly routine. After a brief announcement of the intended purpose of the meeting by one of its convenors, a chairman, vice-chairman, and secretary were duly nominated and elected. Discussion began; a motion or resolution was put before the assembly; after formal debate, it was voted upon. The elaborate minutes of dozens of these meetings, published in local news-

77. *The Constitution and By-Laws of the Jacksonville Mechanics' Union* (Jacksonville, 1840), p. 8, in Illinois State Historical Library; *Patriot*, Nov. 24, 1832; "Records, Odeon, 1868–June 69," pp. 9-12, Illinois State Historical Library, Springfield; *Holland's Jacksonville City Directory for 1871-72* (Chicago, 1871) pp. 23-26.
78. Van Court, *An Address*, p. 8.

papers, reveal a predictable uniformity of public order, even when the debate itself revealed serious differences of opinion.[79]

Of course, Jacksonville's early history had been marked by a succession of raucous and sometimes violent public gatherings, and there would still be occasional heckling and other "disorderly behavior" at public meetings. However, the general pattern beginning in the 1840s was one of predictable order. By this time local leaders and citizens came to accept certain ground rules for public discussion, even when they disagreed violently on the point at issue. Surviving constitutions, bylaws, and minutes show that even the most minor associations were rigorously structured by specific rules of order.[80] At the Odeon Club or among the Odd Fellows, few seriously divisive issues were likely to emerge; nevertheless, this made these groups all the more suitable as schools of group discipline and parliamentary procedure.

Jacksonville's associations, and the social discipline they instilled, helped an extraordinarily mobile and discordant people to live together with a certain stability and order—not because they were basically alike or because they always agreed on fundamental ideals, but because, despite their differences, they accepted certain rules of order in dozens of small societies and, consequently, in the society at large. The associational discipline of order, deference to rules, and self-control was projected onto

79. See, e.g., descriptions of the several public meetings to debate the effort of Republicans to control Jacksonville's Fourth of July celebration after the Civil War, in *Sentinel*, June 2, 9, 16, 23, 30, July 7, 1865. Michael Zuckerman, *Peaceable Kingdoms: New England Towns in the Eighteenth Century* (New York, 1970), pp. 154-86, argues that conflict was intolerable and was therefore suppressed in colonial New England towns. In Jacksonville the procedural rigor of public meetings was designed only to control acknowledged conflict within the community.

80. See, e.g., "Records, Odeon 1868–June 69," and "Jacksonville Singing Society Constitution, 1828," Illinois State Historical Library, Springfield; *Constitution, Mechanics Union*. See preface to General Henry M. Robert, *Robert's Rules of Order Newly Revised*, ed. Sarah Corbin Robert (Glenview, Ill., 1970), pp. xxxvi-xlii, for the story of one man's effort to establish uniform procedural rules for all voluntary associations in the nineteenth-century city. Rowland Berthoff, *An Unsettled People: Social Order and Disorder in American History* (New York, 1971), pp. 254-74; Noel P. Gist, *Secret Societies: A Cultural Study of Fraternalism in the United States* (Columbia, Mo., 1940); Oscar and Mary Handlin, *Dimensions of Liberty* (New York, 1961), pp. 89-112; and Walter S. Glazer, "Participation and Power: Voluntary Associations and the Functional Organization of Cincinnati in

the larger society through institutional reforms and legislation. These mechanisms of social control, to which we shall turn next, were constructed by middle-class reformers who saw it as their duty to extend to the lower classes the social discipline they already had accepted voluntarily.

1840," *Historical Methods Newsletter* 5 (1972): 151-68, have all informed the discussion of voluntary associations in this chapter. A recently published book by Stuart Blumin, *The Urban Threshold: Growth and Change in a Nineteenth-Century American Community* (Chicago, 1976), includes an excellent discussion of the social functions of voluntary associations that complements the interpretation presented here.

Moral Government

> This community is responsible for every soul
> lost by drunkenness. . . .
> —*The Morgan Journal*[1]

THOSE WHO SUBMITTED to the discipline of voluntary institutions also reached out to reform and control those beyond the pale of church and lodge by enlarging the instruments of public authority. The expansion of local public institutions sprang from two interlocking concerns: community leaders' growing interest in the safety and aesthetics of the town's physical order, and nineteenth-century reformers' interest in the control of moral behavior through manipulation of the environment.[2] Both were linked to the boosters' overriding obsession with Jacksonville's growth, especially after 1850. The expansion of public authority resulted from other forces converging at the same time. The rise of the Republican party in the mid-1850s offered ideological justification for the aggressive use of government to promote prosperity and communal morality. The sudden influx of foreigners and blacks frightened the native middle class into a rapid expansion of coercive instruments of external social control. Finally, middle-class recognition of the liquor problem as a fundamental source of disorder in American society prompted community leaders to abandon moral suasion and voluntarism for a more stringent policy of

1. *Journal*, July 13, 1865.
2. See David J. Rothman, *The Discovery of the Asylum: Social Order and Disorder in the New Republic* (Boston, 1970).

194

prohibition. Together these forces transformed Jacksonville's local government from a minimal provider of janitorial services into an important mechanism of social discipline.

PUBLIC AUTHORITY AND THE PHYSICAL ORDER

Before 1850, local government intruded very little into the daily lives of Jacksonville's citizens. The town charter, approved in 1830, provided for the annual election of a five-member board of trustees; this body had limited powers to tax, improve streets, regulate public nuisances, and enforce laws. A few early ordinances touched on moral behavior by way of protecting the Sabbath, but these laws were enforced with indifference by the town constable, whose principal duties were collecting taxes and rounding up the hundreds of loose swine and dogs that roamed the muddy streets. The only prominent symbol of public authority was a large brick market house, constructed in 1834 at public expense to provide stalls where local farmers and butchers sold their products. The market house was a perfect symbol of local government; it maintained a minimal framework within which the forces of the private marketplace ruled.[3]

Charter amendments approved by the General Assembly in 1849 broadened the legislative powers of the trustees and encouraged the expansion of municipal services.[4] The sudden rise in property values which accompanied the railroad boom of the 1850s and a simultaneous flurry of new construction on the public square brought new attention to the problem of fire, the most basic and constant threat to the physical order of Jacksonville. Casual reliance on volunteer bucket brigades may have been satisfactory before the prosperous 1850s, but, as one editor warned in 1855, "Jacksonville has too much property at stake to remain defenseless longer."[5]

3. See Don Harrison Doyle, "Chaos and Community in a Frontier Town: Jacksonville, Illinois, 1825-1860" (Ph.D. dissertation, Northwestern University, 1973), pp. 266-280, for a fuller discussion of early municipal government.

4. The general law of incorporation is in *Laws of Illinois . . . 1830* (Vandalia, 1831), pp. 82-87; see also *Laws of the State of Illinois* (Springfield, 1840), pp. 106-9; *Laws of the State of Illinois* (Springfield, 1841), p. 328; William F. Short, ed., *Historical Encyclopedia of Illinois . . . Morgan County* (Chicago, 1906), p. 682.

5. *Sentinel*, Aug. 10, Dec. 21, 1855; Aug. 1, 1856.

Eastern insurance companies now sold policies through local agents to help cushion losses from fires, and the business community pushed harder for organized, effective protection in order to help lower insurance rates and prevent uncovered losses. Merchants formed the core of the Union Fire Company, a volunteer unit that rushed to any fire with their engine (the "Water Witch"), buckets, ladders, and other fire-fighting equipment. By 1858 the Union Fire Company was backed up by another volunteer unit; like its predecessor, the Rescue Fire Company No. 2 bought its equipment with funds solicited from proprietors on the square and some public monies from the board of trustees.[6]

At first these fire companies were elite social clubs in which the leading citizens demonstrated their "public spirit" while they protected their property. The volunteers responded faithfully to every alarm, but their effectiveness was limited by inadequate equipment and a frequently low water supply. These obstacles were beyond the capacity of private resources and voluntary service to surmount, and public responsibility for the protection of life and property was gradually enlarged.

During the summer drought of 1860 a series of disastrous fires prompted the town board to confront the basic problem of water supply. It authorized four cisterns to be built around the square, and provided the Union Fire Company, and later the Rescue Fire Company, with new three-hundred-foot hoses. The town also assumed the expenses for maintenance of equipment and of the Fireman's Hall; the board appointed a fire warden to supervise equipment and cistern maintenance and to direct firemen and the public at the scene of a fire.[7]

An 1862 fire ordinance, passed immediately after disastrous fires at the Female College and the Presbyterian Church, enforced a stricter code of fire safety. Fire wardens were now appointed in each of the town's four quadrants. They and their

6. Donnelley, Loyd & Co., *History of Morgan County, Illinois: Its Past and Present . . .* (Chicago, 1878), pp. 352-53.

7. "Minutes, Town Board" (title varies), May 5, June 5, July 6, 27, 1860; Mar. 5, Apr. 2, July 2, Nov. 23, Dec. 3, 1861; Oct. 7, 1862, MSS in City Clerk's Vault, Jacksonville Municipal Building, now available on microfilm at Illinois State Historical Library, Springfield; *Journal*, Mar. 15, 1860.

assistants were required to inspect at six-month intervals the stoves and chimneys of all dwellings, and to impose five-dollar fines on citizens who refused to cooperate. The wardens were also authorized to require citizens to join bucket brigades and to "suppress any tumult or disorder" at the scene of fires. Every property-owner was expected to keep a two-gallon tin bucket on each floor of his dwelling. The trustees installed an enormous fire bell atop the Fireman's Hall in order to alert the volunteers more quickly. They added pumps near the cisterns and purchased more hoses to increase the range of the fire engines. A new fire ordinance in 1865 extended preventative measures by strengthening public regulation of building construction. A "Fire Limits" ordinance required all buildings facing the public square to be of brick or stone; codes on the spacing of interior studs and window casements were also enacted. Spurred by the fundamental threat of property destruction, public authority quickly enlarged.[8]

That authority also expanded in response to a new stress on physical order in Jacksonville's streets and public places, a movement compelled by both practical and aesthetic values. Clean streets and sidewalks improved the health of residents and the flow of trade. They signified a "go-ahead spirit" alive in the community, and local boosters came to appreciate the oft-noted beauty and order of the town as a genuine attraction to prospective residents and institutions of charity and learning.

After 1850 this pursuit of physical orderliness focused on the public square and emanated outward. The square had always been the gathering place of rural visitors; there on Saturdays and holidays the "drinking and fighting classes from the country" held foot races and wrestling matches and gambled and drank openly.[9] Encompassing the square was an undefinable social boundary, one that Jacksonville's polite society, particularly respectable women, rarely crossed. Merchants on the square were keenly aware of the influence of this rough mas-

8. *Sentinel*, Dec. 27, 1861; Apr. 4, 1862; "Minutes, Town Board," Oct. 7, 1862; Aug. 18, 1863; Mar. 1, 1864; Mar. 1, 1865; *Revised Ordinances . . . of Jacksonville* (Jacksonville, 1866), pp. 23-25, in Illinois State Historical Library, Springfield.

9. *Journal*, Nov. 9, 1866; Truman Augustus Post, *Truman Marcellus Post: A Biography Personal and Literary* (Boston, 1891), p. 50.

culine element on their clientele, and their advertisements reveal a deliberate effort to reassure women shoppers that they would be welcome and comfortable in their stores. Some wealthy women managed to avoid the square altogether by sending servants on shopping excursions. Mrs. Elizabeth Duncan lived securely in her College Hill home, thankful that she was not "compelled to live in town." Once, however, when preparing a cake for afternoon company, she was forced to go to town for eggs. Near the square she was astonished to see the approach of a large procession of townspeople celebrating the Fourth of July, a holiday she ignored entirely. "It frightened me so much," she recorded that night in her diary, ". . . I felt quite faint and was sick all day."[10]

Few of Jacksonville's middle-class women were as squeamish as Mrs. Duncan, but they still may have felt uncomfortable on the square. The editor of the *Journal* denounced the rude young men who loafed about the square, ogling bypassing women and issuing lewd cat calls. "If they cannot be compelled [to leave the square] is there not some latent sense of decency in them which can be roused into activity, so that they will voluntarily desist from a habit, so very disagreeable to others?" The *Journal* also took it upon itself to recommend a series of rules to govern sidewalk etiquette, with specific suggestions on correct manners when passing others and when stopping to talk or window shop. In reply, the Democratic *Sentinel* warned their "country friends" "when they preambulate our sidewalks" to "conduct themselves in due reverence to the *Journal's rules*, for fear some higher law 'police regulation' may be enforced against him." They criticized their rivals also for their presumptuous "parental supervision over everything public or private."[11] The *Journal*, it was true, spoke more consistently for those who wanted to enlarge public regulation over private behavior.

The first task in this campaign to purify the public square was to cleanse and order the physical environment. With the incep-

10. Elizabeth Duncan Putnam, ed., "Diary of Mrs. Joseph Duncan (Elizabeth Caldwell Smith)," *JISHS* 21 (1928): 44, 48; Frank J. Heinl, *Centennial: J. Capps & Sons, Ltd.* (Jacksonville, 1939), pp. 15-17.

11. *Journal*, Feb. 20, 1860; *Sentinel*, Nov. 2, 1855.

tion of the Jacksonville Gas Light and Coke Company in 1856, the town board quickly approved the installation of lamps around the square and along the principal streets leading away from it. This amenity enhanced the safety and convenience of the center of town and helped reduce the crime and violence that had flourished in the dark streets and alleys.[12]

Earlier ordinances requiring merchants to lay sidewalks across the fronts of their lots left a hodgepodge of rotting, rat-infested plank walks mixed with brick and stone pavements that sank into the mud each spring. The revised ordinances of 1861 required uniform ten-foot walks in front of all lots facing the square, to be constructed with "good brick or stone" with a high stone curbing. Sidewalks were still officially the responsibility of the individual lot owners, but the new ordinances allowed owners along any given block to petition the town board to authorize construction of a common walk. As more owners took advantage of this option, public responsibility for sidewalks gradually expanded.[13]

The trustees also assumed a stronger role in cleansing the square and the town's public thoroughfares of filth and loose animals. The 1861 ordinances increased the fines for leaving refuse or dead animals in public places and gave the street supervisor more power to enforce the law. A cholera scare in the summer of 1866 excited new efforts to sanitize the city. The trustees issued stern warnings that citizens should clean their yards of all "unwholesome things," and appointed a public health inspector to investigate unhealthy conditions in privies and cellars. The board also renewed the campaign to cleanse and beautify the streets and the public square as an example to private citizens. Cows were banned from all streets, and forty acres of pasture were rented at public expense as a place to impound loose animals. The fences and gates around the square were repaired to keep out animals, and the shade trees were pruned and boxed to discourage posting of advertisements and political posters. Squirrels were later imported to the "Courthouse Park" (as it now came to be known) to add

12. "Minutes, Town Board," July 6, Sept. 7, 1857; *Sentinel*, Dec. 9, 1864.
13. Ibid., May 10, 1861: "Minutes, Town Board," passim.

to the enjoyment of the square. License laws also banned auctioneers from the square, and new stone crosswalks allowed pedestrians to cross the still unpaved streets around it. Ladies and their children were now invited to enjoy the green beauty of the park.[14]

On one corner of the square the old courthouse, always an architectural eyesore, grew shabby by the 1860s. Local editors pleaded for its replacement by a new county building, "one that will be in harmony with other city improvements, and reflect credit upon the wealth and enterprise of the people of Morgan." After a prolonged squabble involving the town's jurisdiction over the square and the location of the new courthouse, the old building was torn down at the end of 1869. A new one went up west of the square, a move justified by the economy of constructing a single-front building and by the supposed need to remove it "from the bustle and noise incident to the business centre of the city."[15] An unstated purpose was also to complete the purification of the square—to remove the hubbub of politics, which buzzed about the courthouse steps, from what had now become a central symbol of Jacksonville's tranquil beauty and refinement.

PUBLIC AUTHORITY AND THE PROBLEM OF POVERTY

The expansion of public authority touched the people as well as physical property of Jacksonville. Beginning with dependent populations (the poor and children), public authority extended to the criminal and debauched in new ways in the 1850s, in each case offering a combination of reform and control. The presence of poverty was only reluctantly confronted by officials, for it brought into question a fundamental faith in a burgeoning capitalist society that offered wealth to all with ambition and good character. Prior to the Civil War, the poor were considered to be the charge of the churches, private philanthropists,

14. *Journal*, Apr. 25, 1866; *Sentinel*, July 3, 1863; June 13, 1867; "Minutes, Town Board," Apr. 22, May 6, Oct. 6, Dec. 1, 1865; Apr. 17, 21, 28, Aug. 15, 1866. See Charles E. Rosenberg, *The Cholera Years: The United States in 1832, 1849, and 1866* (Chicago, 1962), pp. 213-25.

15. *Sentinel*, Nov. 3, 1865; Aug. 8, 1867.

and, as a last resort, the county poorhouse and farm on the east side of town. The disabled, elderly widows, and young orphans were all considered members of the "worthy poor," deserving of charity but, nonetheless, expected to work toward self-reliance.[16]

With the Civil War the problem of poverty and the public response to it were quickly reassessed. After Lincoln's first call for volunteers, the town board generously approved a petition from several prominent citizens by allotting $3,000 for "the support of the women and children of Citizens who have volunteered in defence of our Country." As the war 'dragged on and the burden of supporting distressed soldiers' families increased, the board appealed to the churches, "requesting them to form societies in aid of the support of the Poor of said Town." "Benevolent ladies" in all the churches sponsored a succession of Saturday evening "mite meetings" in the Odd Fellows Hall to raise funds for the poor. Eventually they formed the Ladies Aid Society and served as an ongoing liaison between town officials and the poor. The children of Locust Grove School also performed at a large benefit exhibition held in Strawn's Hall. Voluntary organizations seemed to supersede the church when the scale of charity was enlarged by the carnage of war.[17]

The limits of private charity were soon strained by the war, and public responsibility expanded by necessity. In winter, 1862, the town board responded favorably to two leading businessmen's petition to purchase fifty cords of firewood "for the benefit of the poor of the Town." Private donations of wood and provisions to the poor also became important demonstrations of loyalty, and the rival political parties proudly paraded wagonloads of gifts to soldiers' families during their rallies. After a community drive to supply firewood to the poor in 1863, a list of contributors was printed in the Democratic Sentinel (with proud reference to the large numbers of Democratic donors).[18]

16. See Robert H. Bremner, *From the Depths: The Discovery of Poverty in the United States* (New York, 1956), pp. 42-45: Walter I. Trattner, *From Poor Law to Welfare State: A History of Social Welfare in America* (New York, 1974), pp. 44-93.

17. "Minutes, Town Board," Apr. 20, Dec. 20, 1861; Nov. 17, 1866; *Sentinel*, Apr. 26, Dec. 20, 1861; Apr. 10, May 8, 1863; *Journal*, Apr. 9, 1863.

18. "Minutes, Town Board," Feb. 4, 1862; *Sentinel*, Dec. 18, 1863.

As charity became entangled in the politics of war, the traditional distinctions of worthy poor versus undeserving indigents seemed to lose meaning. The wives and children of Jacksonville's loyal fighting men were in need of community support; who would deny them? Besides, their sheer numbers made judgments of worthiness difficult.

By the end of the war the burden of public and private charity began to weigh heavily. Even the Republican newspaper complained of "the unusual number of soldiers' families, of southern refugees and freedmen . . . dependent upon the charities of an already overtaxed people." Benevolent families were urged to give employment—not alms—to the poor, and thus to avoid a permanent burden of charity on the community: "Let us all endeavor to aid the poor among us to profitable employment so that by well directed energy and industry they may, ere another winter comes, be prepared to meet its wants without depending upon charity."[19]

But a growing number of the poor were thrown upon the charities of the poorhouse. By the end of the war the facility was bursting with widows and orphans, and the flow of new arrivals showed no indication of subsiding. Early in 1866 the county sold its forty-four-acre tract on the eastern edge of town to two subdividers, who advertised it as the next rival of the College Hill neighborhood. With profits from the sale the county was able to purchase a much larger poorhouse, surrounded by more farmland to occupy its growing clientele.[20]

Private and public charity cooperated in the creation of a new female orphans' asylum opened in 1870. Elizabeth Ayers, wife of a wealthy banker, purchased the building of the defunct Berean College on East State Street and deeded it to the city as an orphans' home and city hospital. The orphanage sheltered young females from the poorhouse and promised "to qualify them for useful and honorable positions in society."[21] In a community that made public charity one of its principal industries, Jacksonville's own "worthy poor" now became the responsibility of combined private and public institutions.

19. *Journal*, Mar. 9, 1865.
20. Ibid., Jan. 18, 1866; *Sentinel*, Feb. 2, Mar. 23, 1866.
21. Donnelley, *History of Morgan*, pp. 398-99; *Holland's Directory, 1871-72*, p. 12.

The "Well Ordered School"

Public authority also reached out to control local children in the 1850s. Education had always been a central force shaping the community; the Yale Band founded Illinois College in order to train western teachers to supply the state's desperately needed schools. But despite the proliferation of denominational seminaries and colleges, the lower levels of Illinois' educational system remained crude and incomplete before 1850. Earlier legislation to support a public common-school system was defeated by rural hostility and general indifference.[22]

Those who wanted education in communities like Jacksonville relied upon ad hoc subscription schools. They hired itinerant young men who used teaching to tide them over for a winter before embarking on a more lucrative carrer. William Thomas, an aspiring young lawyer, opened Jacksonville's first subscription school in 1826. He had traveled from Bowling Green, Kentucky, "as far as my money and horse would carry me." "Not being able to obtain other employment, out of which to pay for board, and being out of funds," Thomas recalled, "I engaged to teach school for three months upon the old plan of obtaining subscribers for scholars." Some twenty-five families sent their children to the dark log meetinghouse south of the square; children of varying ages and widely different levels of preparation were thrown together in one small room, with slabs to sit on and rough wood planks nailed to the inside walls to serve as desks. All the students recited their various lessons simultaneously, creating an incredible level of noise and confusion. Amid this havoc Thomas was expected to instruct his students in the basic skills of reading, writing, and spelling. Teachers in early Illinois who ventured beyond this rudimentary curriculum to grammar, mathematics, science, literature, or history were frequently challenged by suspicious rural parents who saw no practical use in these subjects.[23]

22. Theodore Calvin Pease, *The Frontier State, 1818-1848*, The Centennial History of Illinois, vol. 2 (Chicago, 1918), pp. 66-68; Paul E. Belting, "The Development of the Free Public High School in Illinois to 1860," *JISHS* 11 (1918-19): 269-369, 467-565; William L. Pillsbury, "Early Education in Illinois," in Superintendent of Public Instruction of the State of Illinois, *Sixteenth Biennial Report* (Springfield, 1886).

23. Donnelley, *History of Morgan*, pp. 339-43; Robert W. Patterson, *Early Society in Southern Illinois* (Chicago, 1881), pp. 23-25; *Semi-Centennial and Anniversary Exercises of*

Most families saw the subscription school as an unsatisfactory stopgap preceding a full system of public common schools. During the 1830s the influx of Northerners into Illinois and the emergence of more towns brought new energy to the movement for public-supported common schools. With its heavy investment in Illinois College, Jacksonville soon became a spearhead for educational reform. The *Common School Advocate*, a newspaper founded in Jacksonville in 1837, served as an important voice for the movement. A State Teachers Association, established in 1837 at a convention called in Jacksonville, joined the cause and advocated teacher training and certification.[24]

Jacksonville's educational reformers also led the effort to bring women into the teaching profession. A group of women, most of them wives of local clergymen and college professors, formed the Ladies' Association for Educating Females in 1833. Together with the Jacksonville Female Academy (established in 1830) it sought to fill the void of competent male teachers with trained and dedicated women. As Edward Beecher explained in the annual report before the Ladies' Association (polite women were not allowed to speak in public), a woman is "best suited to the work" of teaching, since "that period of human life in which the mind is most susceptible of deep and lasting impressions is almost exclusively under her care and influence." "Add to this," Beecher concluded, "the relative cheapness of the terms on which they can be employed, and does not the voice of wisdom say, let them be educated and qualified for this important work?" This last argument was attractive to tax-shy Illinoisans: women were paid about half to two-thirds the salary paid to male teachers. It was the feminization of a large part of the teaching force by the 1850s that made mass education feasible in Illinois.[25]

---

the Jacksonville Female Academy (Jacksonville, 1880), p. 267; James Haines, "Social Life and Scenes in the Early Settlement of Central Illinois," Illinois State Historical Society *Transactions* 10 (1905): 44.

24. Belting, "High School," pp. 481-87; Pease, *Frontier State*, p. 432; Frank J. Heinl, "Jacksonville and Morgan County: An Historical Review," *JISHS* 18 (1925): 20.

25. Margaret King Moore, "The Ladies' Association for Educating Females,

Beginning in 1849, a series of state laws allowed local communities to receive state education funds more easily and to levy their own school taxes. In 1850 Jacksonville organized its first graded public district school in the Masonic Hall. Classes soon overflowed with students, and more rooms had to be rented to satisfy the demand for free education. A new schoolhouse was quickly constructed on the west side of town, and by the mid-1860s two more district schools were built, both in the eastern section. The community schools were attached loosely to county and state supervisory agencies that defined standards, certified teachers, and guided the reform of public education. Jacksonville's superintendent, Newton Bateman, a graduate of Illinois College, began on the county level to tighten qualifications for teachers in the 1850s. Following his appointment as state superintendent, he continued his reform campaign on a broader scale.[26]

The periodic reports by the county and state superintendents voiced the new consciousness of public education beginning in the late 1850s. One central obsession pervading every report was the schoolhouse environment, again revealing the interest of reformers in the influence of the physical order upon moral behavior. The old multipurpose schoolrooms with their stuffy, dark interiors were now rejected as "dilapidated and forlorn specimens of barbarity" which produced "slovenly and unhappy inmates." The new "model district school" had a "neat and attractive appearance" with "all the attractions of a pleasant and happy home." This model school featured a separate cloakroom for students of each sex. Inside a spacious, well-lighted room were neat rows of iron-mounted desks; each student was assigned to a specific place. This "neatness, order and taste" influenced the students' habits. The "well ordered school," one report claimed, was reflected in its "inmates'" "progress of

1833-1937," *JISHS* 31 (1938): 171. Salaries are reported in Superintendent of Public Instruction of the State of Illinois, *Biennial Reports* (Springfield, 1856-70). See Michael B. Katz, *The Irony of Early School Reform: Educational Innovation in Mid-Nineteenth Century Massachusetts* (Cambridge, Mass., 1968), pp. 56-57.

26. Donnelley, *History of Morgan*, p. 378; Charles M. Eames, *Historic Morgan and Classic Jacksonville* (Jacksonville, 1885), p. 185; *Journal*, Sept. 5, 1866.

study, accurate recitations . . . courteous manners, refinement and true politeness."[27]

In place of the common school where children of all ages were "promiscuously" mixed in one room, progressive communities like Jacksonville adopted graded school systems. This system recognized varying levels of learning and development among children of different ages and abilities. It was also praised as a more efficient method of teaching. "A systematic division of labor is as applicable to school as to all other affairs," the argument went, and teachers as well as students began to concentrate on one level in a sequential process of education. This "systematic division of labor" reflected the new conditions of the marketplace, for it anticipated the child's experience in the competitive "race of life":

> The poor man's children enter the school room on an exact equality . . . with the rich man's child. The latter, robbed of all extraneous advantages and supports . . . find that application to study and good deportment will alone suffice to maintain a respectable standing. . . . Once classified in a graded school, the pupil has a double incentive to keep up with, or outstrip his classmates—the hope of being promoted to a higher class in case he excels, and the fear of being degraded by being assigned to a lower one, provided he does not maintain his standing.[28]

The school also provided a disciplined environment for students, who now were taught not only the basic rudiments of reading and writing but a certain moral training as well. Although the early subscription school in Jacksonville had promised to "pay strict attention to [the student's] moral deportment," the public school system which emerged in the 1850s took on the duty of moral instruction with new ardor. The rise of the public school coincided with a growing intolerance for undisciplined youth. Editorials criticized idle young men who loafed about the square, and they scorned children's games as yet another nuisance disturbing the public order. "Even in our city, orderly and quiet as it is," one indignant editor snorted in

27. Superintendent of Public Instruction, *Second Biennial Report, 1857-58*, p. 25.
28. Ibid., pp. 42-44.

1855, "our best pavements are continually blockaded with juveniles making them their sporting places to the great impediment of pedestrians. This is intolerable in any place, and the powers that be should see that it is abated."[29]

Reformers advocated the school as a vital instrument of social discipline for youth, an essential supplement to what they saw as the eroding authority of traditional institutions in the family and church. Teachers and their administrative superiors were given new powers to exercise this discipline, with corporal punishment if necessary. In the late 1860s elaborate rules were introduced in Jacksonville schools to regulate students' punctuality, absenteeism, and a whole range of social behavior. Under the old subscription school system, teachers worked at the parents' sufferance and therefore had to "keep fair weather with all," as one reformer complained. The public school system now possessed more autonomous power.[30]

The exercise of this new power did not go unchallenged. When an angry father took a local teacher to court in 1855 for punishing his son, the school's authority was debated, and inevitably the debate took on political overtones. The Democratic *Sentinel* reprinted a furious letter responding to the *Journal*'s defense of the teacher and denounced the growing authority of the public school: "It is a *petty monarchy* which would even seek to enter into the secrets of the family, and sway its controlling ceptre there. . . . This sympathizer with nigger cruelties calls upon the Trustees of our School to sustain the teacher in this barbarous act."[31] In the late 1860s the introduction of a strict code of discipline punishing unruly or tardy students brought forth another torrent of criticism through the *Sentinel*'s pages.[32]

The Democrats also continued to criticize the growing tax

29. *Sentinel*, Mar. 23, 1855.

30. *Illinois Intelligencer* (Vandalia), Dec. 5, 1829. See David Tyack, "The Kingdom of God and the Common School: Protestant Ministers and the Educational Awakening in the West," *Harvard Educational Review* 36 (1966): 447-69; and Michael B. Katz, *Class, Bureaucracy, and Schools: The Illusion of Educational Change in America* (New York, 1971), pp. 3-55.

31. *Sentinel*, Oct. 26, 1855.

32. Ibid., Feb. 12, 1869.

burden of Jacksonville's school system, which increased four-fold between 1857 and 1870. The increased expenses derived from the enormous investment in new buildings and modern equipment required by a fully graded school system. The creation of a city school system in 1867 expanded the number of public primary schools to five (one six-grade school for each of the four wards, plus a colored school with grades one and two only), in addition to a high school. An expensive new administrative bureaucracy, including a principal for each school and a handsomely paid superintendent, added to the tax burden.[33]

One of the central goals of public school reform was to extend the benefits (and the discipline) of the school to all classes in the community. Illinois reformers denounced private academies as harbingers of aristocracy. Without free public education, they argued, "there will be two classes of society, and all the odious features and miserable distinctions of aristocracy, will be en-grafted upon our free institutions." Public schools were also promoted by native Protestants as a means of socializing the children of foreigners. However, the capacity of public schools to incorporate all segments of the community was limited. On the one hand, Irish Catholics, Germans, and Portuguese wanted to set up their own schools and perpetuate their own distinctive culture. And, though the doors of the public school theoretically were open to all, working-class families could not always afford to forego their children's contribution to the family income, particularly in the cases of families with teenagers.[34] Yet within these limits the public school emerged as an institution of central importance to the community. It taught the values of self-reliance and social mobility necessary to a capitalist social system, and it transmitted covert lessons in social discipline, self-restraint, and deference to a hierarchical structure of authority. In this sense the school embodied the community's effort to balance voluntarism and coercion.

33. Ibid., Apr. 1, 15, 1870; *Holland's Directory, 1871-72*, pp. 18-19.

34. James Hall, "A Few Thoughts on Education," *Illinois Monthly Magazine* 1 (1830): 111-12. See Ruth Miller Elson, *Guardians of Tradition* (Lincoln, Nebr., 1964); Richard D. Mosier, *Making the American Mind: Social and Moral Ideas in McGuffey's Readers* (New York, 1965). Robert H. Wiebe, "The Social Functions of Public Education," *American Quarterly* 21 (1969): 147-64, provides a perceptive overview of school reform.

Captain Slick and the Public Order

The expansion of public authority after 1850 also transformed the methods of law enforcement. Early Jacksonville had never relied upon systematic police protection. When Sheriff Charles Zabriskie chased three thieves all the way to Canada in the winter of 1844, a lavish "citizens' supper" was held at a local hotel to applaud his heroic deed. A congratulatory resolution passed at the occasion proclaimed:

> In a community like ours, where no regular system of Police is established, and where the rights of property are consequently in some degree insecure; and citizens are not unfrequently made to suffer from the acts and villany of depredators and felons, it is an honorable enterprise and worthy the applause of all honest men, to *volunteer* like our respected guest, in pursuit of the fugitive offender, and like him, to be instant and active, bold and persevering, wary and untiring. . . . Every good man has felt that both his property and public morals, are more safe since his return; he has slept more quietly. . . .

Zabriskie had indeed earned this praise (even if it was a bit overblown), but it is curious that this triumph of the law was seen as the "voluntary" act of a heroic individual, who only incidentally was carrying out his prescribed duties as an enforcer of the law. The elaborate celebration in honor of his accomplishment also suggests that it was a rare and unexpected effort.[35]

Much of what could pass for law enforcement was, in practice, left in private rather than official hands. Morgan County had a tradition of vigilante justice extending back to the early 1820s, when the "Regulators of the Valley," a group of stalwart

---

Our Savior Catholic School claimed 185 students in 1866 and 400 in 1871. The German school enrolled only about 30 students in the 1860s. *Holland's Directory, 1871-72*, pp. 19-20; Eames, *Historic Morgan*, p. 185; "Statistical Record, Salem Congregation, Jacksonville, Illinois," in Salem Lutheran Church, Jacksonville. According to the census manuscripts from 1850 through 1870, roughly three-quarters of all school-age children (5-17) attended school for at least part of the year. Native business and professional families had attendance rates hovering around 80%; immigrant blue-collar families sent about 60% of their children to school, and probably for shorter periods during the year.

35. *Illinois Statesman*, Feb. 12, 1844.

pioneers, guarded the interests of law and order in the then-untamed frontier. Their activities became legendary among the older settlers, who fondly remembered the violent retribution of vigilante justice. This tradition was embodied in a mythic figure called Captain Slick, a buckskin-clad Kentucky back-woodsman. "Captain Slick," one of his admirers explained, "is the great police officer for the court which takes cognizance of *equitable* matters—that is to say, of offenses undefined and un-punished by statutory provisions. Suspicions which amount to certainties in the public mind, but lack legal proof to establish them, are duly considered by the captain." Once the accused was determined to be guilty, "the offender is carried into the woods tied to a tree, and scourged with hickory rods. . . ."[36]

Neither the vigilante tradition of Captain Slick nor the over-burdened town constable was sufficient for the task of moral government. By the early 1850s a full-time police force sup-planted both and enforced the widening powers of local gov-ernment with new efficiency. By 1853 the board of trustees created a police force with ten full-time "assistant constables," all endowed with "the same power of the town constable in inforsing the ordinances." Three years later a new ordinance "to Establish and Regulate the Police Department" drew firm lines of authority and specified the duties of the police force, providing for close supervision by the town board and requir-ing of the police "a strict performance of their duties . . . to preserve order, quiet, and peace, throughout the town."[37]

Local newspapers then began weekly reports of all crimes. Editorials alternately scolded the police and their supervisors for negligence or applauded their efforts to maintain order, always pleading for an efficient and rational system of law enforcement. "Several little chunks of rows have occurred in the streets this week," went one familiar complaint. "The most effective way to preserve the peace is to touch pugnacious gentlemen in their pockets. Let every violation of the peace be followed by the immediate and certain infliction of a fine, and such cases will be scarce."[38]

36. *Patriot*, Aug. 31, 1833; Eames, *Historic Morgan*, pp. 20-23.
37. "Minutes, Town Board," June 13, July 12, 1853; June 2, 1858; *Sentinel*, May 23, 1856.
38. Ibid., May 23, 1856.

Occasionally the rational exercise of the law was not enough. When John Sprague was found guilty of molesting a young girl and fined one hundred dollars, the girl's father sought vengeance in a more traditional manner. Between two and three hundred people gathered on the square to witness, without interference, the angry father inflict upon Sprague "a severe chastisement with a carriage whip, 'well and faithfully' laid on." "We are opposed to mob law," commented the *Journal*, "but even in this there are exceptions to the rule. . . ."[39] "The rule" usually involved a growing reliance upon the official mechanisms of law enforcement, found in an enlarged and increasingly systematic police force.

The Civil War further enlarged the presence of police as enforcers of the public order. When the population swelled with hundreds of young soldiers camped at the county fairgrounds, the brothels and saloons, already established with the arrival of the railroads, flourished anew. Ordinances quickly gave the police additional powers to raid vice dens and fine their proprietors, but the demand for pleasures of the flesh seemed always to exceed the best efforts of the police. One notorious brothel in Bostick's Alley southeast of the square attracted a steady stream of "stray soldiers" and other "loafers," who witnessed nightly brawls and several "shooting affrays" before it was shut down.[40]

Drifting bands of robbers also floated from town to town in what some thought were organized rings of thieves. "This city and county are tolerably well filled up with a lot of worthless scoundrels," snorted one observer toward the end of the war. After a series of "startling robberies" in the spring of 1865, the *Sentinel* called for action against the vagrant drifters who "flooded" the town: "These lawless manifestations are alarming, and no citizen can feel safe until the 'city fathers' take energetic steps to ferret out the perpetrators of these acts of robbery."[41]

Civic leaders reacted with determination to the threat of public disorder during the war. More stringent laws were

39. *Journal*, May 24, 1860.
40. *Sentinel*, Dec. 20, 1861; *Journal*, Nov. 7, Dec. 1, 1864; Feb. 23, 1865.
41. *Sentinel*, May 19, 1865; Aug. 6, 1869.

passed against vice dens, vagrants, and criminals of all kinds. Salaries were raised to attract good constables and policemen. Extra police and "secret police" were hired on certain occasions to support the regular department, and the police began a more explicit show of force. Beginning in the summer of 1861, each policeman was required to carry a large billy club, "got up in city style," one approving editor cheered. "They are about the size of a rolling pin, of hard wood, and heavy enough to fell an ox. The war spirit abroad in the land has probably rendered necessary the introduction of this potent instrument of justice."[42] Subsequent complaints of abusive police force and indiscriminant vice raids suggest that the new police powers were exercised freely. The Democratic editor occasionally exploited these opportunities to vent discontent upon the Republican city fathers by denouncing the exercise of such "arbitrary powers." But a consensus prevailed among community leaders in favor of a well-policed "orderly and quiet town."[43]

TEMPERANCE, VOLUNTARISM, AND COERCION

Many saw the problems of poverty and crime as superficial symptoms of a deeper disorder—intemperance—from which all vices ultimately flowed. This analysis of fundamental moral disorder informed the extension of local government after 1850, as it began to exercise control over behavior that had previously been left to the private sphere. The expansion of moral government coincided with the growth of municipal services and the strenuous civic efforts to order and sanitize the physical environment. In a sense, all were efforts to domesticate and control the unruly frontier community and bring it more in line with the image of refinement projected by its boosters.

Before 1850 the temperance movement worked through voluntary associations to persuade and "save" the intemperate masses. Tracts and sermons focused upon the personal costs of intemperance and attempted to convert individuals one at

42. "Minutes, Town Board," June 6, Sept. 4, 1860; Aug. 20, 1861; Sept. 12, Nov. 1, 1864; Apr. 17, May 2, 12, 1866; *Sentinel*, June 28, 1861.
43. Ibid., June 25, 1863; May 16, 1867.

a time. Temperance reform played a major part in the New England mission in the West beginning in the 1820s. Yankee newspaper editor James G. Edwards came to Jacksonville in 1829 and made temperance a central theme in the *Western Observer*; its pages were filled with moralistic accounts of respectable men who fell to poverty and disgrace under the baneful influence of hard liquor. Public lectures, sermons, and published tracts added to this litany of temperance.

Before 1850 the main energy of temperance reform was channeled into voluntary associations formally organized on the community level and loosely attached to national networks. Though each differed in its strategy, these associations all proceeded from the common assumption that temperance was a private, voluntary choice that determined personal fortunes. Added to this concept of voluntarism was a notion that collective discipline could reinforce individual moral strength, and that well-organized campaigns of moral suasion could best advance the cause of temperance in the community and nation.[44]

The Morgan County Temperance Society had been founded in Jacksonville as a unit of the American Temperance Society by 1831. It recruited gentlemen from the clergy, professions, and business to pledge abstinence from hard liquor (except for medicinal use) and to stand before the community as upright examples of the benefits of temperance.[45] National dissension over total abstinence undermined the local unit, but by 1842 Jacksonville's temperance forces regrouped in the Washington Temperance Society, another movement emanating from the East. The Washingtonians proposed to persuade followers through the experience of "reformed drunkards," rather than through the example of already temperate gentlemen. In Jacksonville, however, the society attracted "the members of other societies, the Clergy, the Faculty of Illinois College, members of the bar, Medical Faculty," and other members of the "respect-

44. John Allen Krout, *The Origins of Prohibition* (New York, 1925), and Joseph Gusfield, *Symbolic Crusade: Status Politics and the American Temperance Movement* (Urbana, 1963), both provide good overviews of temperance reform. Michael H. Frisch, *Town into City: Springfield, Massachusetts, and the Meaning of Community, 1840-1880* (Cambridge, Mass., 1972), pp. 36-38 et passim, discusses temperance within a local context.

45. *Western Observer*, Feb. 26, 1831; Krout, *Origins*, pp. 111, 125-52.

able classes." Beyond their periodic meetings (which included testimonials to the evils of "the dangerous appetite"), Jacksonville's Washingtonians worked toward transforming public celebrations of national holidays into quiet, sober events. "No artificial stimulus is necessary to arouse men when their country calls," spoke Richard Yates, addressing the society on Washington's Birthday in 1842; "they can be patriotic without being drunk."[46]

Hundreds of men purportedly pledged and joined the Washingtonian movement in Jacksonville, but its effect was limited, one member explained, because it "lacked that system and organization which were essential to permanency and success."[47] The Sons of Temperance established a brotherhood in Jacksonville sometime after their founding in New York in 1842. This lodge was a more tightly structured secret fraternal organization with "all the elements of strength, efficiency and above all of perpetuity." Jacksonville's lodge quickly grew to 160 members, embracing "the great and the humble, the rich and the poor, men of every party, Christians of every denomination . . . united in a holy brotherhood." The Sons of Temperance, with a local lodge and a state and national hierarchy, acted with "all the force of organization" to guarantee their members' pledge of total abstinence by disciplining backsliders.[48] Joined by the International Order of Good Templars in 1866, the Catholic Total Abstinence Society in 1868, and a number of women's and children's auxiliaries, the temperance associations constituted a durable mechanism for voluntary social discipline in Jacksonville.[49]

The temperance movement took a major theme of evangelical Christian pietism beyond its denominational boundaries and invested in temperance a whole cluster of secular values involv-

46. *Illinois Statesman*, July 3, 10, 1843; Richard Yates, *Address Delivered Before the Washington Temperance Society . . . February 22, 1842* (Jacksonville, 1842), p. 3, in Illinois State Historical Library, Springfield.

47. Richard Yates, *Address Delivered before the Excelsior Division, No. 25 of the Sons of Temperance* (Jacksonville, 1848), p. 7, in Illinois State Historical Library, Springfield.

48. Yates, *Address, Sons of Temperance*, pp. 8, 11, 16; Krout, *Origins*, pp. 209-10.

49. *Journal*, Mar. 29, 1866; W. A. Nixon, comp., *Nixon's Jacksonville Directory for 1868-69* (Jacksonville, 1868), p. 36; *Holland's Directory, 1871-72*, p. 28.

ing social mobility and the sanctity of the family. Nevertheless, all of these associations were built upon the premise that temperance was an individual, voluntary choice. Their movement advanced by means of moral suasion, the conversion of new members, and group discipline to reinforce each member's pledge.

By 1850 the faith in voluntary temperance was quickly eclipsed by a new, more aggressive campaign to coerce temperance by legal prohibition. Building upon the religious and associational foundation of the temperance movement, the prohibitionists now turned to government to impose their discipline upon the community. Prompted in part by the growing number of foreigners outside the pale of pietistic Protestantism, the prohibition movement also sprang from a new faith that government could improve the social order.[50]

After several local victories in 1850, the Illinois prohibition forces sought statewide restrictions during the 1851 legislative session. Under enormous popular pressure, the legislature passed a law prohibiting liquor sales of less than one quart—a plan designed to deprive lower-class imbibers who could afford their whiskey only "by the shot." The "quart law," one Jacksonville critic later complained, is "a law for drunkards. Under its operation, he that wished to disgrace his species could obtain a quart, get drunk, and lie in the street until he gets sober, or is rooted out of the way by the swine." The law was also impossible to enforce. Temperance advocates quickly retreated to the liquor license system, while strict prohibition forces regrouped to battle for a Maine Law to ban all liquor sales in Illinois.[51]

Meanwhile, Jacksonville, followed by other temperate communities in central and northern Illinois, passed local laws restricting or prohibiting the sale and consumption of "spiritus liquors." Jacksonville's local regulation was approved in the state supreme court in a ruling that, in effect, made regulation

50. See Clifford S. Griffen, *Their Brothers' Keepers: Moral Stewardship in the United States, 1800-1865* (New Brunswick, N.J., 1960), pp. 116-51.

51. Arthur Charles Cole, *The Era of the Civil War, 1848-1870*, The Centennial History of Illinois, vol. 3 (Chicago, 1919), pp. 206-7; *Sentinel*, May 25, 1855.

of liquor sales a local option throughout Illinois.[52] Though at first intended to "exclude the sale of spiritus Liquors from said Town and within two miles there off," the ordinance passed in June, 1853, was meant only "to abate the sale of ardent spirits or intoxicating drinks." This ordinance was then amended the next year to allow the Corporation of Jacksonville to sell liquor, but only for "sacramental, chemical, mechanical, or medicinal purposes, and no other." An ordinance passed by the town board in 1855 broadened the range of sins and defined the town's moral perimeter: it banned within a two-mile limit any "billiard table, ball alley, tippling house, dram shop, gaming house, bawdy house or any other common ill governed and disorderly house, to the encouragement of idleness, gaming, drinking, fornication, or any other misbehavior."[53]

Despite its celebrated reputation as a temperate community, Jacksonville was by no means united on the prohibition issue. Most irksome to opponents of the new ordinance was the amendment allowing controlled liquor sales by the corporation itself. According to its opponents, this amendment was nothing more than a clever means of allowing liquor sales to "respectable gentlemen" who supposedly drank temperately in the privacy of their homes. The Democratic *Sentinel* reported sarcastically on the "Progress of Moral Reform in Jacksonville" and exposed the hypocrisy of the city fathers. "The gents could not do without their brandy, so these same temperance loving rulers [established] a corporation grocery. . . . This city grocery is a retail liquor shop, where even a child can get the liquor it wants in any quantity, and at almost any price." "Ikabob, Jr.," the Democrat's rustic spokesman from the countryside, also commented on the curious twist of the temperance movement in Jacksonville: "We found out from your paper that the tempurense men had kenstrewed this ordenense so that they coud have a Town Grosery and still be good tempurense men; and that it wasn't a komon grocery, neither, whare people could go and git drunk but an improved temperunse grosery, that sold

52. Cole, *Civil War*, pp. 207-10.
53. "Minutes, Town Board," Apr. 18, June 13, 1853; Dec. 24, 1854; Feb. 5, 1855.

only to respectibel men when they relly kneeded it."[54] Under heavy legal pressure the board ordered the "town grocery" closed in 1856, and Jacksonville embarked upon a policy of total prohibition.[55]

THE POLITICS OF TEMPERANCE

The temperance issue dominated local politics after the mid-1850s. Each spring factions for and against strict prohibition prepared for the municipal elections. On one level, the contest was between different strategies of encouraging temperance—a virtue that, in itself, no one publicly rejected. On a deeper level, the debate revolved around two different concepts of community. The anti-prohibition side insisted upon the liberty of individuals and minorities and on the sovereignty of traditional restraints of the church and family in all choices involving personal morality. In contrast, the prohibitionists insisted upon communal responsibility for personal moral standards to protect domestic virtue and to promote community progress.

Though Republicans enjoyed a majority of over 60 percent in Jacksonville throughout the 1860s, the party deliberately jettisoned temperance as a partisan issue. The Republican *Journal* was an undying champion of strict prohibition, but it continually argued that temperance was a bipartisan goal. "The ordinary division of political parties," insisted the *Journal* after a prohibition victory in 1860, "is always entirely waived, and the Democrat and Republican work hand in hand, for or against, the strict temperance issue, according as each is personally inclined."[56]

The Republican strategy was built upon local leaders' long-

54. *Sentinel*, May 11, June 15, 1855.

55. Ibid., June 15, 22, Nov. 2, 1855; Apr. 11, 1856; "Minutes, Town Board," Nov. 5, 12, 1855; May 5, 1856.

56. *Journal*, Apr. 5, 1860; Cole, *Civil War*, p. 208. See Paul Kleppner, *The Cross of Culture: A Social Analysis of Midwestern Politics, 1850-1900* (New York, 1970), and Richard Jensen, *The Winning of the Midwest: Social and Political Conflict, 1888-1896* (Chicago, 1971).

standing and rarely broken agreement that partisan politics should not be allowed to intrude upon local government. Parties were organized to promote state and national policies; local communities had their own internal goals of progress and improvement that partisan squabbles would only obstruct. Though slates of candidates were put forward by a citizens' caucus or by newspapers, party labels were almost never used. Editorial endorsements of the candidates stressed their worthiness in nonpartisan terms, as men who would "promote the interests of business, order and temperance." These endorsements also took pains to avoid a partisan appearance. The prohibition slate normally included at least one known Democrat among the five nominees, legitimizing the claim of bipartisan unity in municipal elections.[57]

Proponents of strict temperance linked the liquor question to ideals of community progress, family purity, and Christian pietism, values that appealed to Jacksonville's middle class regardless of party. Boosterism was an underlying motive of local reform even before the temperance issue became dominant. In an emerging frontier society, Jacksonville's image as a "quiet and orderly community" was essential to its effort to attract "respectable" families. As the home of several private and state institutions of education and charity, the community possessed a reputation for moral order which was especially vital to its economic health. The threat posed by the "monster of vices —intemperance," and all its attendant sins, could easily be linked to the overriding interest in Jacksonville's material progress. "The success of the town depends in no small degree upon that of her institutions," warned the *Journal* just before the 1864 town election. "Every blow aimed at the moral status of our town falls with equal weight upon it and our institutions of learning. . . . [and] hinders the march of progress to material wealth."[58]

Prohibition was also portrayed as an essential bulwark de-

57. See *Journal*, Mar. 22, 1860; *Sentinel*, Apr. 11, 1862. The turnout in town elections was normally 50-55%, judging from the polls reported in the late 1850s and 1860s; this was far below the level for openly partisan elections. The low turnout probably strengthened the hand of prohibitionists.

58. *Journal*, Mar. 31, 1864.

fending the family from debauchery and financial ruin. To a middle class increasingly sensitive to the value of protecting and educating its children, this notion of domestic purity had a special appeal. A license law, parents were warned, "would open the doors of vice and extend temptation to youth to enter and spend its evenings in the society of debauchees and idlers. The temptations are sufficiently great now. . . ." The insidious threat of liquor and vice was "creeping in our midst and coiling his slimy poisonous folds among the choicest of our young men, who are to form the character of the future millions."[59]

It was not enough for strong-willed men to pledge abstinence, for the saloon beckoned to unwitting youth and poisoned the moral health of the entire community. Temperance advocates continually reminded sympathizers of their larger responsibilities to the community: "their duty extends beyond the sobriety of themselves and their children. . . . It is not enough that you work by example alone. . . ." "Citizens," another alarming appeal warned, "there are a dozen demons in our midst enticing souls to hell, and making widows and orphans of our women and children."[60]

By placing the temperance issue on a lofty nonpartisan platform, alongside community progress and domestic purity, the prohibitionists reduced the risk of alienating important elements of the Republican coalition, particularly in the German and Portuguese populations. The opposition of Jacksonville's ethnic minorities to strict prohibition, already discussed, created tensions that checked the full force of the temperance crusade.

Democrats worked tirelessly to pull the temperance issue down into the contentious arena of partisan politics, and to force Republicans to stand openly behind their prohibitionist principles. But the Democrats were understandably cautious about running a straight party ticket in municipal elections. Instead, like their opponents, they worked mostly through

59. Ibid.; Yates, *Address, Sons of Temperance*, p. 5. See Bernard Wishy, *The Child and the Republic: The Dawn of Modern American Child Nurture* (Philadelphia, 1968).

60. *Journal*, Mar. 30, July 13, 1865. See Page Smith, *As a City upon a Hill: The Town in American History* (New York, 1966), pp. 145-56.

nonpartisan, ad hoc coalitions to lure disaffected Republicans into an anti-prohibition alliance. Without ever denying the virtue of temperance itself, the Democrats attacked strict prohibition as an infringement on personal liberty and as an upper-class, nativist assault upon foreign, lower-class, and rural citizens.

"The fact is," one opponent of prohibition argued early in the debate, "we are governed too much, both by State Legislatures and town corporations. The object of all governments should be to leave each individual governed, free to act as nature made him in all things touching his own interests, so long as those acts do not infringe upon the rights of others. . . ." "In attempting to promote the temperance cause," an editorial in the *Sentinel* stated, "its over-zealous advocates *may* trample upon the most sacred rights of the people. . . ."[61] The proper authority over personal morality was the family, whose sovereignty government should not violate. These were classic arguments in defense of personal liberties in a democratic society, and they confronted directly the prohibitionists' assumption that local leaders had the right (indeed, the duty) as Christian stewards to define moral standards for the entire community. The Democrats made a special promise to protect the drinking customs of Germans, Portuguese, and the "industrial classes" in general, and urged them to join in opposition to the "swell-head aristocrats" who set themselves up as the "censors of the morals of the community."[62]

Paralleling their defense of personal liberty, the Democrats argued the practical impossibility of enforcement. Prohibition laws, the *Sentinel* explained, "can only be enforced effectively where there is a unity of public sentiment in their favor, and where such a state of public sentiment exists there is little practical use for such restrictions." Indeed, prohibitionists admitted the difficulty of enforcement, but their response was to call for more repressive measures. "It is notorious that our laws are most shamefully violated," the *Journal* proclaimed at an early stage in the town's noble experiment. "The best interests of our

61. *Sentinel*, June 22, July 6, 1855.
62. Ibid., Apr. 3, 1863; Mar. 24, 1865; May 16, 1867.

young and growing city require that something should be done
to stamp the practice with the seal of public disapproval." At a
public meeting following this appeal in 1858, outraged citizens
organized a "Vigilance Committee." The town trustees passed a
more stringent prohibition enforcement ordinance and urged
the police to use the full force of the law against the violators.[63]
Newspapers reported police raids, fines, and confiscations of
liquor, but these acts testified as much to the tenacity of the
bootleggers as to the persistence of the prohibitionists. "It is
continually sold in a score of places all over the city," taunted
the *Sentinel*. "The truth is it is impossible to [enforce
prohibition]. . . . We may guide and control the traffic, but
we cannot obliterate it unless we first obliterate the appetite
of men."[64]

Prohibitionists replied that harsher laws, more police, and
more vigilant enforcement of the law were all that was required.
Would they "add hanging as an additional penalty?" asked the
Sentinel. Perhaps not many would, but the temperance crusad-
ers were willing to follow their "moral imperative" beyond the
limits of jail sentences and fines. In 1869 ardent temperance
men on the city council called out the fire department to douse
a reported blaze in a back alley "whiskey ranch." No fire was
found but, the *Journal* reported with obvious pleasure, the hoses
were turned on and "the shanty was washed out. . . . *Sic semper*
all such holes." The *Journal* applauded this show of force and
went on to recommend a "Temperance Military Company" be
formed to carry on "the prohibition war" against the saloons.[65]

Despite the best efforts of temperance advocates, saloons and
beer gardens continued to flourish. The *Journal* indignantly
reported incidents of drunkenness and violence that abounded
in the vice dens and urged the police on to more diligent
repression. The *Sentinel*, in reply, reiterated the futility of
"coercing men to be temperate" and harped on the expense
of enforcement. The costs of prohibition appeared not only

63. *Sentinel*, Apr. 11, 1862; *Journal*, Mar. 11, 1858; "Minutes, Town Board,"
Mar. 23, 1858.
64. *Sentinel*, May 20, 1861.
65. *Journal*, July 15, 1869; *Sentinel*, Apr. 5, Aug. 1, 8, 1867; July 16, 1869.

in police salaries and legal fees, but in the opportunity lost by refusing to sell licenses to saloonkeepers who operated regardless of the law. "The vote on the license question," argued the *Sentinel* in 1868, "was virtually, whether a revenue should be derived from the traffic, or whether it should go free." Efforts to collect fines from bootleggers had never been successful, and the court costs drained the city treasury further. In 1865 the town trustees tried to settle for half of all unpaid fines, but this only weakened the prohibitionist position still further.[66]

The practical advantages of the license system were tested in the spring of 1861, when an anti-prohibition alliance captured the town board. They campaigned for limited licensing of "malt liquor" sales which, they shrewdly argued, would reduce consumption of "ardent spirits." The license ticket also put together a slate with two Republicans who favored beer licenses and two Democrats who were also on the anti-license ticket (a common maneuver in Jacksonville elections). With a fifth candidate, also a Democrat, the narrow victory of the license ticket gave the Democrats a majority on the board. The new board passed an ordinance licensing all liquor, and, despite stringent provisions against drunkenness and sale of liquor to "habituated drunkards," Jacksonville became legally wet again. By the next election the *Sentinel* pointed proudly to the coffers of the town treasury, now over $3,400 richer from the license sales.[67]

The departure from prohibition only strengthened the resolve of the temperance advocates. Several disastrous fires during the year were claimed to be "traceable to the liquor traffic." The 1862 election saw a return to "unconditional Maine Law" prohibition, and future arguments questioning the capacity to enforce prohibition or the cost of foregoing licensing were refuted with new conviction: "If outlaws are determined to sell liquor, let them do it . . . without the consent of the good and law abiding and order-loving portion of the citizens of Jacksonville." Can license revenues buy back "character lost, reputation and prospects blighted and destroyed"? another *Journal* edito-

66. *Sentinel*, Sept. 4, 1868; "Minutes, Town Board," Feb. 22, 1865.
67. *Sentinel*, Mar. 8, 22, Apr. 5, 19, 1861; "Minutes, Town Board," Apr. 9, 17, 20, 1861; Apr. 4, 1862.

rial queried.[68] These arguments returned the temperance issue to high moral ground, where it could be defended without regard to practical questions of enforcement.

THE CITY FATHERS

The temperance issue tapped the community's social divisions at their deepest level. It strained political alliances within the Republican majority and created an ongoing stimulus to conflict that was vented openly in partisan newspapers. In a town that struggled valiantly to veil internal discord, the temperance issue still seemed to excite irrepressible emotions. We can learn far less about the opponents of strict temperance than we can about its advocates, for the latter almost always triumphed at the polls. Assuming the city fathers, as a group, represent the forces favoring moral government in Jacksonville, we can discover more about the social basis of the local temperance movement by examining these individuals more closely.

An enduring legend in Jacksonville's history is that New Englanders were the lonely champions of moral reform, whether it involved antislavery, education, or temperance. Table 18 (see Appendix) shows that more positions in town government were won by citizens who hailed from the Northeast after 1850, but this was due more to the presence of New Yorkers and Pennsylvanians than to New Englanders. The share of terms served by Southerners declined after 1850, but their numerical influence in local government remained impressive. Indeed, Southerners held a plurality (40 percent) of the terms served between 1850 and 1870. Whatever regional antagonisms festered in the community, the temperance issue united rather than divided northern and southern leaders.[69]

68. Eames, *Historic Morgan*, p. 184; *Journal*, Mar. 24, 31, 1864.
69. Daniel J. Elazar, *Cities of the Prairie: The Metropolitan Frontier and American Politics* (New York, 1970), pp. 151-363, attributes prohibition crusades to the "moralistic political culture" of the Yankee "stream of migration." I am not discounting entirely the importance of sectional political cultures at work in Jacksonville, but Elazar's model seems too static and fails to account for class interests, which I believe brought middle-class Yankees and Southerners together in towns like Jacksonville.

Uniting them, in part, was a common cultural heritage as native Americans and as Protestants; these bonds seemed to overcome sectional differences after 1850, as Jacksonville's foreign-born population grew. Before the introduction of the ward system in 1867 native-born Americans controlled local government with nary a challenge from the foreigners, except for British immigrants, like Alexander MacDonald, who were prominent local merchants. Although the Irish, German, and Portuguese made up nearly one-third of the voting population in the 1860s, they were effectively denied representation on the town board by a system of at-large elections.

The Democrats, speaking for the anti-prohibition forces, fought long and hard for a system of ward representation. Their strategy was to limit the influence of the "swell-head aristocrats" on College Hill and take advantage of neighborhood opposition to prohibition, especially in Madeira, the Irish Patch, and among German residents on the north and east sides of town. In 1857 and again in 1865 Democrats in the state legislature initiated charter amendments introducing ward government in Jacksonville, but each time they were struck down by "conservative law abiding citizens." "The division of the town into wards," one opponent warned, is "unnatural, unequal and inconvenient." "Morality, good order and the best interests of the young and our State Institutions require that there should be the utmost caution and deliberation in the matter."[70] Finally, in 1867, a frenzied boosters' campaign allowed local patriotism to override neighborhood jealousies. Jacksonville adopted a city charter—with ward government, a city school system, and broadened taxation powers—to establish its progressive image as a genuine city. The first election under the new charter assured temperance forces that they could maintain dominance. The Republicans put forward an explicitly partisan slate to mobilize their local majority against pro-license forces. Challenging them was a slate led by Democrats, who lured support from Republicans disaffected by Negro suffrage and prohibition, as well as from Republican "east enders" eager to strike back at the College Hill "radicals" who domi-

70. *Illinois Daily Journal* (Springfield), Feb. 9, 1857; *Sentinel*, Jan. 27, 1865.

nated the local party. The Republicans carried the day except in the First Ward, where Patch residents helped send a "wet" Irishman to the city council. Irish and German strength in the First Ward gave them four terms on the city council by 1870, but never sufficient strength to force official compromise on the prohibition policy.[71]

If moral government in Jacksonville was the manifestation of native Protestant victories in cultural contests, it was not the product of an oligarchy imposing its will upon social inferiors. Local government power was shared widely by a native middle class. Several stalwart trustees served a half-dozen or more terms over the years. Michael Rapp, a harnessmaker from Pennsylvania, served ten terms before 1870, including an unprecedented run of five consecutive years. Normally one, or perhaps two, incumbent trustees or aldermen carried on from one year to the next to provide continuity; the number of terms served by all officeholders averaged less than two. Local office was treated as a mildly burdensome duty to be undertaken without direct compensation by "public spirited citizens."

The middle class, from which Jacksonville's city fathers were drawn, included merchants, bankers, lawyers, and doctors, but it also embraced an impressive number of skilled laborers: carpenters, blacksmiths, brickmakers, and cabinetmakers. Indeed, as Table 19 shows, these skilled laborers enjoyed the largest share (45 percent) of all terms served in the 1850s and 1860s, when moral government was ascendant. Most of these skilled laborers were, in fact, prosperous shopkeepers with substantial wealth; their occupational titles often belied their essentially middle-class stature. Many were also moving up into business occupations, or at least changing their titles to reflect their social aspirations.

Most city fathers had a deep material stake in the community. They came largely from the small portion of the population that could claim property, and their wealth in land far exceeded the average. (See Table 20A.) They also came from the small core of the community that persisted from one decade to the next. (See Table 20B.) Their commitment to Jacksonville was handsomely

71. *Sentinel*, Feb. 21, Mar. 7, 14, 28, Apr. 4, May 16, 1867.

rewarded with gains in landed wealth that greatly outstripped those of other persistent property-owners. Here were men who brought to local government a genuine interest in Jacksonville's future, whose efforts to expand fire control, water service, and schools served their aspirations as upward-striving town boosters.

The temperance crusade was undoubtedly a manifestation of this material investment in Jacksonville's future as a center of education and state charity, but it also emanated from middle-class domestic values which most of the city fathers shared. (See Table 21.) Officeholders were almost all in their thirties or forties, married, with three or more children. While there are several reasons why such men would likely be elected to office, in the context of the temperance crusade their family status takes on another importance. Powerful themes of domesticity pervaded the rhetoric of temperance reform throughout the nineteenth century. Threats to domestic virtue came from all directions: the drunken father pulling his wife and children into poverty and ruin; the innocent son or daughter seduced by liquor or one of its attendant vices; the saloon—the antithesis of domesticity—luring the husband away from the family hearth. The temperance crusade became more than a negation of the saloon and liquor; it was an affirmation of a larger middle-class ethos of domesticity, self-control, social mobility, and public order.

In this sense temperance was, as Joseph Gusfield has argued, a symbolic crusade that rallied the middle class (and those who aspired to it) around an ethos of respectability, hard work, and self-improvement.[72] Even if the effect of Jacksonville's noble experiment in prohibition was as much symbolic as it was practical, the temperance movement provided a logical rationale for the expansion of public authority over the moral behavior of the community. And, within certain limitations of police enforcement and political expediency, this authority gave the city fathers a powerful instrument with which to project their values of moral order upon those who chose not to embrace them voluntarily.

72. Gusfield, *Symbolic Crusade*; *Journal*, Mar. 11, 1858.

Residence of F. G. Farrell, cashier at the First National Bank, 605 West State Street. The homes on College Hill were vital symbols of the prosperity and gentility their owners had acquired. This, and the following eleven illustrations, are from *Morgan County Atlas* (Chicago, 1872).

Residence of C. D. Miller, capitalist, West State Street.

Residence of Mat Stacy, insurance agent and former saddle-maker, Clay Avenue.

Residence of E. M. Sanford, attorney, Clay Avenue.

Residence of D. M. Simmons, merchant of groceries and dry goods, 661 East College Street.

Residence of George M. McConnel, banker, corner of State and Caldwell Streets.

The old homestead of Jacob Strawn, Sr., the "Cattle King," east of Jacksonville.

Residences of James M. Epler, attorney, College Avenue (left), and David Epler, West-minster Street.

Residence of I. J. Ketcham, attorney, Diamond Street.

Young Ladies Atheneum, opened 1864.

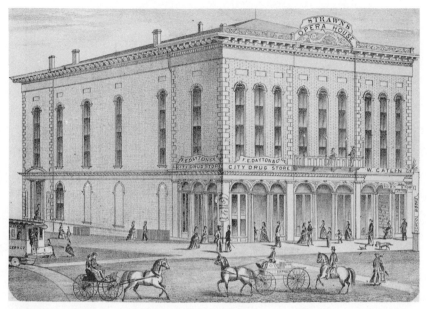

Strawn's Opera House, erected 1861.

Gallaher's block and the Masonic Hall, West State Street.

Localism as Nationalism

> We were evidently in need of some vigorous disci-
> pline. The element of reverence for rightful authority
> was slipping out of the national mind. Our young
> men were beginning to feel that all authority is des-
> potism, all government tyranny, and all submission
> and obedience servility.
>
> —JULIAN STURTEVANT[1]

FOR MOST PEOPLE, Jacksonville was little more than a place
through which diverse streams of migration constantly
flowed. The boosters' ethos of local pride and collective progress checked the tensions of antagonistic cultures and personalities, but it could do little to integrate disinterested transients. Amid the ever-changing population, the social order was
defined by a set of institutions that governed small and large
units within the community. The family and household struc-

---

1. *The Lessons of Our National Conflict: Address to the Alumni of Yale College, July 24, 1861*
(New Haven, 1861), reprinted in *New Englander* 17 (1861): 894-912. Robert H. Wiebe,
The Search for Order, 1877-1920 (New York, 1967), pp. 44-75, has informed my approach in this chapter. Wiebe's concept of the "island community" has been misunder-
stood by those who blandish evidence of geographic mobility and economic ties to the
larger society—e.g., Stephan Thernstrom and Peter R. Knights, "Men in Motion: Some
Data and Speculations about Urban Population Mobility in Nineteenth-Century
America," *Journal of Interdisciplinary History* 1 (1970): 32. Wiebe is describing the
nineteenth-century *perception* that power was located and status defined within the
context of local society before the organization of occupational interest groups on a
national scale in the Progressive era; he is not saying that "island communities" were
actually isolated or self-contained in demographic or economic terms. There is some
evidence to qualify Wiebe's concept as it applies to Jacksonville, but I accept his main
point: cultural perceptions, and not just objective structural conditions, defined the
localism of the "island community."

ture provided the basic unit of organization. Dozens of formal voluntary institutions created a multitude of little societies, each bound in a Lockean compact of common goals and group discipline. Municipal government enlarged its authority beyond the pale of voluntary organization and family authority to define a community standard of moral behavior; however, the city fathers' very efforts to enforce that standard revealed the limits of consensus in a pluralistic community.

Above the contentious rancor of factional conflict, above the diversity of cultures, and above the institutional units of association, Jacksonville's citizens discovered a rare sense of unity in the celebration of national pride and purpose. Nationalism, an abstract emotional tie to the larger society, became concrete experience with the coming of the railroads and the eruption of the Civil War. Still, one of the principal social functions of nationalism was performed within a purely local context. Nationalism was capable of producing a badly needed adhesive for a disparate community.

The Local Uses of Nationalism

Patriotism was constantly displayed in political speeches and local newspapers, but the public celebrations of the Fourth of July, and to a lesser extent Washington's Birthday, became important community rituals of nationalism. Usually the Fourth of July began with a procession; citizens gathered on the public square and marched through the streets to martial tunes of a loud brass band, finally arriving at the grove west of town where the county fairgrounds stood by the late 1850s. A citizens' committee was usually appointed well in advance to prepare the "Order of the Day" and lead the procession. Out at the fairgrounds a barbecue was served; local tradition required that "burgoo stew" be included in the menu. Made with squirrel meat, beef soup bone, pickled pork, canned oysters, and vegetables, all cooked for hours until it thickened, Morgan County's famous burgoo lent a peculiar local flavor to the festivities of the Fourth.[2] Traditionally the Declaration of Independence was read aloud before the citizens broke bread. After the meal a

2. *Sentinel*, July 8, 1870.

long-winded patriotic speech by a local politician gave way to a series of toasts by eminent citizens, each of whom testified to the greatness of their state and nation, and to their own patriotism.[3]

From its beginning as an official national holiday, the Fourth of July was, in many American communities, an occasion for drunken revelry, fighting, and partisan feuding. Jacksonville's newspapers issued repeated warning against defiling this day of national honor. In a pattern that mirrored the evolution of the community itself, Jacksonville's Fourth of July celebrations became the object of concerted attempts to impose virtues of organization, discipline, and sobriety. The *Western Observer* applauded the arrangements committee in charge of the 1830 festivities "for the harmony & good order which prevailed throughout the celebration." Prior to that year, full glasses of wine or other liquor had been consumed for every toast—a practice that must have left few standing in praise of their country after all had volunteered their patriotic tributes. In 1830, however, only the president and vice-president of the day drank from their glasses, "and then but sparingly." A celebration that had previously invited "riot and drunkenness throughout our land" could now be attended by good Christians.[4]

By 1843 the "friends of temperance" organized their own separate celebration of the Fourth, sponsored by the Washingtonians and joined by Illinois College faculty, students, and other business and professional men. In place of "bloody music, the barbarous shouts, and the drunken revels," one witness reported a sentimental scene with the "glistening eyes of thronging infants, the heaving breasts and anxious hearts of mothers . . . leading their little ones to swear them anew on the alter of liberty and of God, so accordant with the true spirit of the anniversary hour of a nation's birth."[5] In other years disagreements over the proper character of Jacksonville's Fourth

3. See Stuart Blumin, *The Urban Threshold: Growth and Change in a Nineteenth-Century American Community* (Chicago, 1976), pp. 32-33, 156-57, and Fletcher Melvyn Green, "Listen to the Eagle Scream: One Hundred Years of the Fourth of July in North Carolina, 1776-1876," in Green, *Democracy in the Old South and Other Essays* (Nashville, 1969), pp. 111-56.

4. *Western Observer*, July 5, 10, 1830.

5. *Illinois Statesman*, July 3, 19, 1843.

of July prevented a procession and barbecue from being organized at all. Many went off to the more raucous celebrations in the rural environs to enjoy their burgoo along with plenty of raw liquor.[6] "Each person will probably celebrate the day by amusing himself on 'his own hook,'" lamented one patriot in 1856. "Alas! What a falling off from the olden time, when the soldiers paraded in their flashy uniforms, their guilt buttons and glittering equipments; . . . and little boys gloried in fire crackers, paper soldier caps, wooden swords and mimic martial revolutions. . . ."[7]

These fond memories were revived in a "glorious Fourth of July" celebration held in 1858. Springfield's citizens, led by the Young American Band and Pioneer Fire Company, were invited to attend, as though to signify that patriotism superseded even the boosters' jealous rivalries. The Springfield entourage arrived by train at six in the morning and assembled with Jacksonville's citizens in front of the Mansion House Hotel on the square; there they were instructed as to the "Order of the Day." The procession was carefully arranged: the city marshals of the day, Stephen Dunlap and Alexander McDonald, handsomely robed in red silk and mounted on horseback, led the parade. The president and vice-presidents of the day followed in a carriage along with the orator of the day, Richard Yates. Beside him sat political enemy John McConnel, displaying bipartisan unity for the day. Another carriage of honored guests, including Abraham Lincoln of Springfield, followed and later shared the platform with Yates and McConnel. Next, Jacksonville's Union Band and Fire Company, dressed in their splendid new uniforms, played martial tunes to accompany the marchers; four black horses pulled their engine, the "Water Witch." Following were the Springfield fire company and band and Jacksonville's Rescue Fire Company No. 2, who also proudly displayed their engine, "Red Rover." Each fraternal society, including the Masonic and Odd Fellows lodges, marched as units in the procession. Behind them were the local German Turnverein and the German Band. The Sons of Tem-

6. *Sentinel*, Aug. 11, 1855; July 11, 1856.
7. Ibid., June 27, 1856.

perance and Templars formed the next unit, marching in sober order to the festive music. Finally came those who did not fit into one of the assorted marching units: "the thronging thousands, both in order and out of order, followed in the wake." Even among this latter group there was a planned order of procession, for pedestrians were allowed to march ahead of citizens in carriages and on horseback.[8]

The mile-long procession followed a prepared route from the square through the east part of town, back to the square, and out West State Street to the new fairgrounds. There all joined in a simple meal of burgoo and bread and listened to a patriotic speech by Richard Yates. Later they applauded a demonstration by the Turners, and in the afternoon watched in amazement as a man ascended in a balloon. A fireworks display that evening capped off the festivities. The Springfield contingent took their leave by nine o'clock to return home by train. "We left the citizens of Jacksonville," wrote the Springfield editor, "shooting, shouting, hurrahing, sweating and rejoicing over the well spent pleasures of the day."[9]

These were simple pleasures, but they allowed a divided people, and even two rival towns, to join in common commitment. The patriotic ideals. being celebrated were ones to which all could pay allegiance. As one citizen explained it, the Fourth of July offered a rare occasion for a segmented community to "meet yearly on the same broad basis of liberty and equality."[10] The strict organization of the procession and the segregation of Irish and German celebrations in the 1860s belied the claims of egalitarian communion on the Fourth, but the nationalism generated by these celebrations did indeed provide an important community bond. They may have served as only a thin plaster over a divided society, but such public rituals of patriotism had a wonderful cosmetic effect on internal fractures. Though an element of rowdy behavior persisted, these celebrations were generally praised in local newspapers for their harmonious order and martial regimentation.

8. *Journal*, July 1, 1858; *Illinois State Journal* (Springfield), July 6, 1858.

9. *Illinois State Journal* (Springfield), July 6, 1858.

10. *Sentinel*, Aug. 16, 1855.

The Fourth of July procession was the perfect symbol of Jacksonville's new social order: always moving, yet organized in formal units, governed by elected officers, joined voluntarily, and bound loosely by a common allegiance to vague values of nationalism.[11] It was as though social order could only be found in formally organized and carefully controlled settings, with clearly recognized figures of authority and well-defined membership and rules.

This pursuit of a formalized social order, evident also in the churches and voluntary associations, found its ultimate expression in the organization of Jacksonville's militia companies. Local militias had been part of the community since the Black Hawk War in the early 1830s.[12] By 1860 three new military companies formed by the young men of Jacksonville were greeted with hearty praise. "We are glad to see a military spirit among the young men of the place, and hope that by judicious management and wise councils they may be able to sustain the companies now being formed to be a source of healthful pleasure to themselves and an ornament to the city." "Let us now have a brass band and an artillery squad," continued the *Journal* editor, "and we can treat the Fourth of July and other Gala days, with all due respect and pomp of circumstance."[13] The young men who conceived these militia companies as "ornaments" to the pageantry of patriotic rituals would soon march off to war, many of them to be slaughtered in defense of the remote concept of nationalism that they had previously celebrated with such gaiety.

JACKSONVILLE VOLUNTEERS FOR WAR

When war came, it was immediately interpreted as a call for local unity and cooperation. Even as it pulled the community

11. Cf. Thernstrom and Knights, "Men in Motion," p. 34: "American society . . . was more like a procession than a stable social order. How did this social order cohere at all?"

12. *Gazette and News*, Sept. 28, 1837; *Illinoian*, Jan. 27, Feb. 17, 1838; "Jacksonville Cavalry and Light Artillery, Minutes," MSS in Illinois State Historical Library, Springfield. See also John L. McConnel, *Western Characters* (New York, 1853), for an amusing sketch of the western militia.

13. *Journal*, Mar. 29, 1860.

into the larger context of national purpose, the war seemed to intensify parochialism. All Union victories were celebrated, but the key role of "Jacksonville's boys" excited the most interest in local newspapers. Now more than ever, national events could be used to explain the causes of economic hardship and poverty in the community; however, these were still interpreted as local problems. In a curious way this intense localism seemed to absorb a growing sense of nationalism, rather than being subsumed by it.

On the evening of April 15, the day the Confederate guns fired on Fort Sumter, Jacksonville's citizens crowded into the new Strawn Opera House to hear their political leaders dedicate the community to war. The meeting was organized "without distinction of party," and both Republican and Democratic leaders addressed the crowd in a carefully balanced program. Each stressed the need for bipartisan support of the Union. "There is no difference of opinion in Jacksonville in reference to the necessity of sustaining the national flag," the Democratic editor summarized. Two military companies were raised with volunteers who enlisted following the mass meeting. "War spirit has been up to the highest notch among our citizens," reported one observer a few days later. "Every day the fife and drum has been heard," and large crowds of townspeople milled about the square, awaiting the latest news over the telegraph.[14]

By the end of May, 1861, Illinois soldiers under the command of an unknown general, Ulysses S. Grant, were encamped at the same fairgrounds that had witnessed so many festive celebrations of nationalism. The women of Jacksonville translated the national crisis into a mission of Christian charity by baking pies and bread and sewing clothes which they delivered to "Camp Duncan" each day. Organized at first through their separate churches, the women quickly formed an independent voluntary organization and later merged with the Sanitary Commission, Christian Commission, and Ladies Loyal League.[15]

14. *Sentinel*, Apr. 19, 1861; Aug. 15, 1862.
15. Ibid., May 13, June 16, July 5, 1861; see also Julia Duncan to Mrs. Putnam, Jacksonville, May 30, 1861; Apr. 18, 1863; Duncan Family Papers, Illinois State Historical Library, Springfield.

In the spring the first two companies of Jacksonville's own young soldiers departed for Springfield with all the ceremony due the occasion. On Sunday, April 26, a community religious service was held in Strawn Opera House, with the volunteers seated prominently in front. The audience in the packed hall listened quietly as Jacksonville's Philharmonic Society played "America," and Professor Sanders of Illinois College delivered a reverent patriotic speech. A second meeting held later that same evening was addressed by prominent clergymen and community leaders. Marshall Ayers, a wealthy Republican banker, made a charitable plea that citizens not persecute their southern neighbors in Jacksonville "who were probably loyal to the Union, but yet held sympathies for the southern people." Enthusiastic applause insured that his appeal to tolerance would be heeded, for a time at least.[16]

By July, 1861, a third company of Jacksonville volunteers was raised under George McConnel and sent to Cairo to help suppress the threat of secession in southern Illinois. The Portuguese also formed a company and paraded proudly through the streets with their new uniforms and rifles. Germans, Irish, and blacks joined their compatriots in Missouri, Illinois, and Massachusetts to fight to save the Union.[17]

As the war dragged on, the continual call for soldiers strained the faith in voluntary military service. In the summer of 1862, under the threat of a conscription bill in Congress, $5,000 in county funds was put up as bounty for volunteers; this would allow $50 for each recruit. An enthusiastic public "war meeting" on the square brought $1,000 more in private donations to sweeten the pot for Jacksonville volunteers. Local doctors and pharmacists even offered free medical care and drug prescriptions to the families of soldiers. As the bounties piled higher, young men streamed into the Union Army; by the end of March, 1862, nearly 650 brave sons of Jacksonville had enlisted.[18]

16. *Sentinel*, Apr. 26, 1861.
17. Ibid., July 5, 26, 1861; Arthur Charles Cole, *The Era of the Civil War, 1848-1870*, The Centennial History of Illinois, vol. 3 (Springfield, 1919), pp. 281-82.
18. Cole, *Civil War*, pp. 275-76; *Sentinel*, July 25, Aug. 1, 1862; Jan. 1, 1863.

After a conscription act was passed in March, 1863, Jacksonville worked furiously to keep ahead of its quotas by attracting volunteers. With generous offers of bounties, family benefits, and carefully organized recruiting rallies, Jacksonville managed to avoid what most saw as the disgrace of requiring a draft.[19] By the war's end the increasing threat of conscription had pressed the community to new efforts at recruiting volunteers. Although a series of well-attended public meetings and benefit performances yielded some $20,000 in private donations to lure new volunteers, by the winter of 1865 the individual bounty had climbed to $500, and these funds recruited only 40 of Jacksonville's quota of 113.[20] Cautious donors now invested in draft insurance policies to pay for substitutes should they be called up. With conscription appearing imminent, a flourishing business in procuring such substitutes quickly appeared in Jacksonville. The town board responded by passing a new ordinance requiring substitute brokers to purchase licenses at the prohibitive fee of $2,000.[21] Volunteer recruitment efforts were redoubled at continual war meetings. "We must have no draft in Jacksonville," pleaded the *Journal* after pointing to the town's proud record of voluntary service. Happily, the events at Appomattox rescued Jacksonville from the shame of having to carry out the draft.[22]

THE WAR AT HOME

As the war transformed vague ideas of nationalism into the concrete experience of sacrifice and death, the community's patriotic ardor at first became all the more intense. The first wartime Fourth of July was celebrated with unprecedented scale and grandeur. A huge procession began unusually early to take full advantage of the day. To neutralize the possibility of

19. *Journal*, Dec. 24, 1863; Feb. 18, Sept. 1, 1864; Cole, *Civil War*, pp. 275-78.

20. *Journal*, Feb. 9, 16, 1865; *Sentinel*, Feb. 10, 17, 1865. The Tenth District, in which Jacksonville was located, was subject to conscription beginning in October, 1864; Cole, *Civil War*, pp. 278-79.

21. *Sentinel*, Feb. 3, 10, 17, 1865; *Journal*, Feb. 9, 16, 1865; "Minutes, Town Board," Feb. 7, 1865.

22. *Journal*, Feb. 9, 1865.

partisanship on this solemn occasion of national unity, all public toasts were this time given by the official reader of toasts. But feelings ran strong, and partisan appeals were difficult to repress. When a long toast "To the Grave of Douglas" was read, complete with extracts from the Little Giant's most memorable speeches, some Republicans began to shift their feet. Their turn came in another toast, "No Compromise with Traitors," the double meaning of which was hardly lost on local Democrats and Southerners.[23]

Behind the veil of patriotic union, sectional tensions flared over the war and its purpose. Pro-southern students at Illinois College lampooned the Home Guard in the fall of 1861, parading about the square with coats inside out, sticks over their shoulders, stovepipe hats, a banner, and brass horn. When some of their classmates proposed to deliver an anti-abolitionist commencement speech in June, 1862, their professor cautiously forbade it; students who protested found their diplomas withheld. Outraged Southerners and sympathetic Democrats gave the students a public forum by renting Strawn Opera House and inviting the public to attend. A student's speech against abolitionism and censorship at the college drew "rapturous applause" from a large audience, according to indignant editorial commentary in the Democratic press.[24]

The antiwar movement took a more militant form in the rural environs. Copperhead southern sympathizers in Illinois organized a secret political society, the Knights of the Golden Circle, even before the war broke out. Its stronghold was in "Egypt" (the popular label for southern Illinois), but pro-Southerners in all parts of the state joined as the war continued, and the nightmare of treason and civil strife came home to Jacksonville. "We had hopes," the *Journal* lamented in March, 1863, "that no such wicked clans of oath-bound, incipient traitors would pollute the air and soil of Morgan County." Within a week the *Journal* issued the alarm: "the Copperheads

23. *Sentinel*, June 28, July 19, 1861.
24. *Sentinel*, Nov. 22, 1861; Charles H. Rammelkamp, "The Reverberations of the Slavery Conflict in a Pioneer College," *Mississippi Valley Historical Review* 14 (1928): 456-57.

are arming." It reported "an extraordinary call for Colts' Revolvers, for knives, guns, buckshots," among the "rabid Copperheads from the rural districts." That fall the *Journal* began accusing Jacksonville Democrats of active sympathy for the Knights of the Golden Circle, claiming that at least one-third of the party belonged to the Knights' "castle" at nearby Woodson.[25]

In September, 1863, heavily armed Knights some two to four hundred strong swarmed into Jacksonville and swaggered about the square. Their mission was to rescue their leader, John Husted, who had assaulted an informant on the Knights at Jacksonville's railroad station and was being held in jail. They arrived the morning of Husted's trial and claimed that another thousand armed horsemen lay waiting at Mauvaise Terre Creek, ready to attack unless they received assurances that Husted would be given a fair trial and would not be bound over to military authorities.

Jacksonville's Republicans anticipated violence. They had already organized their own secret society, the Union League, as part of a statewide organization that gathered intelligence on Copperhead activities and compiled lists with names of suspected anti-Unionists. Union League members in Jacksonville devised a secret alarm: two quick raps repeated three times with a cane on the sidewalk warned of imminent danger. Just a month before the "Husted Raid," Quantrill and his guerilla raiders had sacked Lawrence, Kansas, and murdered many of its citizens. The morning of John Husted's trial the streets of Jacksonville echoed with the repeated warning taps of anxious Union Leaguers. Bank clerks on the square strapped on pistols to warn away the raiders; the *Journal* office, twice burned out by anti-Republican arsonists, barricaded its doors. A telegram was sent to nearby Camp Butler for army support, and orders were given to bring out repeating rifles to defend the town. Inside the courthouse Husted's trial proceeded hastily. He was bound over to circuit court under a $500 bond, and his militant defenders out on the square returned home satisfied that they had secured justice. The *Journal* editor denounced the Copperheads for

25. *Journal*, Mar. 12, Sept. 10, 1863; Cole, *Civil War*, pp. 308-9.

"inducing a sort of semi-reign of terror amongst the Union men here," and then boasted, "the Knights of the Golden Circle scared nobody. . . . Jacksonville still lives."[26]

Tensions generated by the war soon disrupted the celebrations of the very nationalism it was fought to defend. After the elaborate 1861 Fourth of July ceremony, the 1862 holiday found Jacksonville unable to organize even the most routine procession. "No general arrangements have been made for celebrating the day in this city," reported the *Sentinel*, "but the citizens will probably scatter and each enjoy the holiday occasion in his own way." For the first time separate Irish and German celebrations were arranged at picnic grounds outside of town. This, of course, was partly a function of the local temperance issue, but it also reflected the inability of nationalism to overcome internal factionalism during the war.

The next year a committee met nearly a month in advance to plan a traditional community procession and barbecue; however, the meeting broke up when Democrats, according to the partisan account in the *Journal*, "tried to foist upon us" men of "doubtful loyalty" to serve on the arrangements committee. Two separate committees later met to plan their own partisan celebrations; they came together to settle their "unhappy differences" two weeks before the day. A bipartisan committee was appointed and a new program agreed upon, but by the Fourth the alliance had dissolved in bickering. The Republicans met in their own "Union Yankee" celebration at Salem church, east of town; the Irish "celebrated the day in their own peculiar way" out at the fairgrounds; the Germans met at Bacon's Grove; and, the *Journal* snidely added, the Copperheads had their own meeting somewhere nearby.[27]

When the Republicans returned to town after a long day of festivities, some gathered on the square. After a few spontaneous partisan harangues, they decided to cap off the day's festivities by harassing local Copperheads. A band of Republican

26. *Journal*, Sept. 17, 1865; Jay Monahgan, "Morgan County's Dog Fennel War: An Account of the Cass County Invasion of Jacksonville in 1863," *JISHS* 39 (1946): 447-58; J. N. Gridley, "The Husted or Jacksonville Raid," *JISHS* 5 (1912): 207-11.

27. *Journal*, June 22, 25, July 2, 9, 1863.

patriots ran through the dark streets shrieking "demoniac yells" and then gathered outside the home of P. B. Price, a prominent Democrat. They called Price outside, shouted accusations of treason, and, according to the *Sentinel*'s account, made "loud threats of hanging him, tearing down his house, etc." The police intervened before the mob got out of hand, but this was neither the first nor the last time Union patriots would threaten with their own "ruffianly raids." Soon after the Fourth an antiwar Democrat named J. T. Springer was rudely awakened from his sleep when a large mob outside his home invited him to join them in celebrating the Union victory at Vicksburg.[28]

In 1864 the Fourth passed again with "no united movement . . . for the 'due celebration of the fourth' in this city in the old fashioned style." Then, as the war drew to a close in the spring of 1865, there was cathartic rejoicing in Jacksonville. Early reports of the Confederate defeat proved premature, and "heartless copperheads" jeered the Union celebrants. When news of Richmond's fall finally came, an enormous crowd gathered spontaneously on the square. Immediately a group of Jacksonville's "enterprising citizens" huddled by the courthouse to design a "programme for the occasion," but the excitement of the crowd proved beyond their capacity to organize. The *Journal* reported the scene with a mixture of fascination and fear: "Ere any definite arrangements could be agreed upon the enthusiastic multitude becoming wild with joy, broke forth in the most indescribable demonstrations of uproarious, wild almost frantic enthusiasm, setting at defiance all efforts at system, order or arrangements." On through the afternoon and evening the demonstration continued entirely on its own momentum. Flags were displayed, fireworks and guns exploded, boys "and even men" ran through the streets with bells, tin pans, and horns, "rivalling Pandemonium in the noise and confusion they made." By the afternoon the Jacksonville Silver Coronet Band played loudly, the Home Guards paraded, businesses closed, and the courts adjourned. That evening Chinese lanterns illuminated the festivities as the crowd listened to a series of speeches by local politicos, and "many still held revel in various

28. *Sentinel*, July 10; cf. Aug. 6, 1863.

parts of the city till after midnight." With Lee's surrender a few days later, Jacksonville's citizens were far too exhausted to repeat their orgy of patriotism. A few stalwart young patriots loaded an old cannon with a wad of paper and blasted it across the square through a drugstore window. They then carefully turned it around and sent another load through a window of Marshall Ayers's Bank.[29]

"Cannot we, as one people, forgetting parties and past differences unite on this occasion, kiss the old flag and give it anew to the free winds of a brightly dawning Spring?" Thus queried the Republican editor at war's end. The spirit of patriotic unity did seem to come alive again; a bipartisan committee of arrangements formed as early as May 22 to prepare for the first community Fourth of July celebration since 1861. But the reconciliation was premature. Radical Republicans insisted that only "loyal citizens" be allowed to celebrate the Fourth, and on June 3 they called a new meeting to arrange a "loyal" Fourth of July. Voices of moderation prevailed at the meeting, though, and a new bipartisan committee was appointed. The Radicals, still unsatisfied, called yet another meeting, appointed their own committee of arrangements, and pressured fellow Republicans to withdraw from the bipartisan committee.[30]

A community about to celebrate the end of the Civil War and the anniversary of the Union seemed unable to overcome its own internal divisions; by mid-June, however, the spirit of nationalism managed to subsume all the partisan insults and bickering. The two feuding committees each sent out negotiators "with a view to the conciliation of the unhappy differences that had arisen in the public mind in relation to a grand celebration of the 4th of July." A new committee, formed "solely to harmonize the citizens of Morgan," planned a celebration that would smother any remaining differences in the largest and most elaborate pageant ever. Representatives from every precinct in the county were invited to participate in this display of unity. Colonel James Dunlap, a Democrat of southern

29. *Journal*, Apr. 6, 13, 1865; *Sentinel*, Apr. 7, 1865.
30. *Journal*, Mar. 2, June 8, 1865; *Sentinel*, June 2, 16, 1865.

background, was generously awarded the post of president of the day. No less than thirty-two vice-presidents shared the honors. Eight subcommittees were assigned special responsibilities for everything from financing to music and toasts; over them an Executive Committee coordinated plans. Altogether nearly fifty committeemen were involved in this elaborate demonstration of community organization.

The various committees arranged special trains to transport the country folk into town to celebrate the Union's birthday, and detailed plans were made to coordinate the ritual procession through town to the fairgrounds. O. D. Fitzsimmons, chief marshal of the day, was assisted by seventeen assistant marshals and military officers to regulate the enormous crowds. By eight in the morning the procession began to form; soldiers and veterans were placed conspicuously toward the front, behind the officers of the day. Delegations from each section of the town and county were instructed in advance about where to assemble, and at the signal of cannon fire they merged into the procession and marched to the fairgrounds, where the band greeted them with a rousing version of "Rally Round the Flag." There "a united people . . . without distinction of party, policy or place" joined to eat and "to rejoice on that most fitting day together over . . . an undivided and indivisible country."

The crowd, estimated at fifteen to twenty thousand, amassed at the fairgrounds to hear a full day of readings, toasts, and long speeches by politicians, all carefully prepared to maintain the nonpartisan spirit of unity. Lemonade, ice cream, and beer were served, along with the traditional burgoo. Underlining the frivolity of the day, an incredible Wild West exhibition was staged in the late afternoon. Posters tacked up all over the county had promised a genuine buffalo hunt by "wild Indians." As it turned out, the crowd was too large and unwieldy to risk an actual bow and arrow kill of a loose buffalo; nevertheless, people seemed satisfied with a brief Indian war dance and an exhibition of the beast. Buffaloes and burgoo were far better at inspiring patriotic unity than were civil wars.[31]

31. *Sentinel*, June 30, July 7, 1865.

THE REVIVAL OF BOOSTERISM

"We are a homogeneous people," wrote the *Sentinel* editor during the 1865 Fourth of July imbroglio, "and for good or ill our interests are blended. Men of both parties naturally commingle in trade and business, and all are benefitted."[32] The familiar themes of unity and progress found new voice at the end of the war, reaching a crescendo of boosterism by 1867. The very forces of war, politics, and railroads that pulled Jacksonville toward the larger society at the same time intensified a parochial obsession with local improvement.

The town newspapers, always vocal organs of boosterism, now turned inward more than before. The *Sentinel*'s new 1866 prospectus explained that the paper intended to devote "special attention to local news noticing the progress of improvements in the city and advocating generally the local interests of Jacksonville and Morgan County." That same year the *Journal* became Jacksonville's first daily, and it hired a separate editor solely to report local news. "With nearly ten thousand inhabitants, very many wealthy citizens, a thoroughly wide-awake and enterprising business population," the *Journal* proclaimed, "we believe a Daily paper is indispensable."[33] Not only did the newspapers of the 1860s devote increasing space to local affairs; in addition, they reported items formerly left to parlor gossip and the streetcorner grapevine. Reports of weekly real estate sales, new homes under construction, travel plans of prominent citizens, and arrests of those less prominent all reflected a growing interest in the local scene and, perhaps, a certain distance from things once known without newspapers.

Underlying the renewed interest in local affairs was an increasing concern over Jacksonville's future. Initially the war had devastating effects on the local economy; it pulled nearly 3,000 of the town's young men into service and burdened the public with enormous increases in taxes and living expenses. Illinois College, already torn by sectional discord, watched its dwindling student body march off to war and nearly decided to close. The credit system collapsed across the state, the Morgan

32. Ibid., June 2, 1865.
33. Ibid., Mar. 9, 1866; *Journal*, Mar. 22, Apr. 14, 1866.

County Bank failed, and merchants required strict cash payments as the entire economy retrenched.[34]

By the end of the second year of war, the increased demand for Morgan County beef and woolens began to pay handsome dividends. The "cattle kings," Jacob Strawn and John T. Alexander, led Illinois' sudden rise to first rank as a stock-raising state in the 1860s. By 1862 half of the 165 million pounds of beef entering the New York City market came from Illinois, and Morgan County led the state. With the Texas cattle trade shut off by the war, beef prices rose, and Morgan County stock men worked furiously to keep up with Union demand for meat.[35]

Jacob Strawn's prosperous cattle business made him a major figure in Jacksonville. The Strawn Opera House, which he erected in 1861, became a focal point of the community. As the host of touring symphonies, lectures, and theater, the opera house, with its imposing architectural presence on the south side of the square, symbolized the genteel life that Jacksonville's middle class had so proudly nurtured over the years.

By the time of Strawn's death at the end of the war, the growing influence of this self-made man was a measure of Jacksonville's changing economic base.[36] After the war Morgan County's livestock trade continued to flourish, soon attracting complementary industries including a new stockyard, meat-packing factory, and tannery. Chicago would later usurp Jacksonville's role in meat processing, but throughout the 1860s this industry remained an important and growing component of the town's changing economy.[37]

The Union Army's demand for blankets and clothing helped give new life to Jacksonville's woolen industries as well. Joseph Capps and Sons outgrew their modest factory; by 1864 the firm

34. *Sentinel*, Apr. 5, 1861; Mar. 28, 1862; Cole, *Civil War*, pp. 362, 368; Ernest G. Hildner, *Jacksonville: A Survey of Its Past* (Jacksonville, 1960), p. 11; Rammelkamp, "Slavery Conflict," pp. 456, 459.

35. Paul W. Gates, "Cattle Kings in the Prairies," *Mississippi Valley Historical Review* 35 (1948): 383-86, 402; Cole, *Civil War*, pp. 376-77; Clarence P. McClelland, "Jacob Strawn and John T. Alexander: Central Illinois Stockmen," *JISHS* 34 (1941): 177-208.

36. *Journal*, May 26, June 23, 1864.

37. *Sentinel*, Jan. 27, 1865; June 18, Nov. 5, 1869; John C. W. Baily, comp., *Sangamon County Gazetteer . . . with City Directories of Springfield and Jacksonville* (Springfield, 1866), pp. 407-16; *Holland's Jacksonville City Directory for 1871-72* (Chicago, 1871), p. 39.

put up a three-story brick structure on the north side of town to accommodate seven broad looms and 620 spindles. In the prosperous postwar economy Capps was able to expand again. Together with local merchant Alexander McDonald, Capps invested $125,000 in a new factory addition and retail outlet. Now forty looms turned out 5,000 yards each week by 1866. As local growers responded with greater wool production, a second mill, the Home Manufacturing Company, was started by banker Marshall Ayers and others in 1865. "This is a move in the right direction," cheered the *Journal*. "We hope other capitalists will follow suit and supply our city with a full complement of Manufacturing establishments." Nearly $200,000 was invested in wool manufacturing by 1866, "which in ten years may be increased to millions," the *Journal* predicted joyously.[38]

The growth in meat and woolen industries seemed only to whet the boosters' appetites for a true manufacturing economy during the postwar resurgence. Jacksonville had nothing but "old ladies industries," carped one impatient booster in 1866. Everything is "made *someplace* else. All this is wrong. Let us offer a premium to the woman who will purchase and set in operation a knitting machine in Jacksonville; to the man who will start a match factory, and encourage the enterprise we already have and in a few years the noise of machines will be music in our ears."[39]

It was the more familiar music of rails and steam that gave the tempo to the postwar economy. Throughout Illinois the small lines that had been laid out during the previous decade were now consolidated into larger systems; more tracks were also laid, bringing the state to the national forefront in railroad mileage. In some ways this trend strengthened Jacksonville's position in central Illinois. The St. Louis, Jacksonville, and Chicago line subsumed two smaller roads in 1862 and improved connections to both destinations. The next year the Peoria, Pekin, and Jacksonville line was formed from the Illinois River

38. *Journal*, June 9, 1864; Dec. 21, 1865; Jan. 18, 19, 1866. See Frank J. Heinl, *Centennial: J. Capps & Sons, Ltd.* (Jacksonville, 1939), on the growth of the woolen industry in Morgan County.

39. *Journal*, Jan. 18, 1866.

Road that went north from Jacksonville. The Great Western, which connected the town to Quincy and Springfield, merged under the new Toledo, Wabash, and Western by 1865. Through this latter line the powerful Illinois Central Railroad slithered an ominous tentacle into west-central Illinois. A vigorous battle ensued, with the Chicago, Alton, and St. Louis leading the struggle against the "great monopoly" of the Illinois Central "Ring" for control of the "vast and fertile region" of central Illinois.[40]

Meshed with the battle of the railroads was the postwar rivalry of St. Louis and Chicago for metropolitan dominance in the Midwest. Jacksonville strategists were keenly aware of their favorable geographic position between these two giants, and they coyly invited merchants of both cities to compete vigorously for Jacksonville's trade. Together with railroad expansion and rate wars, this competition of metropolitan giants stimulated Jacksonville's postwar economy. However, these same forces would also ultimately set the limits of Jacksonville's growth.[41]

The boosters seemed to sense their destiny, even as the thrust of railroads and local manufacturing generated a resurgence of growth. Quincy, Springfield, Decatur, and Peoria had outstripped Jacksonville, and a recurrent theme of self-criticism now crept into the local press. "The leading men in our city," charged the *Sentinel*, "have been indulging in a Rip Van Winkle slumber, permitting rival cities in central Illinois to grasp from them the elements of success and prosperity within their reach. . . ."[42]

There was also a growing awareness of the limitations inherent in Jacksonville's dual foundations as agricultural market center and the home of educational and charitable institutions. A new state institution was added to Jacksonville's constellation in 1865, when the legislature approved the Illinois Institution for Feeble-Minded Children. Housed in the old Duncan man-

40. *Journal*, Oct. 15, 1863; Dec. 1, 1864; Dec. 21, 1865.
41. Wyatt W. Belcher, *The Economic Rivalry between St. Louis and Chicago, 1850-1880* (New York, 1947); Maurice H. Yeates and Barry J. Garner, *The North American City* (New York, 1961), pp. 41-58.
42. *Sentinel*, Aug. 1, 1867.

sion on College Hill, the school operated successfully on an experimental basis, but was later removed to nearby Lincoln in Logan County.[43]

The State Hospital for the Insane overflowed with patients during the war, and in 1865 Superintendent McFarland pleaded for an additional $75,000 to complete the east wing. But even with this addition the Jacksonville facility had reached full capacity, and McFarland himself urged the legislature to build a new branch in northern Illinois. In 1867 the hospital was once again wracked by scandal, this time because a patient, Elizabeth Packard, protested that she had been illegally committed in 1860 by her husband and cruelly mistreated by McFarland and the attendants. During her confinement Mrs. Packard wrote a scathing exposé of conditions in the asylum; it was later published as a sensational two-volume book, *Modern Persecution.* Mrs. Packard's agitation led to a thorough investigation of the hospital and of Superintendent McFarland. The legislature approved what came to be known as "Mrs. Packard's Personal Liberty Law," which required jury trials to determine the mental state of every patient. Jacksonville newspapers dismissed Mrs. Packard as "deranged," but the hospital, once proudly claimed as "the highest evidence of our civilization," was again a source of disgrace.[44]

Jacksonville's private schools and colleges continued to multiply, but none truly flourished in the 1860s. Illinois College languished, its student body depleted by the war and its endowment withered for lack of united support in Illinois. Some of the professors started separate academies to supplement their meager incomes. Professor Sanders opened the Ladies Atheneum in 1864; it was notable for a controversial curriculum and a strident refutation of the "ornamental" educa-

43. *Journal*, Feb. 16, Mar. 18, 1865; Donnelley, Loyd & Co., *History of Morgan County, Illinois: Its Past and Present* (Chicago, 1878), p. 405; Dr. C. T. Wilbur, "Illinois Institution for Idiots and Imbeciles" [ca. 1865], broadside, Illinois State Historical Library, Springfield.

44. *Sentinel*, Jan. 20, 1865; May 9, 16, Dec. 2, 19, 1867; *Journal*, Feb. 2, 1867; Mrs. E. P. W. Packard, *Modern Persecution, or Insane Asylums Unveiled* (New York, 1873); Henry M. Hurd, ed., *The Institutional Care of the Insane in the United States and Canada* (Baltimore, 1916), II, 192-93.

tion offered at the Methodists' Female College across town. Two years later Professor Crampton, also of Illinois College, opened a commercial college, and in 1870 Sanders added the Illinois Conservatory of Music. These new schools claimed to supplement Illinois College with female education, practical business training, and instruction in music, but they only dissipated the support for existing educational institutions.[45]

The colleges also advertised Jacksonville as a quiet, temperate refuge from the evils of large cities;[46] in this sense the "Athens of the West" provided a contradictory foundation for the more ambitious boosters' visions of growth. "Jacksonville will never become a large commercial place by virtue alone of her literary and state institutions," admonished the *Sentinel* in 1866. Furthermore, agricultural trade and processing "will build up our city to a certain point and no further, and when that point has been reached she must stand still."[47] Industrial manufacturing alone would salvage the town's future, and the boosters began a valiant last effort in August, 1867, to alter Jacksonville's destiny as a small town. The new enthusiasm for manufacturing was sparked by a campaign to attract the proposed machine shops of the St. Louis, Jacksonville, and Chicago Railroad. In competition with other cities along the line, Jacksonville was required to bid for the machine shops with generous offers of land and cash. A bond issue of $75,000 was put before the citizenry in September, 1867, and the boosters' drums beat loudly as the election neared. "The machine shops," promised one, "will be a nucleus that may in a few years be fostered into a growth of giant proportions." Four to five hundred new mechanics would probably be added to Jacksonville's wage-earning population, and the construction of new factories would generate a sustained cycle of industrial and commercial expansion. Dismis-

45. *Journal*, Aug. 17, 1865; *Sentinel*, July 28, 1865; Charles Henry Rammelkamp, *Illinois College: A Centennial History, 1829-1929* (New Haven, 1928), pp. 224-30; Travis Keene Hedrick, Jr., "Julian Monson Sturtevant and the Moral Machinery of Society: The New England Struggle against Pluralism in the Old Northwest" (Ph.D. dissertation, Brown University, 1974), II, 492.

46. W. A. Nixon, comp., *Nixon's Jacksonville Directory for 1868-69* (Jacksonville, 1868), p. 22.

47. *Sentinel*, Aug. 1, 1867.

sing the pessimists who worried about the lack of coal and water power, Jacksonville's industrialists stressed a familiar theme: the sheer power of human will could make up for any lack of natural advantages. "Growing towns and cities usually owe more to the enlightened and active enterprises of their citizens than to adventitious circumstances. . . . There is nothing to prevent Jacksonville from becoming a large manufacturing place if her citizens shall have the forecast to invite and encourage that class of industry."[48] With enough human industry, boosterism might even win an argument with nature.

The din of boosterism was not enough to awaken the "spirit of public enterprise" in Jacksonville, however, and the bond issue failed to pass. A second election was planned for the following December, and Jacksonville's citizens were warned that the prize would go to "some more enterprising community" if it failed. A steady stream of editorials and a large public meeting preceded the second election; critics of the proposed bond complained of the increasing tax burden, and some wondered whether the "Athens of the West" might be better off without the "greasy mechanics" that came with the machine shops. Pointing to the sudden growth of Decatur and Bloomington after they obtained their own machine shops, the proponents insisted the taxes "will be a big paying investment." To the objection about "greasy mechanics," the *Sentinel* answered: "A literary center is a nice thing, and very good in its way, but will never build up a live city unless backed up by the muscle and intelligent skill of the laborer and mechanic." The bond issue carried this time, but too late. The directors of the railroad had already awarded the prize to a more "wide-awake" competitor.[49]

The following year local promoters tackled the next obstacle to Jacksonville's future as an industrial metropolis: the lack of natural sources of power. Coal was discovered in several shafts drilled with local capital, and the prophecies of greatness soared. ("Immense sources of wealth are now lying dormant in the valuable layers of coal beneath our surface soil, requiring only the hand of capital to develop them.") Even the slimy

48. Ibid., Nov. 21, 1867.
49. Ibid., Sept. 19, Nov. 21, Dec. 5, 12, 1867.

Mauvaise Terre might be turned into a source of industrial water power—with proper engineering and another bond issue, that is. "There is nothing to prevent Jacksonville from becoming one of the most important manufacturing cities in the state," blustered one editorial favoring a city waterworks bond in 1868. "All that is lacking . . . is an abundant supply of water." But the boosters' shouts died down when the coal proved too low grade, and the waterworks prohibitively expensive.[50] While other efforts would be made to stimulate manufacturing in Jacksonville, industry never became the basis for sustained growth. The boosters' predictions of future stagnation proved all too true after 1870.

Jacksonville's champions ran their hardest race in a more familiar contest, to become the educational capital of Illinois. After the Civil War the rules of this race were radically changed, with the competition for the state land grant college. As early as 1851 Jonathan Baldwin Turner had led the movement for a public-supported industrial university in Illinois; tied to a millennial vision of universal education and the dignity of the "industrial classes," the "Turner Plan" was also a revolt against the sectarian liberal arts college that had struggled to survive in Jacksonville and across the Midwest.[51] In 1862 the concept of the land grant college became national policy with the passage of the Morrill Act, which promised each state a public endowment from receipts of federal land sales. But in Illinois the establishment of this plan for a public university would be determined by the interplay of local interests, as "rival groups gathered like sharks around the carcass of the land grant, and Illinois Industrial University received its baptism in bloody political waters."[52]

The final decision to create Illinois' new industrial university was postponed until after the Civil War. In the meantime,

50. Ibid., Mar. 14, 1867; Dec. 18, 1868.
51. See Jon Francis McKenna, "Disputed Destiny: The Political and Intellectual Origins of Public-Supported Higher Education in Illinois" (Ph.D. dissertation, University of Illinois, 1973); Mary Turner Carriel, *The Life of Jonathan Baldwin Turner* (1911; reprinted, Urbana, 1961); Winton U. Solberg, *The University of Illinois, 1867-94: An Intellectual and Cultural History* (Urbana, 1968), pp. 1-58.
52. Solberg, *University of Illinois*, p. 60.

contending local interests gathered their forces. Jacksonville's claim to the new university went back to its earliest efforts to make Illinois College a shining beacon on the dim frontier. By the 1860s the college still floundered on a weak endowment; it was torn by sectarian and sectional dissension, and its student body had declined disastrously. Turner, who in 1847 had been forced to resign from the college faculty because of his religious and political views, was convinced that the age of sectarian colleges, narrowly designed to educate the clergy and professions, was doomed. Julian Sturtevant, the beleaguered president of Illinois College, was by this time prepared to agree; he revamped the college curriculum and adjusted his own ideals to accommodate what he hoped would be a merger with the new industrial university in Jacksonville. Turner, at the same time, began arousing the boosters for the last big race to make good Jacksonville's dubious claim as the "Athens of the West."[53]

The race began in earnest in January, 1866, when Turner addressed a series of public meetings in Morgan County. A large committee "of the most influential citizens" was appointed to "present a subject of more importance to the material interests of the county than any ever before introduced." The industrial university campaign received unprecedented attention in newspapers and public meetings; the whole concept of a state-supported industrial university was barely debated, as the boosters focused on the more crucial question of who would get it and what economic benefits were at stake. Even the normally high-minded Turner promised that such a university "would promote the pecuniary interests of the county more than all the rest of the state institutions now located here, put together."[54]

The industrial university would certainly bring direct benefits in payroll revenue, jobs, and rising population and land values. Furthermore, it would provide the key to the sustained growth which Jacksonville's partisans so anxiously sought. The annual state agricultural fair would almost surely come to the

53. Hedrick, "Sturtevant," II, 463-91; Julian M. Sturtevant to Jonathan Baldwin Turner, Illinois College, Dec. 21, 1864, Turner Collection, Illinois Historical Survey, University of Illinois.

54. *Sentinel*, Dec. 29, 1865; May 11, Sept. 20, 1866; *Journal*, Jan. 25, Feb. 8, 22, 1866.

site of the new university; agricultural industries would cluster near it; maybe even the federal Bureau of Agriculture would find Jacksonville's university an ideal center for its headquarters. And surely "a hundred incidental interests" would follow. The industrial university was, above all, a community interest:

> the poor man surely wants it, for . . . it will greatly increase the demand for his labor, and all the incidental products of his garden and his home. The rich want it because it will increase the value of their lands, the sale of their products. . . . Our professional and literary men want it because it is needful to finish our great circle of literary and benevolent institutions. . . . It will add to the value of every property inheritance, and open up higher chances in life to the youth of the county through all coming generations.[55]

At stake in this persuasive argument for community interest was a county bond issue for $300,000 to serve as the base of Jacksonville's bid for the university. Several public appeals in both party newspapers and a series of carefully staged bipartisan meetings gently introduced the bond issue to a tax-weary constituency. Jacksonville's boosters took pains to show rural folk how the tax would fall most heavily on the town's business classes. A Young Man's Industrial League, based in Jacksonville, helped carry the message to rural Morgan with "speeches such as farmers can understand and appreciate."[56]

Unexpected resistance emerged among small farmers, who were overburdened with taxes and wary of the sudden interest of Jacksonville luminaries in educating the farmer and mechanic. The university's model farm might undermine agricultural prices and wages in Morgan. Jacksonville alone, and not the rest of the county, stood to gain from rising property values and "fat professorships and contracts." Jacksonville newspapers dismissed these and other rural doubts as "stupid" and "foolish," but worried boosters issued grave warnings of Morgan County's dismal future if this singular opportunity were rejected.[57]

55. *Sentinel*, Sept. 20, 1866; *Journal*, May 17, 1866.
56. *Sentinel*, Sept. 4, 1866.
57. *Journal*, Oct. 25, 30, Nov. 1, 1866; *Sentinel*, Oct. 25, 1866.

Looming in the background was the aggressive "Champaign Ring" led by a zealous town booster, Clark Griggs. Champaign-Urbana, small twin cities in the eastern part of the state on the Illinois Central line, had the advantage of an early start and strong political allies. Local promoters put together the bogus Urbana-Champaign Institute in 1861 and threw up a tall brick building to house it. Known by its detractors as the "Champaign Elephant," the building was to serve as a lure to the new industrial university and as a refutation of Jacksonville's boast that it alone could provide facilities for immediate instruction of university students. Griggs, with the help of untold financial support from the county and the Illinois Central Railroad "Ring," proved to be a skillful political manipulator; by 1866 he had formulated an impressive legislative coalition in Champaign's favor. Jacksonville, Griggs argued forcefully, had already received enough favors from the state—over two million dollars' worth since 1846, by Jacksonville's own admission. It was high time that eastern Illinois received its due.[58]

Jacksonville's champions insisted on their moral claim to the University, but they covered their bet with the sensible assumption that in Illinois politics hard cash would suffice when moral claims did not. Early returns from the bond election in November quickly relieved their anxiety over rebellious farmers; the unofficial tally showed a landslide in favor of the $300,000 bond. Turner issued joyous congratulations to the people of Old Morgan, and the Republicans graciously extended the "hand of fellowship" to rural Democrats, "co-workers in the cause of liberal education and local improvement." But a final count of the ballots later determined that a scant twelve-vote majority had in fact defeated the bond. This cruel, inexplicable twist of fortune quickly soured the boosters' pollyannaish view of Jacksonville, and a stream of self-abuse poured through the newspapers. "Our people seem to have individual enterprise, but are almost entirely destitute of public spirit," the *Journal* confessed, grudgingly admitting that "wide-awake" Champaign deserved the university.[59]

58. Solberg, *University of Illinois*, pp. 75-79; *Sentinel*, Sept. 20, 1866.
59. *Journal*, Nov. 9, Dec. 24, 1866.

The boosters' faith died hard, though, and by January "Jacksonville spirit" revived. A second county bond issue for $200,000 was put before the people, this time with success. In addition, Jacksonville's citizens passed, almost unanimously, a separate bond for $50,000 matched by private donations from "certain wealthy gentlemen of the city." Mrs. Elizabeth Ayers, wife of wealthy banker Marshall Ayers, kicked in her deed to the old Berean College campus, valued at $75,000. Illinois College threw in its entire campus and endowment; the county also added over 200 acres for the university model farm, bringing the total bid to nearly half a million dollars. Jacksonville was making its last big bet on the town's future greatness.[60]

The boosters, their pockets turned inside out, graciously welcomed the legislative committee that came in February, 1867, to inspect the assets in Morgan County's bid. An entourage of Jacksonville's best citizens, well-dressed ladies, and Morgan County politicos met the special train from Springfield and escorted the visitors to their plush quarters in the Dunlap House. Before visiting the various sites that made up the bid, the legislators were treated to a sumptuous dinner. After their tour of the city, which had been neatly manicured for the occasion, the "distinguished city guests" retired to a reception and gala ball at the Dunlap House. Late that evening Jacksonville's hopeful partisans escorted their visitors back to the train station.[61]

As the rival bids were tallied, it became clear that Jacksonville's long-awaited destiny as an educational center was finally to come to fruition. With nearly half a million dollars in appraised assets, the Morgan County bid was nearly twice the size of Champaign's. Bloomington and Lincoln, the two other contending towns, came in with intermediate bids. But this was a question to be decided in the political arena, where the "high-toned" moral and intellectual atmosphere touted by the "Athens of the West" was no match for the tough maneuvering

60. *Sentinel*, Jan. 3, 10, Feb. 7, 1867; "Pledges to Subscriptions for Securing Location of Industrial University in Morgan County" [1867], MSS in Turner Collection, Illinois Historical Survey, University of Illinois.

61. *Sentinel*, Feb. 14, 1867.

of Clark Griggs and his cronies. Griggs rented several suites in Springfield's Leland Hotel during the legislative battle. In one room the "friends of Champaign County" were served free whiskey and food. In addition, "for the evangelical and temperance portion of 'the ring' and their friends," an insider later explained, "we had a quiet room set apart provided only with a bible, a pitcher of cold water, and a bottle of bay rum (for the hair)." Friendly legislators were also feted with oyster suppers, quail dinners, and theater tickets; some were said to have received more blatant forms of bribery from Champaign County's generous slush fund. Champaign's official bid may have paled next to Jacksonville's, but his savvy knowledge of Illinois politics told Griggs where to spend his money. The "Champaign Ring" also allied with other delegations in a classic demonstration of pork barreling: a new penitentiary was promised to Egypt (southern Illinois), a new statehouse for Springfield, a branch hospital for the insane at Peoria, and a canal for Chicago. For individual allies, Griggs promised lucrative positions on the university Board of Trustees and faculty. One disappointed political crony later confessed that he had planned on becoming a professor of moral philosophy, and that he had even prepared lecture notes "on the theory and practice of early piety."[62]

As the votes came in, Jacksonville's dreams were finally destroyed—Champaign had triumphed. This time Jacksonville's defeat was not blamed on internal flaws of "public spirit" or strategy; instead, local virtue had simply been betrayed by larger conspiracies of "knaves and fools" in government, monopolistic railroads controlled from the East, and a ruthless band of Champaign "sharpers" who won the prize by deceit and bribery. Turner's post-mortem report to the people of Morgan County congratulated them for their efforts and took high ground by offering pity to a state "disgraced" by Jacksonville's defeat. "No men of talent and genius will ever gather around it," Turner said of Champaign's new university, "nothing above the level of the miserable scamps and scalliwags whose votes and services were bought up at the capital. . . . No parent from abroad would trust his son there, unless he wished

62. Ibid., Apr. 4, Mar. 14, 1867; Solberg, *University of Illinois*, pp. 59-83.

him to take lessons in the arts of perfidy, imprudence, hypocrisy and drunkenness."[63]

THE INVERSION OF BOOSTERISM

Community virtue, abused by uncontrollable forces from without, now sought refuge by withdrawing further into a parochial localism, and into the past. There would be other sporadic efforts to promote Jacksonville's growth as a manufacturing and commercial center, but in the spring of 1867, when the state university was lost, all but the most diehard boosters seemed willing to make peace with the verdict that Jacksonville's promise had already been fulfilled. Instead of carping about internal failures or denouncing external conspiracies, they adjusted by inverting the boosters' central themes of harmony and collective progress into a tradition of local history that justified small-town failure as chosen success. They now nurtured the ideal of a small, intimate, self-consciously genteel community; in the process, an unspoken agreement was made to deny that Jacksonville had ever wanted to be anything else.

In April, 1867, John Mathers, recently elected the first mayor under Jacksonville's new city charter, addressed the city council and citizens at large. The new charter had been part of Jacksonville's desperate effort to win the state university, but Mathers made no mention of the bitter disappointment that had come only a few weeks earlier. Instead, he used the occasion to review Jacksonville's past and pay tribute to earlier city fathers. Mathers, who had lived in the community since 1840, recalled the crude beginnings of the town, its one-room log meetinghouse, skeletal government, and meager economy:

> Jacksonville, at that date, was *emphatically* a *new* town, and located in a *new* country. Yet the inhabitants, notwithstanding they were deprived of many of the conveniences and luxuries of life, seemed to be happy and contented, and the kind and social feelings, which generally characterize the . . . settlers of a new country, prevailed. . . . The cause of morality, Christianity, and

63. *Sentinel*, Mar. 14, 1867. The report was signed by the county committee but appears to be written by Turner.

temperance kept pace with the increasing population and prosperity of the town, until it is now . . . recognized as the "Athens of Illinois." Admitting, as we freely do, that we have not increased in population as rapidly as some of our sister cities, yet, our prosperity . . . gives evidence that "the day of small things should not be despised."[64]

Mathers's brief historical discourse was contrived to compensate for Jacksonville's disappointed future by offering a glowing vision of the past. His nostalgic remembrance of the town's beginnings coincided with a new interest in the early history of the community, fed by a series of long newspaper accounts that suddenly appeared by 1867. Based primarily on the recollections of old pioneers, these newspaper articles went into infinite detail on the people and events of "Old Morgan." The deaths of "old settlers" now received unusual attention, with long obituaries and rambling historical eulogies testifying to the virtues of Jacksonville's pioneer generation. "Another old citizen gone," lamented the *Sentinel* in a report of Captain Samuel Hunt's well-attended funeral. "One by one our old citizens are giving place to a new generation."[65]

In reverence to the early pioneers, some of Jacksonville's citizens gathered in 1869 to honor the remains of Isaac Fort Roe, one of the earliest settlers of Morgan County. His body was removed from its original grave and, accompanied by a solemn procession of citizens, was placed in Jacksonville's Diamond Grove Cemetery. There a monument was erected; it stood twelve feet high and was adorned with figures of a pioneer and wagon, symbolizing the spirit of the town fathers.[66]

The old settlers formed a county association on the Fourth of July of that same year. Open to all those living in Morgan County before the famous Deep Snow of '31, some two thousand old settlers gathered in Henderson's grove to celebrate shared memories and listen to maudlin songs and prose testifying to their brave sacrifices and honorable past. As their numbers dwindled, the Old Settlers Society wisely modified

64. Ibid., Apr. 11, 1867.
65. Ibid., July 31, 1868; Mar. 3, 1866.
66. Ibid., Aug. 6, 1869.

their residency requirement and admitted members who had settled prior to 1840. Eventually it evolved into an ongoing local history and genealogical society, open to all who shared an interest in the community's past.[67]

This cult of local history found its ultimate expression in two published county and city histories that appeared in the twilight of Jacksonville's pioneer generation. The first, *History of Morgan County, Illinois: Its Past and Present,* was published by a Chicago firm in 1878.[68] Like hundreds of other local histories that appeared in the late nineteenth century, the *History of Morgan County* was a massive compendium of facts, memoirs, and mythology organized loosely around descriptions of the various institutional units of the community. It combined an encyclopedic compilation of factual data with sentimental tributes to old settlers; Jacksonville's history was described as the unfolding of destiny, guided by selfless, honorable pioneers, and the picture was tactfully allowed to fade after the Civil War. In the back of the book was a city directory, oddly combined with biographical sketches of selected citizens (who no doubt paid handsomely for the honor). Almost invariably these accounts were historical in their approach; they detailed the early arrival of the subject, his rise to wealth and prominence, and his service to the community. While these tributes unquestionably helped boost sales of the book, they also confirmed the myths that pervaded Jacksonville's new consciousness of its past by demonstrating individual success intertwined with community progress.

The perfect expression of local history as inverted boosterism came later, with the publication of Charles Eames's *Historic Morgan and Classic Jacksonville.* Eames, the son of a prominent local merchant, was the editor-owner of the *Daily Journal.* He brought to his history of Jacksonville all the zeal and loyalty which his predecessors in the local press had once applied to the business of boosting Jacksonville's future. Based on a strange

67. Ibid., Sept. 2, 1870; Donnelley, *History of Morgan,* pp. 319-21; "Records, Old Settlers Society," in Morgan County Historical Society Collection, Jacksonville Public Library.

68. Donnelley, Loyd & Co., *History of Morgan.*

assortment of old settlers' interviews, newspaper clippings, official records, and shameless plagiarism from earlier histories, Eames's book reads like a shuffled pack of uninterpreted note cards. His facts garbled, his dates often incorrect, his interpretation of Jacksonville's pioneers usually sentimentalized, Eames's history distorted the past in much the same way (and for many of the same reasons) that the boosters had once distorted the future. His implicit purpose was to invest pride and satisfaction in a community that had tried desperately hard to be something more than it was. The introduction to *Historic Morgan and Classic Jacksonville* dismissed any future hope of industrial boom, and the book carefully avoided any mention of Jacksonville's disappointed efforts to avoid its fate as a small town. "Our city," Eames consoled his readers with a delightful understatement, "has not been in a hurry to climb the hill of fame."[69]

Local history had become a community adhesive as vital and real as boosterism once had been. It confused fact with myth and smoothed over conflict and disappointment with nostalgic sentimentalism, but it served its purpose. History has other uses—equally legitimate, we may hope. The present history of Jacksonville has aimed not at inflating local community pride, but at helping a wider audience understand the form and meaning of community forged within a mobile, diverse, and strange new society. Standing at the midpoint in Jacksonville's early history, one of the old settlers looked back with longing toward the good old days and forward with apprehension toward the future: "Fain would I picture the beautiful intercourse of our domestic circles in those days—one family almost in heart, in interest, in joy, and in suffering—an Arcadian dream, destined to fade away before the advancing stages of more artificial society."[70] The old settler anticipated themes familiar to our own day: the decline of family and community, and the advent of superficial relationships in a cold, inhuman society. But

69. Eames, *Historic Morgan*, p. 41; cf. Robert R. Dykstra, *The Cattle Towns* (New York, 1968), pp. 355-67; Blaine A. Brownell, *The Urban Ethos in the South, 1920-1930* (Baton Rouge, 1975), pp. 191-216.

70. Truman Post, quoted in Julian M. Sturtevant, *Quarter Century Celebration at Illinois College: Historical Discourse* (New York, 1855), p. 40, in Tanner Library, Illinois College, Jacksonville.

Jacksonville's history should serve to remind modern America that despite (or perhaps because of) whatever chaos envelops us, we will invent new forms and new values to satisfy the deep and enduring need for community.

Appendix: Tables

TABLE 1. Population and Persistence, 1830-70

Census	Population	Growth rate	Persistence
1830	466		
1840	1,900	326%	
1850	2,745	44%	
1860	5,528	101%	27%
1870	9,203	66%	21%

SOURCE: U.S. Census MSS, Morgan County, 1830, 1840, 1850, 1860, 1870

TABLE 2. Occupational Distribution of Non-Dependent Population, 1850-70

Occupational category	1850	1860	1870
Business-Professional	20%	23%	22%
Skilled labor	46%	38%	34%
Proprietors	(14%)	(13%)	(10%)
Non-proprietors	(32%)	(25%)	(24%)
Unskilled labor	19%	25%	33%
No occupation reported	15%	14%	11%
N	759	1,628	2,941

SOURCE: U.S. Census MSS, Morgan County, 1850, 1860, 1870

NOTE: "non-dependent population" includes: 1) all household heads and family heads; 2) all gainfully employed persons; 3) all males 20 or older.

Occupational categories are adapted from those in Merle Curti et al., *The Making of an American Community: A Case Study of Democracy in a Frontier County* (Stanford, 1959), appendix II. I have collapsed Curti's 12 categories into 5, and have added a property qualification ($500 combined real and personal property) to distinguish artisan-proprietors from other skilled laborers. The important deviations from Curti's classification scheme are as follows:

"Business-professional" includes property-owning farmers and stock-raisers; manufacturers; hotel, restaurant, grocery, livery, and mill proprietors; and excludes clerks. The professions of law, medicine, clergy, and college professors are combined with semi-professional occupations (e.g., teachers, dentists, journalists, and government officials).

"Skilled labor" includes all with specialized skills in building, metal-wood-leather, food processing, and clothing trades; mechanics, apprentices; barbers, clerks.

"Unskilled labor" refers to general laborers, draymen, railroad laborers, and domestic servants.

The "no occupation reported" category includes some retired persons, gentlemen, and those "keeping house."

261

TABLE 3. Occupation and Persistence

Occupation at beginning of decade	Persistence			
	1850-60		1860-70	
Business-Professional	53%		23%	
Skilled, proprietors	40%		50%	
TOTAL WHITE COLLAR		47%		33%
Skilled, non-proprietors	17%		17%	
Unskilled labor	13%		9%	
TOTAL BLUE COLLAR		15%		13%
No occupation reported	22%		17%	
Total persistence	27%		21%	
N Persistent	207		334	

SOURCE: same as Table 2.

TABLE 4. Occupational Mobility, 1850-60

Occupation, 1850	Occupation, 1860						Mobility[a]			
	Business-Professional	Skilled, proprietor	Skilled, non-proprietor	Unskilled	No occupation reported	N	Up	Stable	Down	N
Business-Professional	72%	6%	4%	1%	17%	79	0	86%	14%	66
Skilled, proprietor	30%	51%	12%	0	7%	43	32%	55%	13%	40
Skilled, non-proprietor	20%	34%	26%	10%	10%	41	59%	30%	11%	37
Unskilled	0	22%	22%	50%	6%	18	47%	53%	0	17
No occupation reported	39%	4%	4%	12%	42%	26	—	—	—	
TOTAL						207	46%[b] 43	62% 99	13%[c] 18	160

SOURCE: same as Table 2.

[a]"Mobility" measures movement among those with known occupations in both censuses.

[b] Since only 94 cases with known occupations in both censuses began below the top rank, 46% (43/94) of those at risk moved upward.

[c] Since only 143 cases with known occupations in both censuses began above the bottom rank, 13% (18/143) of those at risk moved downward.

TABLE 5. Occupational Mobility, 1860-70

Occupation, 1860	Occupation, 1870						Mobility[a]			
	Business-Professional	Skilled, proprietor	Skilled, non-proprietor	Unskilled	No occupation reported	N	Up	Stable	Down	N
Business-Professional	75%	5%	3%	2%	15%	88	0	88%	12%	75
Skilled, proprietor	17%	59%	13%	2%	9%	103	19%	65%	16%	94
Skilled, non-proprietor	16%	30%	44%	3%	7%	68	49%	48%	3%	63
Unskilled	8%	14%	5%	68%	5%	37	29%	71%	0	35
No occupation reported	37%	8%	5%	0	50%	38	—	—	—	
TOTAL						334	31%[b] 59	68% 182	11%[c] 26	267

SOURCE: same as Table 2.

[a]"Mobility" measures movement among those with known occupations in both censuses.

[b]Since only 192 cases with known occupations in both censuses began below the top rank, 31% (59/192) of those at risk moved upward.

[c]Since only 232 cases with known occupations in both censuses began above the bottom rank, 11% (26/232) of those at risk moved downward.

TABLE 6. Distribution of Landed Wealth in Town Lots, 1849-70

	1849[a]	1850[b]	1860[b]	1870[b]
Owners as % of non-dependent population	25%	37%	31%	29%
Owners (N)	187	279	508	865
Total value ($000)	$176	$962	$3,496	$8,360
% of total owned by wealthiest 10% of owners	43%	48%	50%	50%
Gini Index[c] of inequality among owners	.57	.65	.61	.63

SOURCE: same as Table 2, and Morgan County Tax List, 1849, Morgan County Courthouse.

[a]Derived from Morgan County Tax List, 1849, Morgan County Courthouse; Jacksonville lots only.

[b]Derived from U.S. Census MSS, Morgan County, 1850, 1860, 1870.

[c]0 = "perfect equality;" 1 = "perfect inequality"

TABLE 7. Wealth and Persistence

Real Property	Non-dependent population			Persistence	
	1850	1860	1870	1850-60	1860-70
$5,000 or more	6%	10%	13%	60%	40%
$1,000 - 4,999	17%	7%	14%	50%	35%
$1 - 999	14%	4%	2%	27%	32%
0	63%	69%	71%	18%	13%
Total				27%	21%
N	759	1,628	2,941	207	334

SOURCE: same as Table 2.

TABLE 8. Wealth Mobility among the Persistent, 1850-60

Quintile rank among real property owners, 1850	Mobility, 1850-60			
	Up	Stable	Down	N
5 (Wealthiest)	0	75%	25%	36
4	32%	52%	16%	31
3	57%	22%	21%	23
2	53%	24%	23%	17
1	70%	0	31%	13
0 (no property)	59%	41%	0	87
Total	53%[a]	42%	24%[b]	
N	91	87	29	207

SOURCE: same as Table 2.

NOTE: Quintile ranks were determined by total non-dependent population data.

[a]Since only 171 cases began below the top rank, 53% (91/171) of those at risk moved upward.

[b]Since only 120 cases began above the bottom rank, 24% (29/120) of those at risk moved downward.

TABLE 9. Wealth Mobility among the Persistent, 1860-70

Quintile rank among real property owners, 1860	Mobility, 1850-60			
	Up	Stable	Down	N
5 (wealthiest)	0	84%	16%	45
4	33%	44%	23%	36
3	53%	21%	26%	38
2	61%	12%	27%	33
1	50%	3%	47%	34
0 (no property)	49%	51%	0	148
Total	48%ᵃ	43%	27%ᵇ	
N	140	144	50	334

SOURCE: same as Table 2.

NOTE: Quintile ranks were defined by total non-dependent population data.

ᵃSince only 289 cases began below the top rank, 48% (140/289) of those at risk moved upward.

ᵇSince only 186 cases began above the bottom rank, 27% (50/186) of those at risk moved downward.

TABLE 10. Sex Ratios and Marriage, 1830-70

	1830	1840	1850	1860	1870
Crude sex ratioᵃ					
Morgan County	108	108	110	110	105
Jacksonville			104	96	94
Sex ratio, population 15 years and older					
Morgan County	105	107	114	114	111
Jacksonville					99ᵇ
% males (20 and older) marriedᶜ					
Jacksonville			62%	62%	67%

SOURCE: U.S. Census MSS, Morgan County, 1830, 1840, 1850, 1860, 1870; published U.S. Census, volumes on population, same years.

ᵃCrude sex ratios = number of males per 100 females.

ᵇEstimated

ᶜIncludes single parents

TABLE 11. Social Characteristics of Household Heads and Boarders, 1850-70

	Household heads	Boarders and servants[a]
Occupation[b]		
White collar (%)		
1850	50	8
1860	50	16
1870	45	17
Blue collar (%)		
1850	31	83
1860	36	71
1870	40	75
Wealth		
Owning $1,000 real property (%)		
1850	36	3
1860	48	4
1870	47	6
Life Cycle		
Under 30 years old (%)		
1850	21	70
1860	18	75
1870	16	68
Single (%)		
1850	5	87
1860	7	88
1870	8	81
Persistence		
1850-60	38	9
1860-70	29	7
N		
1850	439	237
1860	842	522
1870	1,513	1,428

SOURCE: same as Table 2.

[a]For 1850 and 1860 brothers and fathers of the household head are excluded. These kinsmen constituted 26% of all boarders in 1850 and 34% in 1860.

[b]Figures indicate percentages of household heads and boarders in selected social categories. Percentages do not add up to 100 because of those in unknown category.

TABLE 12. Male-Linked Kinship, 1850, 1860

	1850	1860
Adult[a] males with adult male kin	28%	35%
Kin groups > 2	29%	44%
Kinship ties between father and son	63%	73%
(in same dwelling)	(44%)	(62%)
Kinship ties between brothers[b]	37%	27%
(in same dwelling)	(14%)	(13%)
White collar with kin	33%	35%
Blue collar with kin	24%	23%
Under 30 with kin	31%	30%
Kin persistent through following decade	31%	26%

SOURCE: U.S. Census MSS, Morgan County, 1850, 1860, and biographical sketches in Donnelley, Loyd, & Co., *History of Morgan County, Illinois: Its Past and Present* (Chicago, 1878); Charles M. Eames, *Historic Morgan and Classic Jacksonville* (Jacksonville, 1885); William F. Short, ed., *Historical Encyclopedia of Illinois . . . Morgan County* (Chicago, 1906); Old Settlers Society files, Morgan County Historical Society Collections, Jacksonville Public Library.

[a]Includes a few males under 20 who were employed

[b]Excludes brothers with fathers in town

TABLE 13. Ethnic Populations, 1850-70

	Non-dependent population		
	1850	1860	1870
Portuguese	4%	3%	5%
German	2%	6%	6%
Irish	10%	15%	14%
Foreign (other)	9%	11%	13%
Black	4%	3%	6%
Total	28%	38%	44%
N	217	605	1,258

SOURCE: U.S. Census MSS, Morgan County, 1850, 1860, 1870

TABLE 14. Ethnicity and Social Status, 1850-70

	Portu-guese	German	Irish	Foreign (other)	Black	White (native)
White collar						
1850	10%	6%	11%	21%	12%	42%
1860	20%	30%	14%	30%	15%	48%
1870	21%	41%	14%	29%	8%	38%
Blue collar						
1850	85%	83%	84%	67%	47%	42%
1860	78%	63%	84%	61%	68%	33%
1870	64%	54%	80%	61%	86%	48%
With $500 real property						
1850	5%	6%	9%	21%	16%	40%
1860	11%	24%	16%	29%	13%	36%
1870	44%	32%	20%	27%	20%	30%

SOURCE: U.S. Census MSS, Morgan County, 1850, 1860, 1870

TABLE 15. Ethnicity and Residential Segregation, 1870

	Index of dissimilarity[a]	N
Portuguese	48	141
German	18	176
Irish	18	397
Foreign (other)	6[b]	371
Black	16[b]	172
All Minorities	12	1,257

SOURCE: U.S. Census MSS, Morgan County, 1870

[a]All groups are compared with native white population in non-dependent population.

[b]The indexes for the total foreign and black populations in the published census were 21 and 24, probably indicating a higher residential concentration among those with children. *Ninth Census, Volume 1, The Statistics of the Population of the United States* (Washington, 1872), p. 117.

TABLE 16. Social Characteristics of Association Officers

| | | Officers | | | | Total non-dependent | | |
| | | Pre-1860 | | Post-1860 | | | | |
		1850	1860	1860	1870	1850	1860	1870
A.	Occupation							
	Business	39%	41%	30%	25%	12%	14%	14%
	Professional	28%	25%	15%	27%	8%	9%	8%
	Skilled labor	29%	16%	41%	35%	46%	38%	34%
	Unskilled							
	labor	0	0	2%	0	19%	25%	33%
	Unknown	4%	17%	12%	13%	15%	14%	11%
	N	119	75	115	109	759	1,628	2,941
B.	Nativity[a]							
	Northeast	36%		29%	29%	27%	21%	17%
	South	56%		37%	25%	35%	23%	18%
	Midwest	6%		19%	28%	14%	22%	28%
	Foreign	3%		16%	18%	25%	34%	37%
	N	108		115	109	759	1,628	2,941
C.	Life cycle							
	Median age	44	54	37	42	31	30	31
	Under 30							
	years old	14%	0	29%	17%	42%	48%	41%
	Married[b]	97%	97%	73%	81%	62%	62%	67%
	Median number							
	of children[c]	3.1	3.1	3.1	2.7	2.1	2.2	2.0

SOURCES: U.S. Census MSS, Morgan County, 1850, 1860, 1870. Officers identified in newspapers before 1860, and city directories after 1860.

[a]Nativity data for the pre-1860 officers were gathered from the census MSS when available, and from the biographical sketches found in the sources listed for Table 12.

[b]"Married" includes single parents. Total figures based on adult males (20 years and over) only.

[c]Computed only for married couples.

NOTE: See Merle Curti et al., *The Making of an American Community: A Case Study of Democracy in a Frontier County* (Stanford, 1959), p. 420, for comparable data on Trempleau County, Wisc., leaders.

TABLE 17. Real Property Gains among Persistent Association Officers and Total Non-Dependent Population

	Officers		Persistent total non-dependent	
	Pre-1860	Post-1860	1850-60	1860-70
Average wealth				
1850	$ 4,855	—	$2,762	—
1860	$13,296	$ 9,510	$8,345	$4,289
1870	—	$16,243	—	$8,811
Average gain	$ 8,441	$ 6,733	$5,583	$4,522
N	73	73	207	334

SOURCE: same as Table 16.

TABLE 18. Elected Terms in Municipal Government, by Nativity

	North-east	South	Mid-west	Irish	German	Foreign (other)	Unknown	N (Terms)
1830s	9%	54%	0	0	0	0	37%	35
1840s	18%	74%	4%	0	0	0	4%	50
1850s	36%	49%	2%	0	0	7%	5%	55
1860s	36%	33%	12%	4%	1%	7%	7%	67
1850-70	36%	40%	7%	2%	1%	7%	6%	122
1833-70	27%	51%	5%	1%	—	4%	12%	207

SOURCES: U.S. Census MSS, Morgan County, 1850, 1860, 1870; "Minutes, Town Board" (title varies), MSS in City Clerk's Vault, Jacksonville Municipal Building.

TABLE 19. Elected Terms in Municipal Government, by Occupation

	Business	Professional	Skilled labor	Unknown	N (Terms)
1830s	21%	26%	32%	21%	38
1840s	47%	10%	37%	6%	51
1850s	35%	7%	58%	0	55
1860s	30%	9%	34%	27%	67
1850-70	32%	8%	45%	15%	122
1833-70	34%	11%	41%	14%	211

SOURCE: same as Table 18

TABLE 20. Wealth and Persistence of City Fathers, 1850-70

		Trustees		Total non-dependent population
		1850-60	1861-70	
A.	Real Property			
	With real property			
	1850	79%		37%
	1860	100%	91%	31%
	1870		82%	29%
	Among wealthiest			
	20% of owners			
	1850	44%		7%
	1860	51%	41%	6%
	1870		49%	6%
B.	Persistence			
	1850-60	84%		27%
	1860-70		97%	21%
	N	55	67	

SOURCES: same as Table 18

TABLE 21. Life Cycle and City Fathers, 1850-70

	Trustees		Total non-dependent population
	1850-60	1861-70	
Under 30 years old			
1850	25%		42%
1860	0	11%	48%
1870		0	52%
Married[a]			
1850	96%		62%
1860	96%	93%	62%
1870		97%	67%
Median number of children[b]			
1850	3.1		2.1
1860	3.1	3.4	2.2
1870		3.3	2.0
N	55	67	

SOURCES: same as Table 18

[a]"Married" includes single parents. Total figures based on adult males (20 years and over) only.

[b]Computed only for married couples.

Bibliographical Essay

Rather than repeat all the sources listed in the notes, it may be more useful to discuss the most important manuscripts and secondary works, and how they were employed in the process of research. This book attempts to combine analysis of the social structure and the cultural values that defined the community in Jacksonville. I was interested not just in reducing the social structure to a series of quantitative measurements of demography, economy, leadership and stratification, social mobility, family and associational networks, but in understanding the structural skeleton with its cultural flesh intact. This metaphor may suggest a notion of organic unity that is misleading, for the study of any community's cultural values requires a constant awareness of class, ethnic, and generational differences within the population. Still, the study of ideas and values, expressed in rhetoric and behavior, reveals how the social structure was both justified and contradicted by the culture of the community and its parts. The process of research, like the dynamics of the community itself, involves a constant interaction between objective structural conditions and subjective expressions of values. Few of the sources listed below fit neatly into these two categories, but I have attempted to suggest the ways in which many of them can be used to serve this research strategy.

Some of the sources discussed below are peculiar to Jacksonville, but their description may help guide research in other communities. One firm warning to those who follow: the small size of a community—so attractive to twentieth-century social scientists doing survey research—is a frustrating obstacle to historical community studies. In comparison to large cities, small towns generally had fewer newspapers and sparse coverage of local events; personal papers and institutional records are less likely to be preserved and are rarely centralized in a public archive; city directories, local histories, and biographies of leading citizens are fewer, and often poor in quality. Jacksonville's past is far better preserved than that of several other Illinois towns I explored, but much is lost, and the task of locating and gaining access to local records required enormous time and perseverance.

The most important source for this study was probably the local newspapers, conveniently available on microfilm through the Illinois State Historical Library in Springfield (hereafter ISHL). Most newspapers were partisan organs devoted largely to national political news, with cut-and-paste articles from other papers around the nation. Though partisan disputes were vented openly, local conflict was usually suppressed by what Robert Dykstra calls the "taboo on divisiveness." If boosterism discouraged candid discussion of local problems, it stimulated reporting on the misfortunes of rival towns; hence Springfield's newspapers were useful in providing a fuller account of events in Jacksonville. Newspapers also reported on the meetings of local political parties, churches, reform societies, and lodges. These reports helped construct a picture of the town's organizational network; they identified party and association leaders whose names I compiled and linked whenever possible with census data, tax lists, and church membership lists to form a collective biography of local leaders. Finally, the newspapers were filled with hyperbolic booster rhetoric, yet in an important way they served as vital forums for defining and promoting the town's economic goals.

Newspapers rarely gave unbiased views of the world occupied by transients and minorities. The U.S. Census manuscripts, available on microfilm from the National Archives, allow a more objective view of local society at all levels. Beginning in 1850 the census included details on every individual located by the census marshal. The wealth of data in this source cannot be extracted adequately without the aid of a computer, which requires coding all the information and putting it into machine-readable format. In this task Merle Curti et al., *The Making of an*

American Community: A Case Study of Democracy in a Frontier County (Stanford, 1959), appendix II, was very helpful. In addition, *Historical Methods Newsletter* has several articles, too numerous to mention here, which helped refine my adaptation of Curti's coding scheme. Norman H. Nie et al., *SPSS: Statistical Package for the Social Sciences*, 2nd ed. (New York, 1970), helped solve most of the computer programming problems I encountered.

After 1860 Jacksonville was large enough to sponsor sporadic publication of city directories. C. S. Williams, *Jacksonville Directory and Business Mirror for 1860-61* (Jacksonville, 1860); John C. W. Baily, *Sangamon County Gazetteer . . . with City Directories of Springfield and Jacksonville . . .* (Springfield, 1866); W. A. Nixon, *Jacksonville Directory for 1868-69* (Jacksonville, 1868); and *Holland's Jacksonville City Directory for 1871-72* (Chicago, 1871), are all available at ISHL. These are valuable sources which can be allied with census manuscripts to identify ethnic neighborhood patterns, for example. The directories also listed business firms, town officials, and the officers of major associations, which provides a convenient means of identifying leaders.

Another source rich in information on business organization, social mobility, and the ethos of temperance are the R. G. Dun & Co. credit reports in the Baker Library at Harvard. I was not able to exploit the full wealth of information in these records, but they did sharpen my understanding of economic conditions and the moral basis of business success in the nineteenth century. Morgan County Poll Books, available on microfilm from the Illinois State Archives, Springfield, identify the party preference of individual voters, but were unfortunately not used after 1848. To determine the political leanings of Jacksonville leaders in the 1850s and 1860s, newspaper accounts of party activities and biographical sketches in local histories were often helpful, though it was tedious to extract the needed information from them.

A number of manuscript collections of personal and family papers proved invaluable to my research. The collections of the Duncan-Kirby family, Samuel Willard, Newton Bateman, Jonathan Baldwin Turner, and the Hammond family scrapbook, all at ISHL, were especially helpful. Elizabeth Duncan's diary, published in *JISHS* 21 (1928), provides a fascinating view of an elite woman's private life. The Sturtevant-Baldwin letters at Illinois College, also available on microfilm at ISHL, document a New England perception of the problems of religion and education in Jacksonville and the West. The Jonathan Baldwin Turner Collection at the Illinois Historical Survey, University of Illinois Library, Urbana, provides details on Jacksonville's campaign for the state university. The Morgan County Historical Society Collection, in the Jacksonville Public Library, includes a number of useful sources—in particular, the Old Settlers Society files, with biographical sketches done by loyal descendants, and the Carl E. Black scrapbooks, filled with clippings on Jacksonville's past.

Many of the most valuable manuscript materials are scattered throughout the town and require patient searching and diplomatic appeals to gain access. The surviving city records, including the complete minutes of the town board since 1833, are housed in the city clerk's vault at the Municipal Building. Thanks to a revival of the "Jacksonville Spirit" during the Bicentennial, these records are now beautifully rebound and available on microfilm at the ISHL. Church records, including several membership lists, were found in many of the major congregations, and they were generally well preserved. One of the most interesting sets of church documents was not discovered until I (fortuitously) moved to Nashville and located the Central Christian Church records at the Disciples of Christ Historical Society. Some church records not only identify individual members, but also document the turnover of membership, the uses of church discipline, and the struggle to suppress sectarian conflict. The records of several lodges and clubs have survived and are accessible to historians respectful of the inner secrets of the fellowship. The Odd Fellows Lodge, No. 4, generously allowed me to see their minute books, and the Masonic Lodge sent me a brief published history of their organization in Jacksonville. The published Grand Lodge reports for both these lodges, in ISHL, listed members, details on disciplinary action, and data on transfers of membership. In addition, a number of minute books, constitutions, and histories of various clubs were found in ISHL and elsewhere.

Several published memoirs and biographies proved valuable, though the best ones were limited to a circle of Illinois College professors. *Julian M. Sturtevant: An Autobiography*, ed. J. M. Sturtevant, Jr. (New York, 1896), along with many of Sturtevant's essays, provide incisive comments on Jacksonville from a Yankee viewpoint. Travis Keene Hedrick, "Julian Monson Sturtevant and the Moral Machinery of Society: The New England Struggle against Pluralism in the Old Northwest, 1829-1877" (Ph.D. dissertation, Brown University, 1974), is a thoughtful study of the man. Mary Turner Carriel, *The Life of Jonathan Baldwin Turner* (1911; reprinted, Urbana, 1961); Truman Augustus Post, *Truman Marcellus Post: A Biography Personal and Literary* (Boston, 1891); William Coffin, *Life and Times of Hon. Samuel D. Lockwood* (Chicago, 1889); and Robert Merideth, *The Politics of the Universe: Edward Beecher, Abolition and Orthodoxy* (Nashville, 1968), are all very useful accounts of New Englanders in Jacksonville. C. H. Rammelkamp, ed., "The Memoirs of John Henry: A Pioneer of Morgan County," *JISHS* 18 (1925), offers a rustic southern view.

Numerous published histories of Jacksonville's many educational, religious, and state charitable institutions were invaluable aids to my research. Among the most important was Charles Henry Rammelkamp, *Illinois College: A Centennial History, 1829-1929* (New Haven, 1928). Local histories also provided essential, though guarded, information on past events, institutions, and civic leaders. Donnelley, Loyd & Co., *History of Morgan County, Illinois: Its Past and Present* (Chicago, 1878); Charles M. Eames, *Historic Morgan and Classic Jacksonville* (Jacksonville, 1885); William F. Short, ed., *Historical Encyclopedia of Illinois . . . Morgan County* (Chicago, 1906); and the "Jacksonville Centennial Number" of *JISHS* 18 (April, 1925), all document both the truth and legend of the community's past. In addition, numerous articles in the *JISHS* dealt with specific people, events, and institutions, and served as a constant source of reference. Illinois is blessed with an excellent multi-volume centennial state history; especially helpful were Theodore Calvin Pease, *The Frontier State, 1818-1848* (Chicago, 1922), and Arthur Charles Cole, *The Era of the Civil War, 1848-1870* (Chicago, 1922).

The questions I asked of all these sources, and the methods I used to analyze them, were molded by dozens of other books and articles in history and the social sciences, only the most influential of which I can mention here. Most important were several historical community studies produced in recent years. Kenneth A. Lockridge, *A New England Town: The First Hundred Years, Dedham, Massachusetts, 1637-1736* (New York, 1970), and Michael Zuckerman, *Peaceable Kingdoms: New England Towns in the Eighteenth Century* (New York, 1970), are two especially provocative studies of social evolution that anticipate the new form of community that emerged in the nineteenth century. In turn, the social order defined in Jacksonville might be understood as a prelude to the late nineteenth century "crisis in the communities" described by Robert H. Wiebe in *The Search for Order, 1877-1920* (New York, 1967). These books have provided a framework for understanding Jacksonville in the context of larger changes in American society.

A number of studies of nineteenth-century northeastern communities also served as benchmarks for measuring the social order of a relatively young Midwestern town. Michael H. Frisch, *Town into City: Springfield, Massachusetts, and the Meaning of Community, 1840-1880* (Cambridge, Mass., 1972); Sam Bass Warner, Jr., *The Private City: Philadelphia in Three Periods of Growth* (Philadelphia, 1968); and Stephan Thernstrom, *Poverty and Progress: Social Mobility in a Nineteenth-Century City* (Cambridge, Mass., 1964), were all early and important influences on my understanding of Jacksonville. Stuart M. Blumin, *The Urban Threshold: Growth and Change in a Nineteenth-Century American Community* (Chicago, 1976), appeared too late for me to profit fully from the author's perceptive analysis of Kingston, New York. The many similarities between Kingston and Jacksonville, their flourishing associational networks in particular, underlines my opening claim for seeing the process of building new communities as a mirror on the social evolution of their eastern counterparts.

The social history of communities outside the northeast has received less attention, but several books on western towns and cities were valuable guides to my own research. Merle Curti et al., *The Making of an American Community*, mentioned above, is a pathbreaking quantitative study of Trempleau County, Wisconsin, that sets out to test Frederick Jackson Turner's frontier thesis. Richard C. Wade, *The Urban Frontier: The Rise of Western Cities, 1790-1830* (Cambridge, Mass., 1959), is an important effort to intersect the diverging paths of frontier and urban history and to refute Turner. Lewis Atherton, *Main Street on the Middle Border* (Bloomington, Ind., 1954), is a sensitive portrayal of the small town in the late nineteenth century in the silent aftermath of the boosters' lash hurrah. Stanley Elkins and Eric McKitrick, "A Meaning for Turner's Frontier," *Political Science Quarterly* 69 (1954); Daniel J. Boorstin, *The Americans: The National Experience* (Chicago, 1965); Allan Bogue, "Social Theory and the Pioneer," *Agricultural History* 34 (1960); and especially Robert R. Dykstra, *The Cattle Towns* (New York, 1968), were centrally important to the framework of analysis from which this book began. Finally, Page Smith, *As a City upon a Hill: The Town in American History* (New York, 1966), is an engaging overview of the small town.

The works most helpful to my understanding of particular topics include Ray Allen Billington, *America's Frontier Heritage* (New York, 1966), a good interdisciplinary synthesis of theory and research on frontier social, economic, and political development. On community conflict, Dykstra's *Cattle Towns* includes a cogent discussion of social science literature on the subject. Like Dykstra, I found James S. Coleman, *Community Conflict* (New York, 1957), very insightful. Lewis Coser, *The Social Functions of Conflict* (New York, 1954), and Ralf Dahrendorf, *Class and Class Conflict in Industrial Society* (Stanford, 1959), are two other important sociological treatments of conflict.

There is now a substantial body of historical research on geographic and social mobility Thernstrom's *Poverty and Progress*, mentioned above, and *The Other Bostonians: Poverty and Progress in the American Metropolis 1880-1970* (Cambridge, Mass., 1973), are both pathbreaking treatments of mobility. Peter R.

Knights, *The Plain People of Boston, 1830-1860: A Study in City Growth* (New York, 1971); Howard P. Chudacoff, *Mobile Americans: Residential and Social Mobility in Omaha, 1880-1920* (New York, 1971), are also excellent case studies of the subject.

The historical study of family and kinship has begun in recent years to make its much-needed contribution to social history. John Modell, "Family and Fertility on the Indiana Frontier, 1820," *American Quarterly* 23 (1971); Jack E. Eblen, "An Analysis of Nineteenth-Century Frontier Populations," *Demography* 2 (1965); Robert E. Bieder, "Kinship as a Factor in Migration," *Journal of Marriage and the Family* 35 (1973); Modell and Tamara K. Hareven, "Urbanization and the Malleable Household: An Examination of Boarding and Lodging in American Families," *Journal of Marriage and the Family* 35 (1973); and several of the essays in Hareven, ed., *Family and Kin in Urban Communities, 1700-1930* (New York, 1977), were all helpful to my understanding of family life in Jacksonville.

There is an abundance of recent literature on ethnicity. Paul Kleppner, *The Cross of Culture: A Social Analysis of Midwestern Politics, 1850-1900* (New York, 1970), is an important interpretation of ethnicity, religion, and politics. Kathleen Neils Conzen, *Immigrant Milwaukee, 1830-1860: Accommodation and Community in a Frontier City* (Cambridge, Mass., 1976), represents the best of the new research on ethnic social organization.

Two works on the social basis of religion which I found most useful were T. Scott Miyakawa, *Protestants and Pioneers: Individualism and Conformity on the American Frontier* (Chicago, 1964), and Sidney E. Mead, *The Lively Experiment: The Shaping of Christianity in America* (New York, 1963). On political parties, Lynn Marshall, "The Strange Stillbirth of the Whig Party," *American Historical Review* 72 (1967), is an insightful study of political organization. Ronald P. Formisano, *The Birth of Mass Political Parties: Michigan, 1827-1861* (Princeton, N.J., 1971), deals perceptively with society and politics in Michigan; and Robert W. Johannsen, *Stephen A. Douglas* (New York, 1973), is, among other things, an excellent study of political organization in Illinois.

Voluntary associations have not received the attention they

deserve from social historians. Noel P. Gist, *Secret Societies: A Cultural Study of Fraternalism in the United States* (Columbia, Mo., 1940); Oscar and Mary Handlin, *Dimensions of Liberty* (New York, 1961); and Rowland Berthoff, *An Unsettled People: Social Order and Disorder in American History* (New York, 1971), all offer various interpretations of the role of associations in American society. Walter S. Glazer, "Participation and Power: Voluntary Associations and the Functional Organization of Cincinnati in 1840," *Historical Methods Newsletter* 5 (1972), and Blumin, *The Urban Threshold*, both break new ground in the empirical study of associational behavior in the nineteenth century. The social sciences have made American voluntary associations a central concern. The best introductions are David L. Sills, "Voluntary Associations: Sociological Aspects," *International Encyclopedia of the Social Sciences* (New York, 1968), and the articles in William A. Glaser and David L. Sills, eds., *The Government of Associations: Selections from the Behavioral Sciences* (Totowa, N.J., 1966). The research on African voluntary associations is also suggestive; see Kenneth Little, *West African Urbanization: A Study of Voluntary Associations* (Cambridge, U.K., 1965); and Immanuel Wallerstein, "Voluntary Associations," in James S. Coleman and Carl G. Roseberg, Jr., eds., *Political Parties and National Integration in Tropical Africa* (Berkeley, 1964). The more courageous will want to consult the works of Edward O. Laumann; see his *Bonds of Pluralism: The Form and Substance of Urban Social Networks* (New York, 1973).

On the evolution of Midwestern urban government, Bayard Still, "Patterns of Mid-Nineteenth Century Urbanization in the Middle West," *Mississippi Valley Historical Review* 28 (1941), is excellent. The temperance question is analyzed in Joseph Gusfield, *Symbolic Crusade: Status Politics and the American Temperance Movement* (Urbana, 1963). My view of the public school was shaped by the work of Michael B. Katz; see his *The Irony of Early School Reform: Educational Innovation in Mid-Nineteenth Century Massachusetts* (Cambridge, Mass., 1968); and *Class, Bureaucracy, and Schools: The Illusion of Educational Change in America* (New York, 1971). David Rothman, *The Discovery of the Asylum: Social Order and Disorder in the New Republic* (Boston, 1970), helped me understand a wide range of reform movements as well as the emergence of Jacksonville's state institutions.

Several sociological studies also influenced the questions I asked and the interpretations I made of the evidence. Robert and Helen Lynd, *Middletown: A Study in American Culture* (New York, 1928), is a classic of its kind, a wide-ranging analysis of the structure and values of a Midwestern community in the 1920s. Morris Janowitz, *The Community Press in an Urban Setting: The Social Elements of Urbanism*, 2nd ed. (Chicago, 1967), helped me to understand the emergence of the modern community as something more than a decline from intimacy to anomie. Gerald D. Suttles, *The Social Order of the Slum: Ethnicity and Territory in the Inner City* (Chicago, 1968), encouraged me to examine how residents of a community order their own environment amid apparent disarray, and (if Jacksonville will forgive me) it suggested a title for my own book. Finally, Maurice R. Stein, *The Eclipse of Community: An Interpretation of American Studies* (Princeton, N.J., 1960), puts a series of twentieth-century community studies into historical perspective and gives heart to the historian interested in exploring the meaning of community in America in another age.

Index